Crime and Criminology

An Introduction

Rob **White**

Fiona **Haines**

Melbourne
OXFORD UNIVERSITY PRESS
Oxford Auckland New York

OXFORD UNIVERSITY PRESS AUSTRALIA

Oxford New York
Athens Auckland Bangkok Bombay
Calcutta Cape Town Dar es Salaam Delhi
Florence Hong Kong Istanbul Karachi
Kuala Lumpur Madras Madrid Melbourne
Mexico City Nairobi Paris Port Moresby
Singapore Taipei Tokyo Toronto

and associated companies in
Berlin Ibadan

OXFORD is a trade mark of Oxford University Press

National Library of Australia
Cataloguing-in-Publication data:

White, R. D. (Robert Douglas), 1956–.
    Crime and criminology: an introduction.

    Bibliography.
    Includes index.
    ISBN 0 19 553 774 2.

    1. Criminology. I. Haines, Fiona. II. Title.

364

Edited by Janet Mackenzie
Typeset by Desktop Concepts P/L, Melbourne
Printed through Bookpac Production Services, Singapore
Published by Oxford University Press,
253 Normanby Road, South Melbourne, Australia

Contents

List of Charts   iv
Acknowledgements   v

1   The Study of Crime   1
2   Classical Theory   21
3   Biological and Psychological Positivism   37
4   Strain Theory   56
5   Labelling Perspectives   75
6   Marxist Criminology   92
7   Feminist Perspectives   112
8   New Right Criminology   135
9   Left Realism   152
10 Republican Theory   172
11 Critical Criminology   192
12 Conclusion   209

References   214
Index   226

Charts

1.1   A Radical Definition of Crime   **17**
2.1   Classical Theory   **26**
3.1   Positivist Approaches   **42**
4.1   Strain Theory   **59**
5.1   Labelling Perspectives   **78**
6.1   Marxist Criminology   **97**
7.1   Feminist Perspectives   **121**
7.2   Women and Crime   **126**
8.1   Right-wing Libertarianism   **141**
8.2   Conservatism   **143**
9.1   Left Realist Perspectives   **157**
10.1 Republican Theory   **177**
11.1 Critical Criminology   **197**
12.1 Underlying Assumptions of
      Criminological Theory   **211**

Acknowledgements

This book arose out of our work over a period of several years in teaching the introductory criminology subjects at the University of Melbourne. Over that time it became clear to us that an introductory 'theory' text was badly needed, especially one which was specifically designed to expose students to the central concepts and explanations in criminology.

We are grateful to many people in the development of the book. Our special thanks go to Steve James and Santina Perrone who, as fellow lecturers in the subject at various points in time, helped to mould and shape the ways in which the material was actually developed for teaching purposes. We are also grateful to the many tutors and students over the years who each in their own way have assisted us in refining and simplifying the core ideas of the field. Specific sections and passages of the book have been drawn from previous work by Chris Cunneen and Rob White. Thanks are also due to the academic and general staff in the Department of Criminology for their ongoing encouragement and support for projects of this nature. Finally, we are grateful to Jill Lane of Oxford University Press for her constant enthusiasm and genuine interest in putting the book together.

CHAPTER 1

The Study of Crime

This book is about the causes of crime. More specifically, it describes the diverse and at times competing perspectives within criminology, and their attempts to explain why certain types of people engage in certain types of behaviour which have been identified as being criminal in nature.

The aim of this chapter is to introduce the reader to the study of crime, and in so doing to explore a series of issues relating to the definition and measurement of crime. A major part of the chapter describes the criteria which serve to differentiate the many perspectives on crime. In particular, we will explore the different levels of analysis used to explain crime, and the different political perspectives which are brought to bear upon criminological analysis. Thus one purpose of this chapter is to provide a sense of how we can distinguish between different theoretical perspectives by looking at similarities and differences in broad approach.

Criminology as a Field of Study

Before we discuss the nature of crime, it is useful first to say a few words about criminology as a field of study. As we shall see, criminology, like crime, is not a monolith; it contains varied and competing perspectives. This variety of perspectives should be considered in light of the social context of the production of intellectual knowledge.

For instance, the production of knowledge is itself a social and material process. When any kind of knowledge is produced, we must ask who has control over this process — not only the production of knowledge itself, but also the ownership and use of the results of research and scholarship. In a similar vein, specific types of 'knowledge' or 'truth' are not always recognised or visible in the public domain. This can happen for a variety of reasons — because there is no market for it, because of publishing rivalries, or because the 'knowledge' is not deemed to conform to particular academic standards or mainstream political agendas.

Knowledge also has distinctive international dimensions. For example, in the field of criminology each country may have its own unique social concerns, intellectual milieux, political traditions, historical development and, hence, its own theoretical emphases and biases. For example in England, the perspective known as Left Realism and debates over policing have been prominent in recent years, whereas in the USA, major concerns have been expressed over ghetto neighbourhoods and youth gangs. In Canada debates have centred on gun laws and violent crime, while the area of juvenile justice in Australia has been dominated by discussions of family group conferences and diversion strategies.

Cutting across all of these debates in each of the regions, however, have been a series of general issues relating to the nature of crime and the social control of crime. Invariably, analysis of specific issues has employed abstract concepts which are designed to explain why these particular phenomena should be dealt with in any particular way. Major themes of this book are to explore the nature of the more generalised statements regarding crime; to examine the broad social and historical context within which certain theories and concepts have emerged; and to demonstrate the application of these theoretical understandings to selected issues and criminal justice reform.

While 'theory' informs everything which criminologists do, not every criminologist is a theorist. So what should criminologists actually do, and why is theory relevant to their practice? To answer this, we need to appreciate the dual nature of much contemporary criminology. On the one hand, many people adopt what could be called a **vocational** or professional approach to criminology. In this view, the role of criminology is tied to improving the immediate practices of the criminal justice system. This approach seeks to study, analyse and research alternative theories in order to institute reform of some kind. Generally, it is directed at making some aspect of the criminal justice system 'better' at some level — a programme, an institution or a strategy. Often it is linked to attempts to solve a 'social problem' or an administrative difficulty within the existing system.

On the other hand, there is a strand of criminology in which the emphasis is on a **critical** or analytical approach. Unlike the previous approach, this tends not to be a nuts-and-bolts view of the criminal justice system, particularly in respect to making minor changes within the existing institutional frameworks of criminal justice. Rather, it is suggested that one must stand back from policy decisions and ask bigger questions, such as 'What if ...?' This approach delves into the deeper philosophical issues of the day; for example, why do we continue to have and use institutions such as prisons when they demonstrably do not work to prevent offending or reoffending? The approach here is not to suggest improvements to the existing penal system, but to question whether it is valid or viable to begin with. Indeed, an informed opinion might simply advocate the abolition of such institutions in their present shape and form.

It is essential to note, however, that often there are strong inter-links between these two approaches. The variability in criminological perspectives in general is due in part to the nature of the relationship between the practical vocational orientation (with a focus on what can be done here and how to improve the system) and its critical counterpart (with a focus on why things ought to be done in one way or another). We must also be aware of the uncertainties of knowledge. For instance, whatever area of criminology one may concentrate on, there are almost always unintended consequences that emerge from the knowledge we acquire and the reforms we put forward. Knowledge is a guide to the future — it does not fix the future on one single pathway.

Generally speaking, criminology focuses on three main areas:
- the sociology of law, which examines social aspects and the institutions of the law
- theories of crime causation, sometimes referred to as criminogenesis
- the study of social responses to crime, which examines in more depth the formal institutions of criminal justice such as the police, courts and corrections.

As pointed out earlier, the main theme of this book is theories relating to the causes of crime. As will be seen, however, the other domains of criminology often overlap and are inseparable parts of any review of causal theories.

Defining Crime

What is crime? In fact there is no straightforward answer to this question. Instead, we find that there are constantly changing ideas, perceptions and conceptions regarding what constitutes criminal behaviour. To a certain extent, both crime and criminology are uncertain in the sense that one's definition of crime is dependent upon one's particular interests and particular worldview. This becomes clearer when we discuss the various definitions put forward for crime.

There are competing views of crime. Crime is always socially defined. This of course can lead to debate: for example, should crime always be defined by law? Could or should it instead be based upon moral and social conceptions, such as social harm? To illustrate the difficulties surrounding different definitions of crime, we might consider the film *Schindler's List*. In the movie (and in real life) Schindler broke Nazi law in order to assist Jewish people. But was he then a criminal? Who defines the law? What about cases today where people may actively break the law in the name of social justice? There are unjust systems in the world, and it may well be the case that many legal definitions are built on highly contentious and unjust or unfair propositions.

Legal and sociological definitions of crime

There are many diverse conceptions of crime, each of which reflects a different scientific and ideological viewpoint. Hagan (1987), for example, identifies seven different approaches to the definition of crime, ranging from a 'legal-consensus' definition to a 'human rights' definition. For present purposes, we can summarise broad differences in definition in the following way:

- A **formal legal** definition of crime is one which says that what the state identifies as a crime, is a crime. That is, if something is written into the criminal law, and is subject to state sanction in the form of a specific penalty, then that activity is a crime.

- A **social harm** conception of crime says that crime involves both criminal offences (e.g., assault) and civil offences (e.g., negligence), in that each type of action or inaction brings with it some type of harm. Each should therefore attract some sort of penalty.
- A **cross-cultural universal norm** argument states that crime, in essence, does not vary across different cultures. Thus, murder is murder regardless of the society, and we can postulate conduct norms which cut across diverse cultural backgrounds.
- A **labelling** approach to the definition of crime argues that crime only really exists when there has been a social response to particular activity which labels that activity as criminal. If there is no label, there is in effect no crime.
- A **human rights** approach says that crime occurs whenever a human right has been violated, regardless of the legality or otherwise of the action. Such a conception also expands the definition of crime to include oppressive practices such as racism, sexism and class-based exploitation.
- A **human diversity** approach defines crime in terms of the manner in which deviance represents a normal response to oppressive or unequal circumstances. A major focus here is on power relations, and the attempts by dominant groups to restrict human diversity of experience, language and culture.

Our intention here is not to explain fully each type of definition of crime, nor to evaluate the explanatory or practical usefulness of each definition (instead, see for example, Hagan, 1987; Nettler, 1984). Rather, we wish to alert the reader to the fact that there are important differences in how people conceive of crime.

Further to this, the variation in definition often has real consequences upon how different types of behaviour are dealt with at a practical level. For example, we might consider the issue of violence.

> In the home, parents hit children; on the playing field, sportsmen assault each other; at work, industrial 'accidents' occur; in our community, dangerous chemicals are dumped; our governments turn a blind eye to the practices of some police officers; and our governments are responsible for the mass violence of war (Alder, 1991, p. 61).

How violence is perceived and responded to by criminal justice institutions depends very much upon a range of political and social factors. Crime is not inherent in an activity: it is defined under particular material circumstances and in relation to specific social processes.

Historical constructions of crime

While criminologists may argue about the definition of crime, ultimately it is the legal definition of crime which determines how we as a society respond to certain acts deemed to be wrongful. But, we might ask, who actually makes the laws, and why are they made? Whose interests are reflected in those laws and how are they enforced? In line with the broad theme of the variability of definitions of crime, it is also useful to acknowledge that legal definitions of crime themselves change over time. The law itself is thus socially produced and is not static. As it changes, so too does the definition of crime. In this sense we can say that morality itself is variable, at least insofar as it is reflected in the laws of a country.

What is legally defined as crime varies according to social and historical contexts. This is shown in the following examples.

- As of 1530 in England there existed the crime of being a vagabond, which in effect meant that a person was unemployed and idle. Any person so identified could be branded a criminal — figuratively and literally (through burning of the gristle of the right ear with a hot iron). Vagabonds over the age of eighteen could be hanged if they did not obtain suitable employment for two years. Revived in 1743, the Vagrancy Acts expanded the types of persons liable for prosecution to include a wide variety of homeless and poor people (see Chambliss, 1975a). This crime does not still exist, although one could be tempted to draw similarities with the negative status accorded to the young unemployed today.

- In the seventeenth century, the crime of witchcraft was the commonest of all crimes in Europe. Crime here was constructed in terms of religion and referred to conduct allegedly against (the Christian) God. By and large, such laws pertaining to witchcraft targeted women, particularly those displaying eccentric and secretive tendencies, as a means of controlling them and their knowledge (see Inverarity, Lauderdale and Feld, 1983). Such laws of course are not common in the criminal law today. However, in some jurisdictions crimes related to witchcraft are still on the statute books, such as reading of tarot cards. Similarly, some of the public concern about heavy-metal music appears to have vestiges of the moral and religious panics over witchcraft which swept Europe several hundred years ago.

- Property and theft are historically and culturally specific concepts. In traditional Australian Aboriginal and other indigenous communal societies, everything is shared. There is no concept of theft (which is premised on the notion of ownership of personal property), because in these cultures property is communal. Concepts of land ownership likewise differ from mainstream legal conceptions. Some members of indigenous communities hold the belief that they do not really own the land, so it cannot be taken away from them. To put it differently, land is not a possession, it is something that you have a relationship with. Crime in traditional indigenous communities is associated with the abuse of sacred knowledge, custom, spirituality, witchcraft, and ritual — it is not centred upon property as is most Western law (see Bottomley, Gunningham and Parker, 1991).

Crime is thus an offence of the time. In European history it was for a while intimately linked to moral prescriptions, as defined by religious bodies. One reason for this was that, for example, in the 1400s to 1600s, the body that had access to the tools of justice administration was the church. This was because literacy tended to be the preserve of the clergy, who therefore were in a position to construct the laws. Later on, it was the preserve of the state to determine laws. Accordingly, crime became defined as a transgression against the state, not against God. Even today, however, there are vestiges of conflict between the secular and non-secular law, as indicated in legal action taken over the ordination of women in some Christian denominations.

Popular media images of crime

The media have a significant influence on the general portrayal of crime in society. The images which permeate popular consciousness of crime are mainly generated by and reflected in the electronic and printed media. Obviously the media have a tremendous impact in terms of how crime is generally defined in society (see Sarre, 1992; Grabosky and Wilson, 1989; Ericson, Baranek and Chan, 1991).

According to the media, in both fictional and factual types of programmes and reportage, crime tends to be defined primarily as 'street crime'. Such crime is thus associated with personal terror and fear, and violence is seen as central. Crime is sensationalised, with important implications for the fear of crime among certain sections of the population. This fear is heightened by the way in which crime is seen to be random in nature, with anyone and everyone a possible target for victimisation.

As well, there is often the idea that crime is related to morality, and specifically to the decline of that morality. What is 'wrong' is plain for all to see. Furthermore, the 'criminal' is distinctive and identifiably different from everyone else in society. Overall, the idea is that there is a continuing 'law-and-order' problem in society, and that things are constantly getting worse. Against this tide of disorder and lawlessness, the police and other crime-fighters are generally portrayed as 'superheroes', who are infallible and who use violence legitimately in order to counter the violence of the streets.

The media are important not only in shaping our definitions of crime and crime control, but in producing legal changes and reinforcing particular types of policing strategies. For example, the 'moral panics' (see Cohen, 1973) generated by the media on problems such as 'youth gangs' may lead to changes in the law (e.g., introduction of youth curfews) and the adoption of certain police methods (e.g., increasing the use of 'name checks' in particular locales). It has been demonstrated that the interests of the police and the media are entwined; they have a symbiotic relationship in that the media rely upon the police for much of their information, and the police use the media to portray certain images relating to their work.

The media thus convey a sensationalised image of crime, and a protective view of police and policing practices — and they make unusual events usual events in our lives. As Grabosky and Wilson (1989: 11) comment: 'The most common types of crime according to official statistics, crimes against property, receive relatively little media attention. By contrast, crimes of violence, which are very uncommon in actuarial terms, are accorded much greater coverage.'

Similarly, there is a skewed focus on 'street crime' and bizarre events. Meanwhile, the destruction of the environment, domestic violence, white-collar crimes, and occupational health and safety crimes tend not to receive the same kind of coverage or treatment by the mainstream media outlets.

With regard to crime control, the usual implication is that, once a crime has been brought to the attention of the authorities, investigation will lead to generally lead to detection and capture of the offender. This is a far cry from the reality of much police work, and in specific cases of serious street crime a significant proportion of cases do not get to the prosecution stage. In fictional accounts of crime fighting, the police are usually endowed with special qualities (e.g., big guns, martial arts abilities) and violence is central and always justified because of the nature of the 'criminals' at hand. The nature of actual policing is once again misconstrued, and the mundane aspects of interviewing, looking over file material, research, traffic regulation and so on are generally absent. Another facet of fictional accounts is that the police are not accountable to anyone; they can even step outside the bounds of the law, because we all know they are on 'our' side. Thus, the police are always honest and incorruptible, even though evidence in real life, such as the Fitzgerald inquiry into police in Queensland (Fitzgerald, 1989), reveals widespread and systematic corruption.

It is important therefore to separate the images and realities of crime in society. The media shape our perceptions of crime, and in the process they define crime in particular ways. One aspect of this process is that the media often portray crime in terms of distinct **crime waves**. This refers to the way in which increased reporting of particular types of crime (usually street crimes such as assault, rape or homicide) increases the public awareness of this crime. Significantly, there need not have been an actual increase in the crime for a crime wave to occur. The increase exists only in public perception.

Nevertheless, 'crime waves' can and do have real consequences regardless of factual basis. For example, extensive media coverage of child abuse may lead to changes in the law, such as the introduction of mandatory reporting of suspected incidents. Or the fear generated by press coverage of assaults on elderly people may lead to calls for more police, tougher sentences, greater police power and so on. Given the close relationship between the police and the media, major questions can be asked as to who benefits from the selective reporting of specific crimes, especially around government budget time.

Measuring Crime

Given the limitations and problems of relying upon media definitions and treatments of crime, it is reasonable to accept that any statement made about crime should be tested by referring to the 'facts' about crime. This usually means that we need to confirm particular crime trends and consider official data on criminal activity. However, even here there are difficulties with how crime is defined. For what we 'measure' depends upon how we define crime and how we see the criminalisation process.

In fact, criminologists are not united in their approach to crime and crime statistics (see Nettler, 1984; Jupp, 1989). For present purposes, we can identify three broad strands within criminology which deal with measurement issues.

- The **realist approach** adopts the view that crime exists 'out there' in society and that the 'dark figure' of crime needs to be uncovered and recorded. There are limitations to the gathering of official statistics (such as reliance solely on police records of reported offences), and the role of criminology is to supplement official statistics (those generated by the police, courts and prison authorities) through a range of informal or alternative measures. The emphasis is on the **problem of omission** — to uncover the true or real extent of crime by methods such as victim surveys, self-report surveys, test situations, hidden cameras and so on.

- The **institutionalist approach** adopts the view that crime is a 'social process', and it rejects the notion that we can unproblematically gain a sense of the real extent of crime by improving our measuring devices and techniques. This approach concentrates instead on the manner in which official institutions of crime control actually process suspects and thus define certain individuals and certain types of behaviour as being 'criminal'. The emphasis is on the **problem of bias** — to show how some people and events are designated by the criminal justice system as being criminal, while others are not.

• The **critical realist** approach argues that crime measurement can be characterised as having elements of both 'social process' and a grounded 'reality'. The task of measurement from this perspective is to uncover the processes whereby the crimes against the most vulnerable and least powerful sections of the population have been ignored or underrepresented. The emphasis is on the **problem of victimisation** — to demonstrate empirically how certain groups are especially vulnerable to crime and to the fear of crime, and conceptually to criticise the agencies of crime control for their lack of action in protecting these groups.

Thus there are debates within criminology over how and what to measure; these ultimately reflect basic divisions within the field regarding the very definition of crime itself. As the preceding discussions make clear, the study of crime is fraught with a wide range of competing viewpoints and perspectives. It is useful, therefore, to develop an analytical framework whereby we can make sense of these differences and the basis for different points of view on crime and crime control.

Criminological Perspectives

The style of questions you ask necessarily determines the answers you receive. As we have indicated, there are competing definitions of crime: these produce competing answers or explanations of the causes of crime, and these in turn produce different kinds of responses to crime. Criminologists vary in how they approach the study of crime.

Criminological theory can be presented in abstract fashion as being made up of a series of separate perspectives or approaches. Each approach or paradigm attempts to understand a particular phenomenon by asking certain types of questions, using certain concepts, and constructing a particular framework of analysis and explanation. In practice, it is rare to find government departments or academic criminologists who rely solely or exclusively on any one particular criminological framework or approach. Often a wide range of ideas and concepts are combined in different ways in the course of developing policy or in the study of a specific empirical problem.

For the sake of presentation, it is nevertheless useful to present **ideal types** of the various theoretical strands within criminology. The use of ideal types provides us with a means by which we can clarify main ideas and identify important differences between the broad approaches adopted in the field. An ideal type does not exist in the real world. Rather, the intention behind the construction of an ideal type is to abstract from concrete situations the key elements or components of a particular theory or social institution, and to exaggerate these elements if need be, in order to highlight the general tendency or themes of the particular perspective (see Freund, 1969). An ideal type is an analytical tool, not a moral statement of what ought to be. It refers to a process of identifying different aspects of social phenomena and combining them into a 'typical' model or example. For instance, an ideal type of bureaucracy would include such things as impartial and impersonal merit and promotion structures, the following of set rules and regulations, a hierarchical chain of command, and so on. We know, however, that people who work in bureaucracies are not always promoted on the basis of their qualifications, nor is decision-making always rational. But by constructing an exaggerated 'typical' model of a bureaucracy we are able to compare the actual structure of different organisations and how they actually work in the real world.

If we are to construct ideal types in relation to criminological theory, then it is useful first to identify the central focus of theory, and in particular the level of analysis and explanation at which the theory is pitched. There are three broad levels of criminological explanation: the individual, the situational, and the structural. Different theories within criminology tend to locate their main explanation for criminal behaviour or criminality at one of these levels. Occasionally, a theory may attempt to combine all three levels in order to provide a more sophisticated and comprehensive picture of crime and criminality.

Levels of analysis

- **Individual:** The main focus is on the personal or individual characteristics of the offender or victim. Study may consider for example the influence of appearance, dress and public image on the nature of crime causation or victimisation (e.g., tattoos or earrings as indicators of a 'criminal' attitude in men). This level of analysis tends to look to psychological or biological factors which are said to have an important role in determining why certain individuals engage in criminal activity. The key concern is to explain crime or deviant behaviour in terms of the choices or characteristics of the individual person.

- **Situational:** The main site of analysis is the immediate circumstances or situation within which criminal activity or deviant behaviour occurs. Attention is directed to the specific factors which may contribute to an event occurring, such as how the participants define the situation, how different people are labelled by others in the criminal justice system, the opportunities available for the commission of certain types of offences, and so on. Key concerns are the nature of the interaction between different players within the system, the effect of local environmental factors on the nature of this interaction, and the influence of group behaviour and influences on social activity.

- **Social structural:** This approach tends to look at crime in terms of the broad social relationships and the major social institutions of the society as a whole. The analysis makes reference to the relationship between classes, sexes, different ethnic and 'racial' groups, the employed and unemployed, and various other social divisions in society. It also can involve investigation of the operation of specific institutions, such as education, the family, work and the legal system, in the construction of and social responses to crime and deviant behaviour.

The level of analysis one chooses has major consequences for how crime is viewed, the nature of the offender and how the criminal justice system should be organised. For example, a biological positivist approach looks at characteristics of the individual offender (e.g., genetic make-up) and sees crime as revolving around and stemming from the specific personal attributes of the individual. A situational perspective might consider the interaction between police and young people on the street, and argue that 'crime' is defined in the process of specific types of interactions, behaviours and attitudes. From a structural perspective, the issue might be seen in terms of the relationship between poverty and crime, that is, the elements of social life which underpin particular courses of action. The biological, the situational and the structural approaches would all advocate quite different policies because of their particular perspective. The vantage point from which one examines crime — a focus on personal characteristics through to societal institutions — thus shapes the ways in which one thinks about and acts upon criminal justice matters.

The different levels of analysis apparent in criminology are also partly a reflection of the diverse disciplines which have contributed to the study of crime over a number of years. Researchers, scholars and writers in areas such as biological science, psychology, philosophy, law, sociology, forensic medicine, political economy, education, history and cultural studies have all contributed to the multidisciplinary nature of criminology. Each discipline brings to bear its own concepts, debates and methods when examining a criminological issue or problem. This means that within criminology there is a natural diversity of viewpoints as different writers and researchers 'see' the world through very different analytical spectacles. Such differences are also reflected in the adoption of a wide range of different techniques and methodologies in the study of crime. These include historical records, use of surveys, participant observation, interviews, evaluation of official statistics, study of policy documents and discourse analysis.

Most theories of crime tend to congeal into one of these analytical categories. That is, most lean on one of those particular areas, advancing different theories relating to the causes of crime. For example, the classical theory focuses on choice — the offender chooses to offend or not offend; the response is punishment. This approach focuses on the criminal act. The biological positivist looks at the offender's personal characteristics, and focuses on treatment. Some researchers attempt to integrate all three levels of analysis into their approach. The questions one asks will obviously vary according to the approach or combination of approaches one adopts, as will the consequences.

Political orientations

Differences in broad level of analysis, and in specific discipline-related perspectives, can also be linked to some extent to differences in the political framework of the writer. The political orientation of a writer can partially be gleaned by trying to understand their overall picture of society. For example, consider the following representations of society (see Brown, 1979):

- **The geometric circle:** implies society is harmonious, people share the same values of community and equality. The concept of crime is that perpetrators are deviant, outside the circle, and thus they need to be either pulled back into the circle or kept outside the circle's confines.

- **The triangle:** society is viewed as a hierarchy, since some people are situated at the top, possessing the wealth and power, and the majority are situated at the bottom. This vision of society implies conflict and inequality. The concept of crime is that it occurs in the context of struggles and hierarchies of control and power. Situated within this perspective are both meritocratic and critical views. A meritocratic view of the triangle argues that within the existing structure anyone who plays by the rules of the game is capable of rising to the top of the hierarchy, and that success is a question of ability and hard work. The laws are seen to exist as a means of sustaining the rules of the triangle. A critical view of the triangle translates inequality into injustice. The laws are seen to be unequally applied; it is argued that people on the bottom of the triangle are overrepresented in the criminal justice system, and this representation is questioned.

- **The rectangle or square:** society consists of a variety of inter-related rectangles representing different interconnecting institutions, such as the family, work and school. Crime is studied in relation to how these institutions impact upon and reflect upon crime. The concern here is not with values, as in the circle, but with the smooth running of the interconnected institutions. The issue is one of administrative efficiency and application of the right kinds of techniques to fix the particular social problem.

- **Non-geometric forms such as stick figures:** here the focus is on individuals as opposed to society as a whole, and the emphasis is on examining individual creativity and the way individuals construct their realities. The idea is that reality is socially constructed, and that how people act and react in relation to each other has a major impact in terms of defining behaviour and individuals as being deviant, normal or whatever. How people think about themselves and each other is a significant factor in how they subsequently behave in their interactions with others.

The manner in which we view society influences the way in which we view crime. The various competing perspectives within criminology reflect different points of view regarding the nature of society. We can identify three major paradigms (conceptual frameworks for understanding social phenomena) in criminology. These paradigms inevitably incorporate specific kinds of value judgement. The motivation, conceptual development, methodological tools and social values associated with a specific approach are usually intertwined with one of three broad political perspectives: conservative, liberal or radical.

- **Conservative:** A conservative perspective on society tends to be supportive of the legitimacy of the status quo, i.e., it generally accepts the way things are, traditional ways of doing things and traditional social relationships. Conservatives believe dissenters should be made to conform to the status quo. They believe that there is a 'core value system' to which everyone in society should conform. The function of the main institutions is to preserve the dominant system of order for the good of society generally. The values and institutions of society should apply equally to all people regardless of social background or historical developments.

- **Liberal:** A liberal perspective on society accepts the limits of the status quo, but encourages limited changes in societal institutions. This approach tends to avoid questions relating to the whole structure of society. Instead it emphasises the need for action on particular limited 'social problems'. Specific problems such as sexism, racism, poverty and so on can be resolved without fundamental changes to the economic or social structure. Rather, policies and programmes can be developed which will serve to reform existing institutions and day-to-day interactions. Problems tend to be studied in terms of their impact on specific individuals ('the poor' as the focus of research) and the disadvantage suffered by these individuals or groups.

- **Radical:** The radical perspective on society wishes to undermine the legitimacy of the status quo. Like the conservative perspective, it looks at society as whole, but it sees 'social conflict' as the central concern. Society is seen to be divided on the basis of class, gender, ethnicity, 'race', and so on. (The use of the term *'race'* implies that it is a social rather than a scientific construct, and distinguishes it from any biological connotation the word otherwise may have.) The key issue is who holds the power and resources in any particular community. The focus of the radical perspective is fundamental change to the existing social order. Specific issues, such as poverty, are explained in relational terms (e.g., relationship between the rich and poor), and the solution is seen to involve dealing with the structural imbalances and inequalities that lead to the problem (of poverty) in the first place.

If we acknowledge the centrality of politics in criminological analysis, then we must accept that there is no such thing as value-free criminology. Values of the right (conservative), left (radical) and centre (liberal) are embedded in the criminological enterprise. The political orientation of the particular approach has major implications for how crime is defined. For example, Chart 1.1 presents a radical view of how crime can be defined. As opposed to more conservative

Chart 1.1 A Radical Definition of Crime

Crimes of the Powerful	
Typical crimes	**Examples**
Economic	Breaches of corporate law, environmental degradation, inadequate industrial health and safety provisions, pollution, violation of labour laws, fraud
State	Police brutality, government corruption, bribery, violation of civil rights, misuse of public funds
Crimes of the Less Powerful	
Typical crimes	**Examples**
Economic	Street crime, workplace theft, low-level fraud, breach of welfare regulations, prostitution
Socio-cultural	Vandalism, assault, rape, murder, resistance via strikes and demonstrations, public order offences, workplace sabotage

Source: adapted from Cunneen and White, 1995.

perspectives, this approach emphasises both the crimes of the power-ful, and the crimes of the less powerful. Each particular theory of the causes of crime is generally linked in some way to these broad politi-cal perspectives, and thus each sees crime as informed by certain val-ues and philosophical principles.

A further aspect relating to the politics of criminological theory is that the dominant paradigm or approach that is adopted by govern-ments and represented in criminological circles (professional jour-nals, conferences) varies over time. That is, there are competing general perspectives within criminology, but in different periods par-ticular perspectives will be ascendant over others. For example, the conservative perspectives (within which lie a number of related theo-ries, usually associated with classical and positivist views, and which centre on punishment and control strategies) held considerable sway at the level of policy formulation and action in the 1950s. By the late 1960s, the liberal perspective (centring on labelling and efforts at rehabilitation) informed much of the reform activity related to the criminal justice system. By the mid-1980s there had been a swing back to the right, which persisted into the 1990s, with strident calls for the adoption of tougher measures to deal with issues of 'law and order'. Simultaneous with the conservative push at the level of policy were both liberal and radical critiques of the effectiveness and fair-ness of such measures. Criminological theory is thus always related in some way to specific historical contexts, specific material condi-tions and specific political struggles.

The objectives and methods of analysis used in criminology reflect certain underlying ideas and concerns of the writer. In reading crimi-nological material, then, it is important to examine the assumptions of the writers: the key concepts they use; the methods or arguments used to support their theory, to identify their conceptions of society and of human nature; and the kinds of reforms or institutions that they ulti-mately support. It is also important to identify the silences in a partic-ular theory or tradition. That is, what questions are not being asked, and why not? Finally, it is crucial to consider the social relevance of the theory or perspective. What does it tell us about our society, and the direction that our society is or ought to be heading? Fundamen-tally, the study of crime involves the values and opinions of the criminologist, and this too is part of what the student of crime must be aware of if they are to develop an informed view of the issues.

Conclusion

The objectives and methods of criminology reflect and are affected by a wide range of ideas and concerns. This chapter has provided an overview of how the study of crime is built upon a variety of different definitions, involves recognition of historical and cross-cultural processes, and must acknowledge the impact of popular media images on perceptions of crime. The chapter has also indicated the approaches within criminology to measure crime, and the analytically and politically diverse nature of the criminological enterprise.

The main purpose of this book as a whole is to explore how criminology explains the 'causes' of crime. As such, our concern is not to discuss mid-range theories such as those which explain institutional processes as in the case of Foucault (1977) on prisons or Cohen (1985) on social control; nor is it designed to explain issues relating to the responses of society to criminal behaviour and activity, as in the case of Garland (1990) on punishment and Howe (1994) on penality.

In providing a broad overview of the major frameworks of analysis within criminology, we have structured each chapter in the following way: Introduction; Social Context; Basic Concepts; Historical Development; Contemporary Examples; Critique; Conclusion. By organising the material in such a fashion, we hope to offer the reader a useful guide to the background, development and core ideas of each theoretical strand in a way which also makes comparison between the diverse theories relatively easy.

It is our belief that good criminology is that which is self-consciously reflective of the theoretical and political basis of its understandings and analysis. How we view crime, how we define what is harmful or serious, and how we study criminal activity — all have major ramifications for how we propose to deal with crime at the level of policy, institution and strategy. It is our hope that this book will assist the reader in situating the social, theoretical and practical implications of whatever perspective they may draw upon in trying to come to grips with crime and criminology today.

Further Reading

Einstadter, W. and Henry, S. (1995) *Criminological Theory: An Analysis of Its Underlying Assumptions*, Harcourt Brace, New York.

Hagan, J. (1987) *Modern Criminology: Crime, Criminal Behavior, and its Control*, McGraw-Hill, Toronto.

Jupp, V. (1989) *Methods of Criminological Research*, Routledge, London.

Nettler, G. (1984) *Explaining Crime*, McGraw-Hill, New York.

Taylor, I., Walton, P. and Young, J. (1973) *The New Criminology*, Routledge and Kegan Paul, London.

CHAPTER 2

Classical Theory

Introduction

This chapter provides an outline and review of the **classical theory** in criminology. It describes the historical context within which classicism emerged, and the basic principles and concepts of the classical model. The contribution of this model to present criminal justice issues and institutions will be discussed, as will the strengths and limitations of the perspective.

The foundations of the contemporary criminal justice and legal systems were laid down in the eighteenth century. This was the period when the basic principles and practices of classical theory were developed and institutionalised for the first time in Europe. The emergence of classical thought constituted a radical challenge to the institutional and class relations underpinning the system of justice at that time, and resulted in a departure from previous methods of criminal justice adjudication.

Social Context

The development of classical conceptions of law and the criminal justice system was grounded in the transition from feudalism to capitalism. Major social, economic and political changes were occurring throughout Europe which were revolutionising the institutions of power and social relationships generally. The 'revolutions' were at two levels: in production, economies based primarily on agriculture moved to become commercial market economies and then industrial economies; and in the political sphere, the rule of the landed aristocracy was challenged by the emerging bourgeoisie or capitalist class. Thus, over a period of several centuries to the eighteenth century, there occurred a transition from one mode of production, feudalism, to another dominant mode of production, capitalism.

Under **feudalism**, land, wealth and power were concentrated in the hands of a small group of people — the landed aristocracy — which maintained its rule through a combination of repression (e.g., putting down peasant rebellions) and appeal to tradition and custom (e.g., the idea of a preordained social order with kings and queens at the top). Ideologically, law was maintained by appeal to such notions as the 'divine right of monarchs', which said that monarchs ruled by God-given right. Since law-making was a matter of birthright and religious conviction, the aristocracy was for a time able to rule with absolute power. Disobedience or challenge to that order was repressed. Basic social patterns, in particular the relationship between serf and lord, were cast as 'natural' and permanent social arrangements.

In the feudal era, there was an absence of formal legal status as such. Rights were not acknowledged as being common to all. Rather, any rights that did exist were linked to individual station and class. For example, peasants and (most) women were accorded few formal rights, while members of the aristocracy and the upper levels of the Christian church had special rights associated with their position in society. One's social rank thus determined the nature and extent of the rights one was able to claim or exercise.

The administration of justice tended to be haphazard, localised, irregular and unsystematic (see Hall and McLennan, 1986). Just as rights and laws were moulded around the specific interests of powerful individuals, so too the 'justice' system reflected the personal ties or connections of the powerful (e.g., derived from patronage, familiarity, business associations) and the personal whim of the local ruling class. Men (women were generally not decision-makers, unless part of Royalty) held judicial office as an extension of their wealth and rank in society. Furthermore, there was a proliferation of different types of courts, including local manorial courts, ecclesiastical (religious) courts, and the King's or Queen's courts.

Justice was personalised. That is, decisions regarding whether particular acts were deemed to be criminal or not, and the responses to criminal acts, were essentially a matter of the personal opinion or whim of the presiding judge. Decisions were unpredictable. Persons holding legal office could display mercy if they so desired, but this in itself reflected the absolute power they held in their hands to make decisions. There were few institutional checks or balances on this power. The legal system was highly localised, and revolved around the existing power relationships of the landed gentry and church officials.

The penalties for crime were also highly individualised and varied greatly. Torture and death were not uncommon penalties for even minor offences. The brutal nature of the punishment also reflected the fact that the long-term holding of prisoners in particular sites (e.g., prisons) was not used as a general form of sanction. It also reflected the arbitrary use of draconian or extreme measures when the first priority of the day was maintenance of order and orthodoxy, rather than justice and reform.

The exercise of power was, however, circumscribed by certain customs and traditions which, ultimately, served to legitimate the existing social structure (see Fine, 1984). For instance, while the serf or peasant was bound to do extra work or provide an amount of their produce for the lord, the lord was in turn obligated to protect his vassals from outside threat or harm, and to ensure that certain social responsibilities were maintained (e.g., in time of famine to provide a share of social goods to the poor).

The rise of the state, initially linked to the extension of monarchical power, saw the legal and criminal justice systems start to change. Over time, if we take the English case, the monarchs were able to fuse local traditions and customs into a general form of law administration — and hence the development of a 'common law' system of justice. In other European centres such as France, extensive centralised laws were established (e.g., the Code Napoléon) which were to provide a national structure for the legal system. Each system of law served to entrench and consolidate the power of the monarch over that of local land-owners (e.g., barons), so that the monarch was then able to rule much more absolutely than had previously been the case.

The next stage of legal development was linked to the formation of the capitalist class, beginning with the age of **mercantile capitalism** (i.e., merchant trading in the context of nation-states). The absolute power of the monarch constituted a fetter on the activities and aspirations of this new class. For example, the ability of monarchs to grant monopoly trading rights to selected companies (e.g., Hudson's Bay Company in North America) was seen to be unfair, restricting the trading activities of the mercantile capitalists. Furthermore, given that the law was still essentially reflective of personal whim and establishment prerogatives (since decision-making at both national and local levels resided in the hands of the landed aristocracy), a political revolution was necessary to change basic relations of power.

This manifested itself in the form of a series of armed struggles and revolutions, including the French Revolution and the American Revolution. The power of the monarchy was circumscribed or replaced by new institutions (e.g., parliaments), and the aristocracy was pushed to the side as the only or major ruling force in society. For economic reasons (i.e., long-term planning purposes) as well as political reasons (i.e., holding of decision-making power), a new form of law and criminal justice system evolved. A central feature of this system was that it was bureaucratic in nature (rather than personalised), and it provided a more systematic and impersonal method of judicial administration.

The concept of **individual rights**, as opposed to customary and traditional bonds, was central to the political, economic and social project of the bourgeoisie. The new class, the capitalists, called for the universalisation of rights (at least to those who had wealth and property), against a regime based solely upon hereditary privilege. Accompanying the demand for recognition of the 'rights of man' was an insistence that the state no longer simply rule on behalf of a monarch, or the aristocracy. Rather, the role of the state was now to preserve the **rule of law**. In this system the state apparatus acts as a distinct public authority to guarantee 'equality under the law' in relation to freedom, rights and obligations. In this conception of law, not only were all equal in the eyes of the law, but the law-makers themselves were likewise bound by the laws they devised.

The claim for universal and equal rights was relevant to the political domain and, as well, to the law and courts. The idea was that all social attributes such as class, rank and social background should be ignored once a person entered the court. People should not be subject to arbitrary judgement and a justice system based upon different rights for different classes of people. Once in court, participants are transformed into 'abstract legal subjects' who, regardless of background, should be treated equally (O'Malley, 1983).

Economically, the demand for individual rights was important in a number of ways (Fine, 1984). First, it helped to bolster the idea that 'private property' was a right which did not have to be seen in relation to customary or traditional obligations. For example, ownership of land had been linked to certain social obligations for those living on the land; it was now asserted that the use of property was something which was absolutely and exclusively a matter for the owner to decide. An owner could decide to plant cash crops for the market, rather than subsistence crops for the peasant residents. Any obligations to help the poor, or find work for the peasant who had been dispossessed of land, were effectively transferred from private hands to the state.

Second, the notion of rights was used to justify a breaking of bonds between peasants and the landed aristocracy. No longer tied by tradition or custom to the land, peasants were allowed the legal right to freely sell their labour. Coupled with the new legal basis of private property, which soon led to the closing of land to the peasant class, the position of individuals as 'free labourers' served to swell the cities as urbanisation gathered pace. This provided the capitalist class with a huge reservoir of labour from which to choose, and with which production could be magnified in ways hitherto not seen in the history of humankind. The 'freeing' of people from the land was, in fact, crucial to the later development of full-scale industrialisation.

The classical approach in law and criminology was thus born of momentous changes occurring across the political, legal, social and economic domains. At the core of these changes was the relationship between individual rights, the state and equality. The rights of human beings, it was felt, should be protected against arbitrary uses of power. Likewise, a rational system of production and exchange (i.e., the capitalist market) demanded a legal system which was predictable, systematic and regular. Such a system, involving competition between producers, should also ensure that the power of the state be limited, particularly in regard to issues surrounding private property and personal accumulation of wealth.

Basic Concepts

Classical theory is premised upon the notion of individual rights, human capacity to reason and the rule of law (see Chart 2.1). The theory assumes a particular view of human nature, and of the relationship between individuals and the state.

In the classical view, human beings are seen as being essentially self-seeking and self-interested individuals. What we do with our personal talents, skills and energy is a matter of individual initiative and choice. That is, the classical theory has a **voluntaristic** view of human nature which emphasises free will and individual choice. We are thereby seen as ultimately responsible for choosing what to do with our time and energy, and for the consequences which may arise from our actions.

Chart 2.1 Classical Theory

Definition of crime	*Legal* • violation of law • rights and social contract
Focus of analysis	*The criminal act* • specific offence • the criminal law
Cause of crime	*Rationality* • individual choice • irrational decisions
Nature of offender	*Voluntaristic* • free-will, self-interest and equal capacity to reason
Response to crime	*Punishment* • proportional to the crime • fixed or determinate
Crime prevention	*Deterrence* • pleasure-pain principle • reform of the legal system to make it more accessible
Operation of criminal justice system	*Legal-philosophical approach* • basic principles

Rather than analysing the customary or other links between people, the theory emphasises the status of human beings as **rights-holders**. Individuals are deemed to have an equal capacity to reason and to act in accordance with what is rational from the point of view of their own self-interests. Institutionally, each individual is to be granted equal rights under the law. The fundamental objective of the law is to protect individual rights, and to allow the free exercise of choice among individuals as far as this is possible without leading to social harm.

In order to guarantee both individual rights and some semblance of order, classical theory considers the role of the state to be central. Specifically, the theory rests upon the notion of a **social contract** between individual rights-holders and the state. In this model, there is an implied consensus or agreement: individuals in society give up certain rights to the state in return for the protection of their rights and the security of their person and property from other individuals, and from the state itself. If human beings are seen as essentially self-interested and self-seeking, then there needs to be some kind of mechanism which will, in effect, protect us from the self-interested behaviour and actions of others. Hence, the role of the state is to regulate human interaction, and to be a site where rights in general can be protected by not allowing their infringement in specific instances.

The legal manifestation of the social contract is expressed in the phrase **the rule of law**. The rule of law means that everyone is to be treated equally, without fear or favour, in the eyes of the law. It further means that even the law-makers are bound by the law set down for the general populace. Thus, the first principle of the justice system is equal protection of rights. A crucial assumption here is that the social contract will protect each individual against the excesses and corruption of institutions and other individuals by treating all people the same way. For this to occur in practice, it is necessary to have a criminal justice and judicial system which is systematic, predictable and regular.

The law is seen to be intrinsically good, and to reflect the reasoned beliefs and values of the law-makers. The theory assumes a consensus in society regarding what is considered 'good' and what is 'bad', and this is reflected in the specific criminal laws. Crime is defined in the first instance as simply a **violation of the law**. Adherence to the law in general, and to specific laws in particular, is seen to be an essential component of the social contract which protects individual rights generally.

In this framework, criminality is seen as primarily a matter of making the wrong choice, by violating the law. Put simply, individuals are to be held **responsible** for their actions. Since each person is seen to have equal capacity to reason, and given that every effort be made to make citizens familiar with the law, and with its punishments, crime is in essence a matter of free choice. The source of criminality thus lies within the rational, reasoning individual. Crime is the result of individuals either making a calculated decision to do wrong (by weighing up the potential rewards and negative consequences) or engaging in what might be seen as irrational behaviour (by not using their reason adequately or properly).

The social contract is maintained in practice through the use of **punishment**. The purpose of punishment is to deter individuals from violating laws, which in effect means an interference with the person or property rights of another. **Deterrence** should be directed both at the individual (specific deterrence) and at members of society at large (general deterrence) through the use of a range of sanctions or penalties appropriate to the offences committed. Punishment was based upon a **pleasure-pain principle**, in which the pain of the sentence would outweigh any pleasure to be gained from committing the crime.

The response of the criminal justice system is focused primarily on the **criminal act**. The rule of law demands that each violation of the law be treated in the same way. That is, like cases should be treated alike. To put it differently, the emphasis is on equality in legal proceedings (everyone is equal in the eyes of the law), and equality in punishment of offenders (similar crimes are punished in the same way).

The uniformity of the law is guaranteed by set penalties for particular offences. The punishment is thus meant to fit the crime. For the sake of equality, penalties should be fixed prior to sentencing, and be administered in accordance with the actual offence which has been committed. Punishment therefore is to consist of **determinate sentences** which clearly link specific offences with specific penalties, and which are applicable to anyone who has committed the offence in question.

Historical Development

The two leading figures in the development of classical criminology were Cesare Beccaria and Jeremy Bentham (see Taylor, Walton and Young, 1973). The work of Beccaria provided a profound critique of the existing systems of law and criminal justice. He opposed the arbitrary nature of judicial decision-making that was characteristic of the courts of his day, and he was critical of the unduly harsh and barbaric forms of punishment, which included extensive use of the death penalty and the routine use of torture.

According to Beccaria, the basis for all social action should be the utilitarian concept of the greatest happiness for the greater number in society. Translated into the criminal justice sphere, this meant that crime should be considered an injury to society as a whole (and not explained in terms of 'sin' or dealt with solely on the basis of 'privilege'). The purpose of punishment is not simply social revenge or retribution, but to ensure the greatest overall good for everyone. This means that punishment should be oriented toward deterring individuals and others from committing crime, rather than wreaking vengeance.

It was felt that prevention of crime was more important than the punishment itself. To this end it was important to make sure that everyone knew the laws. Human beings were seen as essentially rational. For punishment to work in a deterrent sense, therefore, it needed to be rationally applied (rather than be seen as draconian or unfair). It also needed to be applied in a systematic manner, one which was not subject to the individual whim (including personal granting of mercy) of the judiciary. Furthermore, the deterrent effect of punishment would only be attainable if there was a certainty of punishment, which in turn could be provided only by the establishment of a professionalised police and judicial system.

Ethically, the utilitarian principle demands that the punishment should fit the crime. Hence, the use of torture and the death penalty was condemned insofar as these represented gross violations of individual rights and were disproportionate to the offences actually committed by offenders. Alternatively, incarceration was viewed as a form of punishment which would be particularly effective given the goals of punishment in the classical framework. As Beccaria (1767: 43) put it:

> The end of punishment, therefore, is no other, than to prevent the criminal from doing further injury to society, and to prevent others from committing the like offence. Such punishments, therefore, and such a mode of inflicting them, ought to be chosen, as will make the strongest and most lasting impression on the minds of others, with the least torment to the body of the criminal.

Such an approach necessarily was founded upon a heightened importance attached to formal law, which should set out clearly the range of penalties pertaining to particular kinds of infringements. Judicial discretion should be limited to the area of deciding the 'facts' of the case; it should not extend to selection of penalty once guilt had been ascertained.

The classical view was further developed in the writings of Bentham. Likewise seeing human beings and society within a framework of utilitarianism, Bentham argued that all behaviour is reducible to that of seeking pleasure and avoiding pain. Criminal behaviour, in particular, was also seen as reflecting this universal tendency or generalised pleasure-pain principle (see Gottfredson and Hirschi, 1990).

Given the human beings were seen as having free will, and to have equal capacity to reason, the central question for criminal justice revolved around how to make crime painful and how to reduce the rewards for criminal behaviour. The criminal law reflects a social contract between individuals and the state, a contract which is based upon a rational exchange of rights and obligations. Enforcement of the criminal law should be based on making adherence the most rational thing to do, in the light of the fact that violation would almost certainly mean the experience of negative sanctions. In a nutshell, punishment should offer more pain than the transgression of the law is worth.

To commit or not commit a crime was thus seen as a matter of free choice. Self-interest dictated, however, that if punishment outweighed the potential gain, then crime itself would be the result of either irrational or bad choices. Those who did commit a crime should be punished because the responsibility for doing so in the first place ultimately rests in their own hands.

Although cogent in abstract principle, classical thinking met considerable challenges when put into practice. Essentially, these challenges came from three directions. The first challenge was to make such general principles serve the interests of justice and equality when faced with a specific defendant in court. Some defendants clearly did not conform to the abstract concept of being rational and equal. Questions could be raised about the rationality of children and people with mental illness, for example. To cope with the reality of life in court, reforms took place (sometimes known as the 'neo-classical' reforms). These developed rules to cope with extenuating circumstances where individuals could be deemed not to be totally responsible for their actions.

The second challenge came from the growing bureaucratisation of the state. As capitalism grew, so did the need for a co-ordinating bureaucracy to ensure the smooth running of commerce. The state fulfilled such a role. The courts, as part of the state, had to fulfil the bureaucratic criterion of efficiency as much as those of justice and fairness. Where the criteria of efficiency and justice were incompatible, conflict resulted. Changes to the state which result from the demands of bureaucracy have been labelled 'corporatisation', where procedures are put in place to increase efficiency, rather than to emphasise qualities such as justice.

The third challenge to classicism came from vested interests. Those in positions of power viewed classicism as a challenge to their entrenched authority, which they wielded through considerable discretion in application of the law in practice. Codification of legal principles therefore threatened the autonomy of the aristocracy, who naturally resisted such changes. The system which resulted, particularly in the UK and Australia, represents a hybrid of classical and pre-classical models.

Contemporary Examples

The classical perspective is reflected in many aspects of the contemporary criminal justice system, despite the three challenges outlined above. Classical thinking is evident in legal doctrine which emphasises conscious intent or choice (e.g., the notion of *mens rea* or the guilty mind), in sentencing principles (e.g., the idea of culpability or responsibility) and in the structure of punishment (e.g., gradation of penalties according to seriousness of offence).

Philosophically, the classical view sees its modern counterpart in the supporters of a 'just deserts' approach to sentencing. In this perspective, four basic principles are proposed (see Pettit and Braithwaite, 1993):

1   No one other than a person found to be guilty of a crime must be punished for it.
2   Anyone found to be guilty of a crime must be punished for that crime.
3   Punishment must not be more than of a degree commensurate to or proportional to the nature or gravity of the offence and culpability of the criminal.
4   Punishment must not be less than of a degree commensurate to or proportional to the nature or gravity of the offence and culpability of the criminal.

Such principles clearly rest on a classical foundation. They encapsulate notions of free will and rationality, as well as proportionality and equality. As we have said, these notions form part of the 'just deserts' understanding of criminal behaviour: it seeks to focus on the offence not the offender; to deter the offender from reoffending according to the pleasure-pain principle, and to ensure that justice is served by equal punishment for the same crime. 'Just deserts' philosophy eschews individual discretion and rehabilitation as aims of the justice system. Justice must be done (i.e., proportional punishment must be meted out), and must be seen to be done (i.e., there should be no exceptions).

The 'just deserts' model has formed the basis for much sentencing reform within Australia. The focus of these reforms has been to rationalise the sentencing structure by specifying more clearly the appropriate penalty for the offence. In reality this has been seen to reduce the discretion of the judiciary by controlling penalties more closely in legislation, dictating length of sentence (or more accurately period of incarceration), and removing or reducing parole and other periods of non-incarceration. However, it should be noted that maximum penalties may also have been reduced, so the actual term served more closely reflects the original sentence handed down by the judiciary, and the sentence provided for in legislation. The aim is not necessarily to increase penalties (although this may in fact be what happens); rather, the aim is for the penalty to be reflective of the offence and to be administered without favouring one individual over another.

Such sentencing reforms revisit many of the debates which surround application of classical principles. In particular, debates concern the fairness of a system which has curtailed considerations of extenuating circumstances of the offender and reduced judicial discretion to a large degree. Those who argue for the need to rehabilitate the offender are particularly troubled by the change in legislation, rehabilitation being irrelevant to both classical and 'just deserts' thinking.

It is perhaps misleading, however, to focus on sentencing as the primary concern of classical theory. Classical theorists were equally concerned with codifying and simplifying the law so that it was easily understood by the majority of people. Both these aims have had limited success. Codification, the passing in legislation of what exactly constitutes an offence, has not occurred in all states in Australia. Victoria, New South Wales and South Australia do not have criminal codes. This means that a number of offences — such as manslaughter, for example — are not clearly defined in law but rely on common law judgements.

Simplification of law to make it open and accessible has faced similar obstacles to codification. While there have been some attempts to simplify law, and make it accessible to all, many aspects of law remain obscure and impenetrable to the majority. Furthermore, legal expenses often prove prohibitive to all but the wealthy when it comes to pursuing justice through law. To some extent, though, there have been advances in making the law accessible to the general populace. The provision of legal aid, the Community Legal Centre movement, and the provision of small claims courts and tribunals throughout Australia can be seen to have at least some origin in these concerns of the classical perspective.

Critique

The limitations of classical theory have been signalled throughout the chapter. Here they will be summarised for clarity. Concerns with classical theory can be broken down into two groups; namely, problems with fairness in the case of individuals, and neglect of inequalities in the broader social structure (see Young, 1981; Taylor, Walton and Young, 1973).

The problem of fairness in individual cases formed an early critique of classical theory and led to the first wave of neo-classical reforms. Despite such reforms, the problem still remains where a system focuses on the offence not the offender, coupled with principles of equality and fairness when responding to such criminal behaviour. People are not endowed with equal capacity to reason (e.g., children, people with intellectual disability or mental illness). The decision to offend may or may not be the result of an irrational choice, and the theory gives no insight into how to deal with cases where offending results from an incapacity of reason.

The second critique follows from the first and is concerned with the classical concept of rationality. If offending results from a temporary irrationality, how is it that the distribution of crime (as measured by official statistics) is not spread equally through the social structure? Such measures place the bulk of offending amongst those with low incomes. The findings suggest that for some people offending may be entirely rational in a manner that is not amenable to the deterrence resulting from punishment. In a world of deep social inequalities, universal equality cannot be realised by treating everyone equally before the law. Rational choice may lead some to offend precisely because of social inequalities. Equality before the law masks this reality.

On a broader level, it has long been recognised that there are clear differences between formal law (that which is written) and substantive law (that which happens in practice). The way law was written tended to assist some individuals who understood the law and knew how to exploit it, while disadvantaging others who did not have the same access to lawyers nor understand the way law works in practice. It is a common complaint that a powerful individual or organisation appears able to avoid the 'spirit' of the law, while complying with the 'letter' of the law.

The legal process is itself influenced by the broader social inequalities. Some people are more equal than others, and this in turn affects the legal process. The wealthy have access to legal advice which in turn affects how they are dealt with by the justice system. Furthermore, punishments may be proportional to crime, but will be experienced in markedly different ways — the rich may retain income and wealth, while the poor lose out on income and future work opportunities.

Despite these problems, classical theory had a real and positive effect on the justice system. It did promote a more open, systematic system of justice when compared to the previous system based on the arbitrary whim of the aristocracy. Classical principles argue for the rights of an individual within the system, and place limits on judicial discretion. Finally, the theory espouses a humanitarian approach to punishment when compared to the barbaric practices of the previous era. For example, classical theorists such as Beccaria argued against capital punishment, which was very much a radical proposition for the era.

Conclusion

Classical theory was developed at a time of great social change, namely the transition from feudalism to capitalism. Just as that transition challenged the pre-eminence of the aristocracy in economic matters, so classicism challenged the discretion of the aristocracy in matters of crime and justice. Classical theory sought to promote the rights of individuals as equal and rational. According to this perspective, people are inherently self-seeking and endowed with free will. This free will, coupled with a rational system of laws which deters individuals from offending, will ensure few have the motivation to offend. Under this system punishment will be meted out without reference to who the offender is, in a manner that ensures the pain of punishment outweighs the gain from the offence.

Classical thinking had a profound effect on the justice system, and can be seen particularly clearly in current debates concerning 'just deserts' principles in sentencing. However, the focus on the offence rather than the offender has problems where individuals lack the capacity for reason, or where offending can be seen to reflect the wider inequalities in society. Classical theory can have the effect of masking the reality of these broader inequalities in the social structure, and in this way entrench such equalities through a pretence of equal access to justice through the legal system.

No system has ever reflected the total demands of the classical system. In Australia the justice system can be seen as only a partial reflection of the classical model, still retaining large areas of pre-classical processes and procedures, such as case law, in which the law is made not by the parliament but by the judiciary. Even where classical principles hold in practice, there have been continuing neo-classical revisions (i.e., acknowledgement of individual differences).

The classical thinkers initiated a period of lasting debate and controversy over how we should understand crime and criminal behaviour. Although ostensibly focused on the offence not the offender, the very process of raising issues concerning law and offending inexorably leads to closer scrutiny of the reasons for offending. It is the reasons for offending which form the basis of the theories in the next chapter, namely the positivist perspective.

Further Reading

Beccaria, C. (1767) *An Essay on Crimes and Punishment,*
    J. Almon, London.
Fine, B. (1984) *Democracy and the Rule of Law: Liberal Ideals and Marxist Critiques,* Pluto, London.
Gottfredson, M. and Hirschi, T. (1990) *A General Theory of Crime,* Stanford University Press, Stanford.
Taylor, I., Walton, P. and Young, J. (1973) *The New Criminology,* Routledge and Kegan Paul, London.
Young, J. (1981) 'Thinking Seriously About Crime: Some Models of Criminology', in M. Fitzgerald, G. McLennon and J. Pawson, J. (eds) *Crime and Society: Readings in History and Theory,* Routlege and Kegan Paul and the Open University, London.

CHAPTER 3

Biological and Psychological Positivism

Introduction

This chapter discusses **positivism** as a central theoretical and methodological approach in the history and contemporary practice of criminology. As will be seen, the development of positivistic perspectives constituted a major break with the classical tradition which saw crime as primarily a matter of individual choice. For the positivists, crime is explained by reference to forces and factors outside the decision-making ability of the individual. Thus, the classical and the positivist viewpoints are often seen as being directly counterposed.

The rise of positivism represents a shift from what was seen as armchair theorising or philosophising, to a more rigorous, hands-on, scientific enterprise. The chapter explores the origins of the 'science' of criminology, and discusses two major approaches within positivism: the biological and the psychological. Central to each of these perspectives is the idea that crime can best be explained by examining individual differences between people, and by demonstrating how these differences are, in turn, linked to certain biological and/or psychological factors which predispose certain people toward criminal behaviour.

Social Context

Positivism as a perspective is associated with a very different view of society and human nature from that expressed in classical criminological theory. It emerged in the nineteenth century, a period of further consolidation of capitalism and the capitalist mode of production in Europe. This was a period which witnessed major technological developments and the entrenchment of mass production (rather than agricultural production or merchant trading) as the dominant form of production and source of profit.

The nineteenth century saw the further concentration of peasants and villagers into large cities, the creation and expansion of the factory system, the introduction of new production technologies and sources of energy (such as the steam engine), and expanded communication and transport networks (e.g., extensive railroad and highway construction). Changes in basic production techniques and relations, and the flow of 'free labour' into employment in the industrial sphere, saw the emergence of a new social class — the working class or proletariat.

The rise of the proletariat as a distinct and growing class was accompanied by major industrial, social and political conflict and upheaval. The previous centuries had been marked by periodic struggles between the aristocracy and the peasantry (in the form of peasant rebellions), and between the established ruling class (the landed gentry) and the bourgeoisie (capitalists). Now the dominant class, the capitalist class, was faced with opposition from the working class over the conditions and nature of work, and in some cases over the very ownership and control of production in society.

Life was hard for the members of the working class: child labour was not unusual, and a thin line separated those who worked for a living from those who were condemned to the poorhouse. Living conditions and working conditions were harsh, dirty and crowded. Meanwhile, the capitalists as a class were amassing huge fortunes and adopting opulent lifestyles. The contrast in circumstance and opportunities was stark.

Not surprisingly, the nineteenth century was also a time when the working class began to organise itself industrially, politically, and in some cases militarily. Although banned by law, workers began to combine into industrial organisations, the trade unions. Simultaneously, the material conditions experienced by the working class meant that there was greater analysis of, and sympathetic hearing for, the idea of forging a new type of 'classless' society. This was reflected in the proliferation of alternative working-class publications, pamphlets and daily press, and in the formation of socialist, anarchist and labour political organisations and parties. Over the course of the century a number of compromises were made by the ruling capitalist class. These included, for example, the legal recognition of industrial unions, and the extension of the vote to male members of the working class.

The nineteenth century in Europe was also a time of new thinking about the nature of human beings, and of society generally. The European powers had been involved in carving up the world's resources for several centuries — from Latin America to Africa, the Indian sub-continent to Asia, the Europeans had been extracting resources and exploiting the labour of indigenous people since the 'voyages of discovery' in the fifteenth century. This was justified initially by the simple expedient that 'might makes right'. However, the justification become more sophisticated with the advent of theories of social and biological evolution.

In particular, the great leaps forward in technology and industrial development, combined with reliance on and appreciation of the importance of 'science', meant that the European nations asserted their pre-eminence in the global economic and political structure on the basis of a presumed national and biological superiority. Science and technology ensured the expansion of European influence and power into all corners of the globe. Domination was seen as a natural outcome of the fruits of a European 'civilisation' founded upon innovation, invention and technological superiority.

Simultaneously, the work of natural scientists such as Charles Darwin, and especially his general theory of evolution (based upon notions of natural selection and competition), were (mis)appropriated to justify and explain the dominance of the white European over the rest of the world's populace. Colonialism and imperialism were thus seen as a consequence of the natural biological superiority of the white European. White supremacy was thus justified and intertwined with notions of a racist biological determinism, one in which white Europeans were at the top of human hierarchy.

The visible presence of class conflict and social misery in Europe, the rise of scientific interest and industrial innovation, and the idea of evolution and stages in human development were all to influence the establishment of positivism as an approach to human affairs. Positivism was founded upon the belief that society ('civilisation') is progressing ever forward, and that the social scientist can study society, provide a more accurate understanding of how society works, and ultimately provide a rational means of overcoming existing social problems and ills by using scientific methods.

Social scientists were interested in promoting a positive view of the social order, and in providing positive interventions in social life to make things better. This required systematic study of existing social problems, and the development of a wide range of techniques and strategies to deal with issues relating to schooling, poverty and family life.

Institutionally, the development of positivism was closely associated with the rise of the **professions** during the nineteenth century. The passing of legislation in Britain which banned the use of child labour in factories, for example, was accompanied by the introduction of compulsory schooling and expanded welfare concern over the plight of the children of the poor. Under the rubric of positive reform, a wide variety of 'experts' — medical doctors, psychiatrists, health workers, teachers, criminal justice officials and social workers — began to devise 'scientific' ways to raise children better, to professionalise parenting, to deal with personal troubles and individual deficiencies, to deal with young offenders and, generally, to engineer wide-scale social reform.

Liberal reform rested upon the idea of progress, humanitarianism and the active construction of a more caring and supportive society. The main tool of investigation used by professionals and reformers in fostering particular forms of social change was the scientific method. Indeed, the persuasive power of the professionals relied upon the notion that their judgements and strategies were derived from science. That is, people no longer relied upon appeals to God, revelation, faith or opinion to devise appropriate institutional responses to social problems; rather, social change was to be managed rationally by use of the scientific criteria of logic and empirical study.

The intrinsic appeal of such an approach is understandable, especially since science and technology played a crucial role in industrial capitalism and a high level of bureaucratisation and specialisation were a necessary part of an advanced industrial economy. The model of the natural sciences had worked well for capitalist production techniques and manufacturing processes. Now it could be put to use in the social arena as well.

The adoption of concepts and methods from the natural sciences was manifest in several overlapping ideas about the nature of society. For instance, borrowing from the biological sciences, positivist social scientists often viewed society as a type of organism. It was made up of different components, which worked together in order to ensure the proper functioning of the system as a whole. If any one of these components was or became 'dysfunctional', then correction was required to restore the social equilibrium. This could apply to specific institutions (e.g., school, family, work) and to particular individuals or groups in society (e.g., the poor, sole parents, unemployed). Social scientists had the tasks of identifying the nature and source of dysfunctions, and attempting to devise programmes and strategies to alleviate them.

The positivist method in doing so was guided by certain assumptions regarding the applicability of natural science methods to the study of society. Three premises in particular underpinned the scientific approach as conceived by the positivists (see Taylor, Walton and Young, 1973):

- Social scientists are seen to be neutral observers of the world, and their work is 'value-free'. This is because the world was seen to be 'out there', as an external reality, and the role of the scientist is merely to record the 'facts'.
- The key method of the positivist is that of classifying and quantifying human experience and behaviours through a range of objective tests. This means developing various ways to measure human activity.
- As with the natural world, the social world is seen to obey general laws of operation. The task of the positivist is to uncover the causal determinants of human behaviour (i.e., to identify 'cause' and 'effect' relationships), and thus both to predict and to modify future behaviour outcomes.

The development of positivism is thus related to efforts to adopt natural science methods and concepts in the study of society. This meant accepting certain ideas about the human experience, and attempting to quantify and classify this experience in the expectation that expert intervention could forestall or rectify particular kinds of social problems.

Basic Concepts

Positivism is based on the idea of a scientific understanding of crime and criminality (see Chart 3.1). It assumes that there is a distinction between the 'normal' and the 'deviant', and attempts to study the specific factors which give rise to deviant or criminal behaviour.

One of the hallmarks of the positivist approach is the notion that behaviour is **determined**. That is, the activity and behaviour of individuals are primarily shaped by factors and forces outside the immediate control of the individual. Behaviour is thus a reflection of certain influences on the person, whether biological, psychological or social in nature.

Chart 3.1 Positivist Approaches

Definition of crime	*Natural* • violation of social consensus • extends beyond a legal definition • deviant behaviour with respect to social norms
Focus of analysis	*The offender* • characteristics of offender
Cause of crime	*Pathology* • individual deficiency • not a matter of individual choice
Nature of offender	*Determined and/or predisposed to certain types of behaviour* • biological and social conditioning and individual differences
Response to crime	*Treatment* • diagnosis on individual basis • indeterminate to fit offender
Crime prevention	*Diagnosis and classification* • early intervention
Operation of criminal justice system	*'Scientific' approach* • measurement and evaluation • essentially neutral

It is believed that offenders vary: **individual differences** exist between offenders, and these in turn can be measured and classified in some way. Rather than seeing people in terms of equal capacities, or equal rights, the positivist view emphasises difference, which reflects varying conditions affecting each person.

The focus of analysis therefore is on the nature and characteristics of *the offender*, rather than on the criminal act. Offenders can be scientifically studied, and the factors leading to their criminality can be diagnosed, classified and ultimately treated or dealt with in some way. It is the job of the 'expert' to identify the specific conditions leading to criminality in any particular case.

In addition to identifying the specific attributes of offenders, the positivist also sees crime and deviance as something which likewise can be studied in a scientific manner. In other words, the incidence of such behaviour is not assumed to reside only in official violations of the law. This is because the social or **moral consensus** in society (which can be described and measured independently of the law) can be violated without necessarily being detected or processed formally in the criminal justice system.

Furthermore, given that deviancy is seen to lie within the (abnormal) individual, and is not always reflected in who actually ends up in court or in the hands of the police, the extent of deviant behaviour is an open-ended empirical question. As such, it requires research into that **natural crime** which hitherto has been undetected but which nevertheless is occurring in society. It is necessary then to measure the **dark figure** of unrecorded crime and deviant behaviour, through the use of techniques such as large-scale questionnaires, interviews and various other measures.

A central proposition of positivism is that a moral consensus exists in relation to what constitutes deviant and normal behaviour. Given this, positivists generally see behavioural problems in terms of **individual pathology** or deficiency. Those who do not conform are seen as having personal difficulties related to biological, psychological or social factors. The task of the expert is to identify these factors and to correct or fix the deficiency.

Rather than being oriented toward punishment, the positivist approach is directed toward the **treatment** of offenders. Offending behaviour is analysed in terms of factors or forces beyond the conscious control of the individual. To respond to crime therefore means to deal with the reasons which caused the offending behaviour to occur in the first place.

Since each individual offender is different from all others, treatment must be individualised. This translates at an institutional level into arguments in favour of **indeterminate sentences**. That is, the length of time in custody should not depend solely on the nature of the criminal act committed, but must take into account the diagnosis and classification of the offender (e.g., severe or not severe problem, dangerous or not dangerous), and the type of treatment appropriate to the specific individual.

Historical Development

The origins of positivist perspectives in criminology lie in two interrelated developments in the latter part of the nineteenth century. One strand of scientific research attempted to provide **biological** explanations for criminal behaviour; the other focused on **psychological** factors associated with criminality.

Biological positivism

Biological positivism was first popularised through the work of Lombroso (1911; see also Taylor Walton and Young, 1973). Borrowing heavily from evolutionary theories, Lombroso attempted to distinguish different types of human individuals, and to classify them on the basis of racial and biological difference. In a form of 'criminal anthropology', the argument here was that a general theory of crime can be developed on the basis of measurable physical differences between the criminal and the non-criminal. Specifically, Lombroso wanted to establish a link between criminality, and the assumption that individuals exhibit particular traits which roughly correspond to the various stages of human evolution.

For Lombroso, the criminal was born, not made. The idea of a 'born criminal' reflected the notion that crime is the result of something essential to the nature of the individual criminal. In the early formulations of this view, discussion focused on the concept of the 'atavistic criminal', that is, a person who was biologically inferior in that they represented a reversion to an earlier human evolutionary period. To put it in crude terms, the atavistic criminal was, developmentally, closer to an ape than contemporary human beings. Such a person could be identified through a series of physical stigmata, including abnormal dentition (protruding teeth), asymmetric face, large ears, supernumerary fingers and toes, eye defects, and even tattoos.

Lombroso later modified his views somewhat, although the element of biological determinism remained. For example, he developed a typology of criminals which divided the population into the 'epileptic criminal', the 'insane criminal', the 'occasional criminal' and so on. In explaining female delinquency and criminality, the argument was put forward that, due to the essential nature of the female sex (which was seen as passive), the female offender in fact was biologically more like a man than a woman.

The emphasis on biological factors in explanations of crime was reflected in a number of subsequent studies. Indeed, the search for a single physiological cause of criminality has persisted to this day. Certainly the 'science' of phrenology was popular in criminology for a number of years around the beginning of this century. This doctrine assumes that the shape and size of the skull correspond to the functions and ability of the brain. A study undertaken in 1912 at the University of Melbourne provides an illustration of this kind of research (Brown and Hogg, 1992). The study was conducted on 355 male inmates of Pentridge prison. The skulls of the prisoners were examined and estimates of the cubic capacity of their brains were made in an attempt to correlate the size of skull to intelligence. It was concluded that cattle stealers had the lowest brain capacity, and that forgers and embezzlers had the highest.

Attempts to measure intelligence, and to argue that criminals were innately less intelligent than the general population, were also popular. In 1910, for example, Charles Goring (1910) published the results of his work which involved examining some 3000 convicts. He concluded that people with criminal tendencies were endowed with less intelligence and were of a smaller stature than other people. To measure intelligence, he simply talked to people and decided for himself whether or not they were intelligent.

Another type of study is that which looks to physiology or body structure as a key determinant of criminal behaviour. In the 1940s William Sheldon (1940) proposed a theory based on body build (somotype). He wished to establish a link between different body types and criminality. According to Sheldon, human body types can be classed into three broad categories: endomorphic (soft and round), mesomorphic (muscular and strong), and ectomorphic (thin and fragile). Each body type was associated with a particular temperament: endomorphic (relaxed, sociable and fond of eating), mesomorphic (energetic, courageous and assertive) and ectomorphic (brainy, artistic and introverted). It was further argued that mesomorphs were most likely to become criminals. In other words, there was a positive correlation between body type and criminal activity.

As a final example of biological explanation, we turn to research which examined genetic factors (see Taylor, Walton and Young, 1973). According to the XYY chromosome theory, criminality is related to a deviant genetic make-up. The normal female chromosomal complement is XX, the normal male composition is XY. However, an XYY combination was also discovered. It was held that those who had this kind of chromosomal complement were far more predisposed to criminal activity, due to their 'abnormal' height and mental structures. Fundamentally, a central problem nevertheless remained — that is, how genetic differences actually translate into behavioural traits.

Biological explanations of the kind considered above tend to be fairly pessimistic about positive actions to prevent or deal with crime. This is because crime is seen to be the result of something **essential to the nature of the individual.** Thus, we are born with certain biological attributes that we cannot change, but that may lock some of us into a life of crime and anti-social behaviour.

Psychological positivism

Psychological positivism had different historical origins and a different orientation toward the offender and criminal activity. In this instance, crime was seen as the result of **externally caused biological problems** (e.g., war injury) **or internal psychological factors** (e.g., mental illness) **which were treatable.** The criminal was made, not born. And the task of the criminal justice system was to understand the underlying causes of criminality, and to find the appropriate treatment strategy.

This strand of positivism emerged in England from within the criminal justice institutions themselves (see Garland, 1988). Doctors and psychiatrists who worked within the medico-legal framework, and who spent most of their working life with inmates, became ever more sophisticated in their classification and diagnosis of offenders. As practitioners within the criminal justice establishment, they had daily contact with a wide variety of 'subjects'. They discovered that there were major differences between individual offenders, and furthermore, that there was a whole range of offenders who did not seem entirely responsible for their actions.

Given their medical background, it is not surprising that these practitioners saw the issue as one of pathology. If offenders were deemed to be 'sick' in some way, then the obvious solution to crime was to find some way to 'cure' them. Thus, an offender might exhibit the conditions of criminality, but these conditions could be dealt with. This could be accomplished by scientific diagnosis, classification of the condition or illness, and devising the appropriate treatment to fit the condition of each offender.

Such ideas and reasoning were reinforced by the experiences of medical practitioners in treating soldiers who returned from the battle fronts of World War I. Many of these men were shell-shocked and physically disabled. They presented a number of pathological tendencies, ranging from varying forms of mental illness through to anti-social behaviour. Deviancy in this case was clearly related to trauma of some kind. The problem was not with the innate characteristics of the individual, but with the consequences and impact of the trauma on the individual.

Broadly speaking, psychological theories tended to centre attention on the processes of the mind in explanations of criminal behaviour (see Feldman, 1993). They included several kinds of perspectives:

- some made reference to psychoanalytic theory, such as analysis of the conscious and unconscious, and how basic emotional and developmental processes affect behaviour

- some focused on personality traits, such as studies of aggression and passivity, and the psychological structure of personality as these related to behaviour
- some dealt with psychiatric issues from the point of view of childhood experiences, such as analysis which saw deprivation of universal needs during childhood as leading to the formation of certain personality patterns in later life.

Contemporary Examples

Later work was to make a stronger connection between biological and psychological factors in explaining criminal behaviour. The best known of the **bio-social explanations** is that provided by Eysenck (1984). He argued that behaviour can be explained by a combination of psychological and environmental influences. Human beings are not totally determined by their biology, nor are they unaffected by their social circumstances. Behaviour, and in particular criminal behaviour, can be explained in terms of two key variables:

- **The differential ability to be conditioned:** This referred to the way in which genetic inheritance can affect one's ability to be conditioned. That is, the sensitivity of the autonomic nervous system which you have genetically inherited will determine whether you are an extrovert or introvert, and this in turn influences how well you are able to be conditioned in society.
- **The differential quality of conditioning:** This referred to the effectiveness and efficiency of the family in using appropriate conditioning techniques. That is, the content and method of child-rearing will have an impact upon the child's subsequent behaviour.

The argument, then, is that biological potentials (such as the ability to be conditioned, or socialised) are set through inheritance; these interact with environmental potentials (shaped by parenting practices); and together these factors determine the overall propensity of individuals to commit crime.

Today, the connection between biological and social environmental influences is seen in very sophisticated terms. It is a case of 'nature' plus 'nurture', rather than one or the other as the sole or even dominant factor in producing certain types of behaviour. It is generally argued that human beings have a 'conditional free will', and individuals can choose within a set, yet to some degree changeable, range of possibilities (Fishbein, 1990).

Present-day positivists define and identify criminality in a manner geared to establishing those people who are 'at risk' of certain behaviour. There is no longer a one-to-one link between crime and behaviour; rather, certain groups are seen to be more predisposed to crime than others because of biological and social environmental factors. Individuals are not born criminal, they are exposed to baseline biological and psychological processes which shape their personality in childhood. Once the child is introduced to the school, the personality manifests itself in certain types of behaviour. The social influences encountered in the school environment may then further contribute to anti-social behaviour, depending upon initial personality formation.

Contemporary positivists thus see a dynamic relationship between biological factors (inherited predisposition) and environmental factors (external inputs which modify behaviour). Nevertheless, within this more open and less deterministic framework there has been a resurgence of interest in explanations for crime which are heavily weighted toward the biological. Recent research, for example, has examined the contributions of various factors to criminal behaviour (see Fishbein, 1990):

- **Genetic contributions:** These studies have examined the effect of inheritance on criminal behaviour. Particular traits such as intellectual defects or aggression are seen as genetically given, and as being closely associated with criminal behaviour. Comparisons of identical and non-identical twins, and adoption studies to compare biological and non-biological siblings, are means by which one can test the influence of genetic inheritance.
- **Biochemical contributions:** These studies look at the impact of biochemical differences on human behavioural patterns. Hormonal activity, metabolic processes, the influence of toxins (such as lead poisoning) are examined in terms of various behaviour such as aggression, and the overall propensity to commit crime. Another strand of research examines psychophysiological variables such as heart rate, blood pressure, brain waves, arousal and attention levels. It is suggested here that different physiological

processes have implications for neurotransmission and psychological impairment.

- A third area of research examines **psychopharmacological inducements** — such as cocaine, alcohol, amphetamines and so on — and their effects on human behaviour, especially criminal behaviour.

In a number of these areas it is now possible to conceive of some kind of biological 'corrective' being developed to prevent criminal behaviour from occurring. This could take the form of simply removing the source of the problem (e.g., eliminating lead from one's living environment, banning alcohol sales), or in the case of more complex responses, regulating the biochemical and physiological operations of the body through appropriate treatment measures (e.g., drugs designed to restore hormonal equilibrium or ensure a regular heart rate).

Whether it be efforts to re-jig the biological balance (e.g., through drug therapy), or to restore a psychological norm or balance (e.g., through parenting classes) a key emphasis in positivist approaches is that of self-control. In other words, efforts will be made to reinforce external and internal regulatory measures so that individuals will conform to the conventional norms of behaviour.

Critique

Within the positivist aegis then, there exists a plethora of explanations concerning what factors predispose individuals to commit crime. However, virtually all such explanations are concerned with 'street crime', predominantly violent crime, or juvenile delinquency of one type or another. The reasons behind white-collar crime and state crime are left untouched by positivist criminology.

Furthermore, much positivistic research has taken subjects from incarcerated populations, or those adjudicated as criminal by the law. This poses a problem of the conflict of definitions: the reasoning is that, because criminality is the result of psychological or biological abnormality, someone who is adjudicated as criminal by the judicial process must by psychologically or biologically abnormal (Empey, 1982). Thus all incarcerated populations are, by definition, either psychologically or biologically deficient. This problem results from what is known as **circular reasoning** where A (criminality) is supposed to be caused by B (impairment), and all those in prison are tested as impaired, and are by definition criminal. Hence impairment is assumed to cause criminality. This conclusion is false for a number of reasons; among these are:

- it is not clear whether criminality causes impairment, or impairment causes criminality (problem of the direction of causality)
- it is not clear if the imprisonment was the cause of impairment (confounding variable)
- it is not clear whether those in the general population who have the same impairment also offend (i.e. are the two factors simply correlated, or is there a causal connection?).

All explanations of this type thus face considerable challenges in proving the causal connection between biological and psychological factors and criminal behaviour. These challenges concern defining what exactly is being measured (the specifics of a psychological malfunction or chemical imbalance, for example), and designing and undertaking rigorous studies where extraneous variables are excluded. That is, the studies must really measure what they say they measure, and there must be no other plausible explanations for what the study found.

While the problem of circular reasoning outlined above can be eradicated through appropriate use of control groups and application of scientific method, the possibility of undertaking such experiments has considerable ethical implications and they remain rare. Those that are done face considerable difficulty in matching the variables (such as age, educational attainment, employment status) of the control group with the experimental group. Unless these factors are carefully matched, the claims of the study can be severely compromised.

Many studies which purported to find biological or psychological reasons for offending have been discredited because of the inability to control all variables (Feldman, 1993). A good example of this problem is the purported connection between violence and the genetically controlled abnormal metabolism of neurotransmitters that was reported in *New Scientist* (26 February 1994). Further research revealed that compounding environmental factors could not be ruled out, and the strength of the relationship between genetics and criminality was greatly downplayed (*New Scientist*, 25 February 1995).

Much critique of positivist theory revolves around the blurred distinction between sickness and criminality. Largely undiscussed are the underlying assumptions behind definitions of criminality, or more specifically deviation from norms. If criminal behaviour is likened to a sickness, it must, like sickness, be undesirable and in need of eradication. There is an assumed consensus within positivism concerning what constitutes criminality and deviation from norms, without adequate discussion concerning whose norms are used as the benchmark for deviation.

The analogy with sickness brings further problems. There is a tendency within positivism to reduce the reasons for criminal behaviour to a single cause, either biological or psychological. It assumes that adult behaviour and personality are totally determined and reducible to single overarching factors (e.g., childhood experiences). This assumption ignores or fails to acknowledge that life is a process of continual development, renewal, change and transformation.

This reductionism to a single cause can lead to both racist and sexist conclusions. Where offending is linked to biology, the logical extension of the line of reasoning can lead to attempts to correlate certain people (e.g., Aboriginal people, poor people) with certain 'biologically determined' traits (e.g., intelligence as measured by IQ) and so to criminal offending. Without adequate discussion of the assumptions underlying positivism, the search for the causes of criminal behaviour leads inexorably to racist and unwarranted conclusions (see, especially, Gould, 1981).

Once a cause of offending has been isolated, further problems arise. The question of diagnosis, classification and treatment of offenders becomes important. How is treatment to be administered and on what criteria? Treatment may, for example, require biological 'corrections' (e.g., chemical castration) which raise considerable implications in terms of human rights and human dignity. Even where treatment seems to be relatively benign, such as enhancing parenting skills, there still may be gross assumptions concerning what constitutes adequate parenting. Because of the intrusive nature of treatment suggested by positivist theories, both the theories themselves and the suggested treatments require close scrutiny.

With identification of a biological or psychological cause of crime, positivism suggests that early detection of criminal potential is entirely possible if not desirable. This means intrusive intervention in people's lives may take place long before any crime is committed. Such intervention may be extreme, such as sterilisation, or relatively benign, such as pre-school activities in disadvantaged areas. The intrusiveness of the technique must be weighed against the positive outcomes, with each closely analysed. Do pre-school programmes or pre-natal care really affect behaviour in adolescence and beyond? While there is some evidence that this is the case, should they be conceived of as part of a crime-reduction strategy with the stigma that entails, or are they simply a normal part of society's responsibility to its citizens? Some intrusions such as sterilisation are of course unethical and should be disallowed on ethical grounds alone.

Positivism, with its focus on the scientific method, leads to the production of knowledge which by its nature is inaccessible to the general community. Common-sense understandings of ordinary people are seen as unscientific, and therefore not valid. This reduces the accountability of such professionals, and leaves little avenue for democratic participation in policy which results from positivist research. Specialised knowledge tends to entrench power in the hands of medical or para-medical professionals and other experts.

Often such experts are called upon to give evidence in court. This evidence may pertain to predictions concerning the possibility of future offending behaviour of an individual, particularly violent offending. Judges are uniquely sensitive to the concerns of the community regarding the possibility of releasing someone who is a danger to the public at large. To minimise this possibility, specialist psychiatrists or psychologists are called upon to give expert testimony regarding the likelihood of future offending. Such evidence has proved almost impossible to give with any degree of certainty.

The inability to predict dangerousness was dramatically illustrated in New York in the 1970s. A man by the name of Johnnie Baxtrom had been kept in prison after his release date because doctors argued he was dangerous and in need of psychiatric care. All psychiatric hospitals were full, so he remained in prison. Baxtrom challenged the constitutionality of his incarceration beyond the end of his sentence for assault. He won his case, and as a result 967 similarly incarcerated patients were released, all of whom were considered criminally insane.

That is, they were considered a danger to the community. A team of researchers, led by Henry Steadman, followed up each of these people after four years in order to ascertain how many had reoffended. Only 2.7 per cent of the original 967 had behaved dangerously and were either in a correctional facility or a hospital for the criminally insane (Steadman, 1973). Studies such as this pose tough questions to those who incarcerate individuals deemed to be a danger to the community beyond the term warranted by their criminal offence.

These criticisms aside, the impact of positivism has been beneficial. It did signal a shift away from hard-line classical thinking concerning individual responsibility. People can act for reasons which are outside their own control, and such factors may mitigate their responsibility for their criminal behaviour. Further, punishment must fail if it does not take account of factors which are beyond the control of an individual's free will.

Conclusion

Positivism emerged within a specific historical context which promoted the virtues of scientific reasoning over the philosophical approach championed by the classical thinkers. It was assumed that discoveries about the natural world, and natural laws, would find a counterpart within human behaviour, both individual and social. The emphasis of positivism is on the scientist as neutral observer with the task of uncovering natural laws which regulate human behaviour, including criminal offending. Specific methods, such as experimentation and survey design, are seen to be able to reveal specific causes of criminal behaviour within the individual, causes which are either biologically or psychologically determined. Once discovered, reduction of offending is seen as possible through treatment programmes aimed at ameliorating or eliminating causal agents. Sentencing should therefore be aimed at rehabilitation rather than deterrence. Further extension of investigation into individuals who are 'at risk' of offending may be seen as preferable, since offences may be prevented before they even occur.

Criticisms of positivism centre on the characterisation of criminal offending as akin to a sickness. While criminal behaviour may well be defined as deviation from society's norms, such norms are determined socially, not biologically. Further, society's norms may in fact be the norms of the dominant majority, which marginalise the norms of other social groups within society. In this way positivist research may entrench the current social order by accepting dominant understandings of 'normal' and 'deviant'. Further, positivism has a tendency to reduce the complexities of human behaviour to single identifiable causes, and to prescribe treatments which are intrusive, and in some cases unethical.

Recent writing within positivism has tended to move away from overarching generalisations concerning human behaviour. Fishbein (1990) serves as a good example of a recent theorist who seeks to establish the place of biological and psychological factors among others as the reasons behind criminal offending. She accepts, for example, the very real place of sociological factors behind offending. It is to these factors that we now turn.

Further Reading

Garland, D. (1988) 'British Criminology before 1935', *British Journal of Criminology*, 28(2): 1–16.

Lombroso, C. (1911) *Crime: Its Causes and Remedies*, Little, Brown, Boston.

Eysenck, H. (1984) 'Crime and Personality', in D. Muller, D. Blackmann, and A. Chapmann (eds) *Psychology and Law*, John Wiley and Sons, New York.

Feldman, P. (1993) *The Psychology of Crime*, Cambridge University Press, Cambridge.

Fishbein, D. (1990) 'Biological Perspectives in Criminology', *Criminology*, 28(1): 27–72.

CHAPTER 4

Strain Theory

Introduction

This chapter provides an overview of various types of **strain theory**, and includes a discussion of subcultures and the ways in which deviant or criminal behaviour is learned in interaction with others. Rather than focusing on factors relating to the individual, these types of theories are sociological in nature. That is, they point to aspects of social structure and social learning which contribute to the creation of criminal behaviour and attitudes.

While sharing many of the philosophical and political features of biological and psychological positivism, sociological approaches such as strain theory view crime as manifestations of social pathology, rather than individual pathology. For example, tension or strains are seen to be generated by society itself; they do not reside within the individual (as in the case, for example, of a person feeling strained or pressured by circumstance). The chapter discusses the two main wings of strain theory — those which place emphasis on 'opportunity structures', and those which speak about the learning of particular norms, values and subcultural attributes.

Social Context

The social context in which strain theory emerged and developed can be divided into three key periods. The first period was from the middle of the nineteenth century to the beginning of the twentieth, which saw the rise of sociology as an academic discipline. As with comparable social sciences (such as psychology), it was felt that one could apply the approaches and concepts of the natural sciences to the study of society. In particular, society itself could be studied as if it were external to the observer. As with positivism in general, most sociology presumed that there existed a consensus of values and norms across society. As such, it was supportive of the status quo. The role of the social scientist was to intervene in shaping the direction of social development by providing positive solutions to identified social problems.

The sociological method adopted at this time was one which constructed broad categorisations of different types of societies (e.g., pre-industrial, industrial), and which attempted to show how the structure of a society moulds and shapes individual behaviour. Criminal behaviour, in particular, was seen to be a manifestation of a social pathology — the outcome of something wrong in the structures and values of the society generally. Thus if we are to respond adequately to the incidence of crime, then we must go beyond measures which see it as being simply the result of individual malaise. Some type of institutional reform would be necessary if the problem were particularly acute.

The second key period in the development of strain theory was the early 1920s through to World War II. The industrial revolution had fostered the development of the professions (including sociology) and was linked to the idea of expert or technical solutions to problems such as poverty and crime. By the early decades of the twentieth century, the conceptual tools of sociology were being turned to examine problems with a specifically modern character.

In 1917 the Russian Revolution occurred, with long and lasting impact on developments in the West. A series of class struggles and armed conflict occurred throughout Europe in the early 1920s, and the example of a successful workers' revolution was creating alarm in ruling circles in the advanced capitalist countries. Within Russia itself, many people were displaced from their former positions and residences, and later, under the rule of Stalin, a series of purges were carried out which cost millions of lives.

Meanwhile, two further developments were accelerating the tendency toward crisis and war in Europe. On the one hand, one legacy of World War I was a German nation which had suffered impoverishment and deep loss of dignity as a result of the actions of the victors. As in Spain in the 1930s, and later in Italy, there also arose a strong fascist movement in Germany by the early 1930s. Simultaneously, from 1929 the Great Depression was having a devastating impact on workers and farmers in Europe, North America and elsewhere.

The developments in Europe and the newly constructed Soviet Union, combined with the dramatic changes in economic fortunes, were to lead to mass movements of people. Events such as the counter-revolutionary war in Russia, the purge of selected classes and social groups across different political systems (e.g., attacks on Jews in Nazi Germany, forced collectivisation of farmers in Russia), and the difficulties of economic survival under rampant inflation and high levels of unemployment, created large numbers of war, political and economic refugees in Europe. This led to wide-scale migration to countries such as the USA and Canada, as well as Australia and New Zealand.

A crucial question emerged within the ranks of those who were studying crime as a social phenomenon: how did the successive waves of immigration impact upon crime rates? Furthermore, the issues of unemployment and poverty were put on the agenda in a more systematic and theoretically informed manner by sociologists. These issues were particularly of interest to researchers in the USA. While such people were unlikely to suggest a Russian-style revolution as an appropriate or desirable response to the depression in the heartland of world capitalism, clear links were now being drawn between unemployment and crime. The economic position of the individual in society was now seen as an important factor in the commission of crime.

The third period of note with respect to the development of strain theory was the post-war period of the late 1940s and into the 1950s. By this time, many of the advanced capitalist countries had entered a long boom period of economic growth. People in these countries were generally optimistic about the future; living standards were rising steadily; and capitalism was indeed appearing, for many, to be the 'best of all possible worlds'. The problem, however, was how to explain persistent crime rates even in the face of apparently good general economic and social conditions. The answer, here, was to examine more closely the distribution of opportunities in society, and also the ways in which people interact with and learn from each other. As with the general orientation of strain theory, the intellectual task was to formulate concepts which would best express the social nature of crime.

Basic Concepts

The starting point for strain theory is the notion that crime is essentially a **social phenomenon** (see Chart 4.1). It is based upon a sociological understanding of individual and group behaviour, one which sees specific activity such as crime as somehow being related to and shaped by wider social processes and structures.

Rather than looking at aspects of personal psychology or individual biological traits, strain theory argues that crime is socially induced. Thus, a 'criminal' or 'deviant' is a product of a specific kind of social order. In essence, the activities and values of the offender are seen to be **determined** by wider societal forces and factors, and they have few conscious choices regarding their available social options.

Chart 4.1 Strain Theory

Definition of crime	◆ natural ◆ violation of consensus
Focus of analysis	◆ structure of opportunities ◆ nature of social learning ◆ youth subcultures
Cause of crime	◆ social strain, viz opportunity structure ◆ learned behaviour
Nature of offender	◆ determined (by) social pathology
Response to crime	◆ provide opportunity to reduce strain, resocialise offender
Crime prevention	◆ expanding opportunity and fostering healthy peer group activity
Operation of criminal justice system	◆ essentially neutral ◆ individual rehabilitation combined with social programmes

Crime tends to be defined in conventional terms. However, rather than viewing it as solely that behaviour which formally violates the legal code (as evidenced by court conviction records), this approach sees crime and deviancy in wider terms. In particular, crime is seen as ⸴ any **violation of the general consensus** of values and norms in society. Furthermore, given this definition, and given the high levels of activity which go undetected by the formal criminal justice system, it is important to measure **natural crime** by alternative means, such as victim surveys and self-report studies.

The basic proposition of strain theory is that crime is due to social disjuncture or social processes which represent a **social strain** within a society. The strains or sources of tensions are social, not individual in nature. That is, the cause of crime is located in social structures and/or value systems which in some way are socially pathological. It is this wider **social pathology** which best explains crime as a social problem.

The main focus of analysis in strain theory is on strains associated with 'structural opportunities' and 'cultural processes'. The cause of crime is often seen to lie in inadequate or inappropriate means or **opportunities** to achieve certain goals relative to other people in society. Hence this aspect or type of strain theory is sometimes referred to as 'opportunity theory'. It is argued that restricted or blocked opportunities can lead some people to pursue alternative means, including criminal avenues, to gain desired social goods.

A second broad approach examines how, through various social circumstances, people associate with others who share their **cultural understandings** regarding acceptable and unacceptable behaviour. The emphasis in this kind of approach is on how criminal behaviour is learned in social situations. Analysis is undertaken of particular **subcultures** and how norms and values are transmitted from one person to another. This type of analysis is sometimes called 'social learning theory' or 'subcultural theory'.

The response to crime according to strain theories is to **enhance opportunities** in order to reduce social strain. This can take the form of educational programmes, employment projects, and leisure and recreation outlets for particularly 'disadvantaged' individuals and groups. A related crime-reduction strategy is to **resocialise** the offender into conventional goals and means. This may involve removing them from their previous associates in order to minimise the learning and/or affirmation of deviant norms and values. Overall, the stress is to combine **individual rehabilitation** with a series of social programmes.

From the point of view of crime prevention, strain theory leans toward measures which **expand educational, employment and social opportunities,** and which **foster healthy peer-group activity.** The focus is on developing strategies and policies which involve some degree of institutional reform, rather than solely changing or modifying the individual in some way. Since deviance or criminality is related to problems faced by groups of individuals in disadvantaged situations, then the solution to crime must be to remedy the disadvantage as far as possible.

Historical Development

Contemporary strain theories have their origins in the emergence of sociology as an academic discipline and a recognised field of intellectual endeavour. One of the central figures in this process was French sociologist Emile Durkheim, who was writing around the beginning of the twentieth century. His work was of great importance in that he consistently presented analysis of society, and of social problems, in a manner which demonstrated the close relationship between social structure (the organisation of society) and the norms and values of society (social and cultural life).

Durkheim's analysis was premised upon the notion that there are 'social facts' which can be studied and used to describe social phenomena (see Lukes, 1973). These social facts are seen to be independent of the wishes or actions of individual people. While external to the individual, nevertheless a certain phenomenon has a marked impact upon their behaviour. Thus, for example, one can quantify such social facts as the distribution of population in a certain area or district, or one can ascertain the prevailing norms, rules, regulations, religious beliefs and legal codes of a society. In either case, these kinds of phenomena represent social facts, which can be measured, and which exist as independent entities in their own right.

It order to analyse a particular social phenomenon, it is necessary to acknowledge that different societies give rise to different structures, different beliefs and sentiments, and thus different behavioural patterns. In his famous study of suicide, for instance, Durkheim (1979) demonstrated empirically that suicide rates vary according to whether or not a country is predominantly Catholic or predominantly Protestant in its religious orientation. The point here is that suicide could not be explained simply or solely in terms of individualistic choices or psychological factors. It is a social phenomenon.

More generally, Durkheim employed two basic conceptual tools in analysis of society (Lukes, 1973). On the one hand, it was argued that society is structured around a particular kind of 'division of labour', with specific types of work tasks and roles. A distinction is made between **mechanical solidarity** and **organic solidarity** as indications of the division of labour. The first describes pre-industrial types of society in which individuals tend to share the same skills, work tasks, customs, beliefs and religion. The second describes an industrial society, which is far more heterogenous in terms of wealth, ethnicity, religions, beliefs, and which has a high level of work specialisation.

On the other hand, each society was said to be characterised by a particular form of **collective conscience** (or consciousness). This referred to a set of beliefs and sentiments common to a whole society which forms a determinate system. In a nutshell, what we collectively think is greater than any one individual, and the collective conscience has the feature of shaping and regulating our behaviour as an independent, powerful external force. In a society characterised by mechanical solidarity, the emphasis tends to be on rigid conformity and cultural homogeneity. Alternatively, the organic solidarity of industrial society is one in which people are linked though law and interdependence, rather than similarity of life experience.

In applying these concepts to the specific area of criminology, Durkheim was able to argue that the nature of the society in which one lives will determine the manner in which deviants will be dealt with (see Inverarity, Lauderdale and Feld, 1983). A society with mechanical solidarity tends to generate **repressive justice**, which reaffirms the common beliefs and values by distancing the deviant from the wider collectivity. Conversely, a society with organic solidarity tends to generate **restitutive sanctions,** which aim to restore the social disruption by reintegrating the deviant back into the network of interdependencies.

Fundamentally, the organisation of society as shaped by its division of labour and its collective conscience will determine the nature of crime and the regulation of criminal behaviour. Durkheim argued that where you have an unhealthy division of labour (e.g., one based upon force not choice) or an unhealthy regulation of the collective conscience (e.g., norms not well established) then there is greater likelihood of widespread crime.

A normal, healthy division of labour occurs where occupational relationships are in accordance with individuals' aptitudes. In such a situation, two potential types of deviant can be identified: the biological deviant (who is impossible to predict or prevent), and the functional rebel (who acts as a constructive force for limited social change). Where there is an unhealthy or pathological division of labour, there will be conflict between the individual and the social. That is, it will be difficult to regulate the behaviour of individuals in a society under such circumstances.

Societies vary in their ability to impose social regulation, and this is due in part to the nature of the division of labour. The collective conscience may not be developed sufficiently, or may be skewed in some way, and this can affect behaviour as well. The general condition of society (not the individual) may be one where norms and values are in flux or even partially destroyed. We may thus have a situation in which shared beliefs and values have broken down, and where moral guides to and constraints on behaviour have weakened.

Applying these ideas to the specific area of crime and deviancy, it is argued that a healthy society is one which is characterised by a collective conscience which regulates behaviour smoothly. An unhealthy society is one in which values are not well established, or where they work against the aims of integration and regulation (see Taylor, Walton and Young, 1973).

Durkheim drew a distinction here between 'anomie' and 'egoism', both of which revolve around social norms. In its more restricted sense, the concept of **anomie** refers to a lack of social regulation in which the unrestricted appetites of the individual conscience are no longer held in check: we have a state of normlessness in which society fails to impose norms which inhibit such behaviour. Alternatively, an unhealthy society may be characterised by **egoism**, a situation in which value has been placed on the unrestricted pursuit of individual desires. The problem in this instance is that the norms themselves can produce deviant behaviour.

The importance of Durkheim as a founding thinker within the strain theory tradition is that he established that crime is essentially a social phenomenon. It is inextricably related to the nature of society itself. And criminality is thus a product of a specific kind of social order.

Moreover, it was Durkheim who emphasised that crime is due to social disjuncture or social strains in a society. These are linked to both the division of labour (later seen in terms of opportunity structures) and the collective conscience (later seen in terms of cultural norms and learned behaviours).

Crime and opportunity

These themes were picked up by later theorists in several different ways. In the 1920s and 1930s, for example, Shaw and McKay (1942) explained crime in terms of **social disorganisation** theory. The main focus of their work was on the links between a particular kind of urban environment, and the nature and extent of crime associated with this. More specifically, the researchers were interested in undertaking a form of 'social ecology' which examined crime in terms of the changing composition and settlement patterns of the city.

Based in Chicago, Shaw and McKay were writing at a time of great change. The political turmoil and economic hardship experienced by many people in Europe translated at a practical level into mass migration to other parts of the world and, in particular, to the USA. Shaw and McKay were interested in the way in which the successive waves of immigration were linked to the incidence of crime in American cities. Accordingly, they studied the settlement patterns of migrants, noting the movement first into the spatial grid of the inner-city neighbourhoods and then into outer-city areas.

The process of settling into a new country was accompanied by high levels of chaos and tension, and whole communities were characterised as being in a constant state of change, flux and social disorganisation. Shaw and McKay examined documents relating to the life histories of juvenile offenders in these areas. They found that crime tended to be associated with particular neighbourhoods, and that it flowed from the cyclical process of social change involving shifts in basic social organisation, toward disorganisation and reorganisation. They argued that delinquency can be viewed as part of the natural process of migrant settlement, because customary social controls that normally produce conformist behaviour are disrupted in such circumstances.

To put it differently, Shaw and McKay believed that behaviour is regulated via customary social norms and values. In a situation of high social disorganisation, characteristic of concentrated immigrant settlements in the inner city, young people are not subject to the same kinds of controls that customarily produced conforming behaviour in their country of origin. Furthermore, young people in these circumstances will also tend to associate with like-minded individuals who are sharing the same kind of transitional experiences. Since the neighbourhood is in a state of flux, the behaviour of such young people will tend to also include delinquent acts (see Shoemaker, 1984).

While Shaw and McKay initially concentrated on the issue of a disorganised and transient population, the impact of the Great Depression prompted them to refine their analysis. They began to speak not only of the link between immigration, settlement patterns and crime. They also acknowledged the social strains caused by poverty and unemployment. Economic deprivation meant that, even where mainstream goals had been internalised, people were denied opportunities to achieve those goals. Thus a depressed and stratified economic structure could engender conditions which lead to a greater incidence of crime.

While depressed economic conditions, and overall diminished job opportunities, seem to provide a reasonable explanation for some types of criminal activity, how are we to explain the incidence of crime in periods of economic growth? This was the dilemma facing sociologists and criminologists in the 1950s.

The first two decades after World War II were characterised by low unemployment levels and high standards of living in the advanced capitalist countries. It was a time of general economic prosperity. Politically, the 1950s was stamped by the contours of the Cold War into which the two superpowers — the USA and the Soviet Union — were locked along with their allies. This manifested itself in virulent anti-communist campaigns in the West, such as the public attacks on the left by the US House Committee on Un-American Activities led by Senator Joe McCarthy, and in Australia the attempts by the Menzies Government to ban the Communist Party of Australia. It was a time of general political conformity.

It was in this climate that Merton (1957) sought to offer an explanation for the continued existence of crime in the USA. In seeking to explain the prevalence of crime, he embraced the notion that crime rates are related to society's ability to establish norms that regulate the behaviour of the populace. Merton argued that crime can be understood in relation to two main variables: the **culturally defined goals** of a society; and the **institutionalised means** whereby one can attain these goals. Mal-integration occurs when there is a disjuncture between the cultural goals and the institutional means.

Merton argued that all individuals basically share in the same cultural goal — the American Dream of wealth, status and success — but they have different institutional means available to them. In particular, some people experience blocked opportunities, and thus are unable to achieve their goals through normal or legitimate means.

In such circumstances, people are perceived as having the capacity to make meaningful choices as to how to negotiate their futures. That is, depending upon the opportunities available to them, people decide to accept or reject the cultural goals, and to accept or reject the institutional means to attain commonly accepted goals. The decisions one makes are determined or shaped by one's position or status in society. For example, those people at the lower end of the socio-economic ladder will experience a greater likelihood of blocked opportunities than those from better-off or wealthy families. This has an impact on behaviour.

Merton developed an abstract typology of responses to the means/ends equation. The typology described individual adaptations to goals and means. Using contemporary examples, we can say that people can respond in five different ways to the structure of opportunities available:

1 **Conformism:** those who accept the culturally defined goals (e.g., financial success) and the institutionalised means of attaining them (e.g., education).

2 **Innovation:** those who accept the culturally defined goals, but who lack the institutionalised means to attain them. They therefore resort to innovative means to attain the goals, such as turning to crime (e.g., robbing a bank).

3 **Ritualism:** those who accept the culturally defined goals, but who know they cannot attain them. Nevertheless, they continue pursuing institutional means (e.g., staying at school when no jobs are available), regardless of the outcome.

4 **Retreatism:** those who reject both the culturally defined goals and the institutionalised means of attaining them. They retreat from society in varying ways (e.g., substance abuse).

5 **Rebellion:** those who substitute their own cultural goals and institutionalised means in place of the conventional goals and means in society. They create their own goals and means of achieving them (e.g., ecologically sustainable hippie lifestyle).

From the point of view of strain theory, the choices available to people reflect problems stemming from the structure of the society itself. That is, it is the relationship between cultural goals and institutional means which ultimately determines the kinds of opportunities and choices which are available to different groups of people.

Crime and culture

The structure of opportunities constitutes one part of the criminal behaviour puzzle. The other part, according to some theorists, is the ideas that people hold regarding what is acceptable or not acceptable behaviour. Specifically, attention was directed to issues of **culture** and the ways in which young people in particular learn certain ways of doing things and certain attitudes towards others.

The work done by Sutherland and Cressy (1974), for example, was directed at explaining the nature and development of youth subcultures. They argued that crime was cultural in nature, in the sense that it is **learned behaviour**. People in particular neighbourhoods, or particular social situations, learn about criminal behaviour by interacting with other people. The most significant interaction occurs within intimate personal groups, which of course includes peer groups.

Sutherland and Cressy developed the concept of **differential association** to describe a process in which behaviour is differentially associated insofar as some individuals will associate with carriers of criminal norms, while others will not.

They discussed the process which occurs when a criminal association does take place. The learning of criminal behaviour includes:

- the techniques of committing a crime (e.g., how to hot-wire a stolen car)
- the motives, drives, attitudes and rationalisations associated with crime (e.g., stealing only Porsche cars, because 'the owners can afford it anyway')
- definition of the legal code as favourable or unfavourable (e.g., regarding the legal code relating to car theft as unfavourable, since people have car insurance anyway).

Differential associations may vary in frequency and duration, priority and intensity. Those persons who become delinquent or persistent offenders do so because of a greater number of definitions favourable to violation of the law over definitions unfavourable to violations. This in turn is shaped by group interaction. For example, an individual may associate with a delinquent group, and then later change that orientation by associating with a non-delinquent group.

The essential point of the theory is that criminal behaviour is learned. Because learning takes place in the context of specific types of group formation, and particular types of definitions of behaviour and attitudes, the issues of peer-group pressure and offending cultures are seen as of central importance.

The idea that people learn to associate certain classes of conduct, either legal or illegal, with the group's approval or disapproval, has obvious links to analysis of subcultures *per se*. That is, deviant or criminal behaviour is collective in nature, and is based on shared experiences and perceptions. From within the strain theory tradition, various writers have argued that the strain between cultural goals and institutional means is reflected in specific class cultures.

Albert Cohen (1955) argued that working-class subcultures can be seen as a product of a conflict between working-class and middle-class cultures. That is, such a subculture is an alternative cultural system which develops due to the blocked opportunities and low self-esteem experienced by working-class young people. Instead of measuring 'success' in conventional terms, then, the group focuses on alternative goals that are more directly related to their own class experiences. Whereas Merton's typology spoke of the disappointed individual, Cohen saw crime and delinquency in terms of collective behaviour associated with the different aspirations, expectations and lived experiences of two different class groupings.

Going one step further, Cloward and Ohlin (1960) put forward the view that in fact all classes have the same basic cultural goals (wealth, success, security), but that the working class as a class is disadvantaged in gaining these desired ends. Crime is indeed collective in nature (you learn from your peers), and some groups of working-class children who consider their opportunities to be blocked will adopt criminal or alternative opportunity structures as a result. In other words, illegitimate opportunity structures will develop in those situations where the culturally defined goals are still sought, but legitimate opportunities are blocked or absent. The issue here is not a conflict between middle-class and working-class cultures, but the relationship of certain subcultural practices to specific class backgrounds (i.e., a sense of injustice at the lack of opportunities).

Other explanations of subcultural form were provided by both Matza (1964) and Downes (1966). These writers argued that working-class young people neither rejected nor inverted the dominant culturally prescribed values of society. Instead, they saw working-class youth subcultures as simply accentuating particular 'subterranean values' (risk, adventure, fun) which are part of normal society, but which are sometimes taken too far. In response to restricted access to opportunity, the response of young people is to resort to forms of 'manufactured excitement' of their own.

Contemporary Examples

The appeal of strain theory is that it attempts to provide a sociological explanation for the causes of crime. As we have seen, crime is usually related to blocked opportunities, combined with the activities of particular subcultural groups.

In Australia, the strain theory perspective has regained prominence as many different groups — social workers, criminologists, youth and community workers, psychologists, medical practitioners, teachers — have argued that there exists a strong link between high youth unemployment and criminal activity. Most of the contemporary discussion emphasises the impact of blocked employment or educational opportunities on certain groups of young people (e.g., indigenous young people, low-income youth, young homeless), and the cultural effects of such blocked opportunities in terms of peer-group association and activity.

The relationship between unemployment and crime has been analysed in terms of gender, which shows that high unemployment among females is not mirrored in the female crime figures which remain low, although most female offenders are unemployed at the time of the arrest. As Alder (1986) put it, 'unemployed women have got it heaps worse'. The relationship has also been explored from the point of view of ecological analysis insofar as urban areas experiencing high rates of unemployment tend to have higher crime rates. Furthermore, rural areas hit by recession, and where unemployment has particularly affected indigenous people, have shown a greater propensity to exhibit social features such as anti-social and self-destructive behaviour (Wilson and Lincoln, 1992).

Recent comment by Braithwaite and Chappell (1994) has focused on the dual nature of the unemployment–crime nexus. On the one hand, it is argued that in general there is a strong causal relationship between unemployment and crime. On the other hand, there is also a causal relationship between crime and unemployment. Unemployment can cause crime when people make their living primarily in the criminal or illegal economy, and thus end up forging all of their key friendships and 'business' relationships and contacts in the underground economy. The result is that such people are virtually excluded from the competitive labour market due to their prior associations and lack of interaction with conventional groups and institutions.

As we shall see, a number of elements of 'strain theory' are also apparent in other perspectives as well. For example, the notion that there are distinct criminal subcultures is an important component of republican theory.

Critique

Strain theory focuses almost entirely upon working-class crime. Despite understanding the need to gauge levels of crime not reported to police within communities, strain theorists largely accepted the 'shape' of the official crime statistics, namely that the majority of offences are perpetrated by the working class. An exception to this was Sutherland (1983), who undertook ground-breaking work in the area of white-collar crime. The majority, however, accepted that the crime in working-class neighbourhoods was that which needed explaining and eradicating.

This reflected an acceptance of a consensus of values in society. Ultimately all people in society wanted to achieve the same goals and share the same lifestyle (again there are exceptions to the general view; see, for example, Walter Miller, 1958). In this way, strain theory accepts the status quo. Rather than seeing the goals and aspirations of society as moulded by those in positions of power, strain theory sees such aspirations as a genuine consensus of values. Others argue that this is not necessarily the case at all. The acceptance of the genuine nature of the consensus is subject to challenges today, for example, by many churches, which argue against the materialistic nature of the American Dream. Still others argue against the notion of any consensus by looking at entrenched conflicts of values and interests, as indicated for example in the work of Marxist, feminist and radical environmentalist writers.

The concept of a general social consensus has several consequences. First, it denies pluralism of values in society. By definition, since there is consensus, a conflict of values must mean that one group's values are wrong. Second, strain theorists tended to accept that the gender roles in society were part of this consensus. Working in the 1950s, Cohen, for example, felt that the major strain in the lives of young women was the tension associated with wanting an ideal husband (Naffine, 1987). It did not occur to him that the roles of young women in the 1950s were imposed, or that, given the choice they might have a genuine desire to pursue a career outside the home. Furthermore, Cohen's view was distinctly middle-class, since many working-class women needed to work to bring money into the family home. In working-class areas the strain of unemployment could be as great on working-class women as on their male counterparts.

It can also be argued that by accepting the status quo, in terms of 'core values', strain theory fails to take account of structural inequalities. By this is meant the way the capitalist system by its very nature renders some people 'marginal' and so criminalises their activities. As theories in later chapters suggest, the system itself can be responsible for labelling some people and their activities criminal, while leaving alone other individuals whose activities are equally, or even more, harmful to society as a whole. The process of criminalisation is such that only those who challenge the status quo are labelled as criminal.

Without tackling issues relating to the inequalities of the system itself, some argue that strain theory simply attempts to adapt the individual to a system where structurally he or she has no place. Furthermore, there is often in-built resistance to this kind of change. Periodically, for example, the system will actively react against any (limited) attempts to 'adapt' marginalised groups and to provide them with equal opportunity. A good example of this 'reaction by the system' or 'backlash' is shown by the eventual collapse of the 'War on Poverty', a major initiative by the Kennedy, and later the Johnston, administration in the USA. The aim of the initiative was to empower the poor in order to enable them to assimilate into the opportunity structure of American society. Part of the reason for the lack of effectiveness of this programme was the resistance by those in power to the new realities created by the movement toward empowerment. While various factors led to the demise of the 'War on Poverty', including some ill-conceived programmes it spawned, the resistance by the status quo, and particularly politicians who were now faced with an organised, aggressive inner-city urban population, was certainly a major factor in sealing its fate.

Finally, it can be argued that strain theory oversimplified the link between lack of opportunity and crime. Subsequent studies have shown the link between unemployment and offending to be a very complex one. There are also numerous additional factors, such as attachment to school, family and peers who also offend, which are not accounted for in many of the theories discussed above. While there may indeed be some generalised strain which underlies offending, how this affects individuals, and why some individuals respond with offending behaviour and others do not, is not explained adequately by strain and subculture theories. Having said this, these theories did highlight aspects of offending that were clearly absent from psychological and classical perspectives. They raised the level of debate away from a focus on the individual, to the influence society has on the behaviour of the members of the working class who offend. In doing so it established a strong link between societal context and the nature of criminal or deviant activity. Furthermore, it recognised that criminal activity for those who lack opportunities is meaningful for those involved, given their reduced opportunities and/or peer-group supports. Finally, it opened the way for more progressive reforms politically, and against knee-jerk punitive approaches or intrusive psychological rehabilitation.

Conclusion

From a strain theory perspective, crime is seen to be more a matter of 'normal' people in 'abnormal' situations, rather than disturbed individuals acting out their pathology (Gibbons, 1979). This is clearly a sharp break from individualistic perspectives which locate deviant behaviour squarely in the choices or defects of each offender. These theories took as a base the sociological concepts of Durkheim, which steered them away from looking at individual characteristics, towards concepts such as anomie and social solidarity which could not be reduced to an individualistic frame of reference.

Within the aegis of strain theory there is a wide range of perspectives that share some similarities, yet also clearly differ in their detail and emphasis. Early theorists such as Shaw and McKay emphasised the disorganisation of the poor and lack of cohesive identity which lead to offending. Later theorists, such as Merton, emphasised the strain between goals and means, and the way criminal means would be used to attain goals in the absence of legitimate avenues, such as access to employment and career. Sutherland and Cressey shifted attention to the interaction between individuals which leads to offending behaviour, and looked to the way criminal associations supply the techniques, motivation and rationalisations necessary to act criminally.

Subcultural approaches, such as the work of Cohen, and Cloward and Ohlin, took association between individuals a step further and emphasised the formation of subcultures as a response to the lack of opportunity supplied by society to working-class youth.

The relationship between lack of opportunity, alienation and criminal behaviour is, if anything, more important in the current economic climate. Levels of youth unemployment are high, and the inequalities between rich and poor continue to grow at an alarming rate. If strain theorists are right then the levels of youth crime, and levels of gang formation, should also increase. While studies reveal relatively little in the way of organised criminal gang activity within Australia, and reasonably stable youth crime rates (see Cunneen and White, 1995), the underlying conditions themselves are cause for concern.

Strain and subcultural theories saw movement of analysis of criminal behaviour away from concentration on the conditions of the offender, to the circumstances of criminalisation itself — that is, crime as a social process in response to the inequalities in society. What was left unchallenged was the legitimacy of basic structures of society, and the way society itself influenced the way some activities were criminalised, and others not. This 'labelling process', the process of being seen as criminal, is the subject of the next chapter.

Further Reading

Cloward, R. and Ohlin, L. (1960) *Delinquency and Opportunity: A Theory of Delinquent Gangs*, Free Press, Chicago.

Cohen, A. (1955) *Delinquent Boys: The Culture of the Gang*, Free Press, Chicago.

Merton, R. (1957) *Social Theory and Social Structure*, Free Press, New York.

Shaw, C. and McKay, H. (1942) *Juvenile Delinquency and Urban Areas*, Chicago University Press, Chicago.

Sutherland, E., and Cressy, D. (1974) *Criminology*, Lippincott Company, New York.

CHAPTER 5

Labelling Perspectives

Introduction

The aim of this chapter is to discuss how **labelling perspectives** view issues relating to crime and criminality. Borrowing conceptually from sociological approaches such as 'interactionism', the labelling perspective introduces us to the idea that to understand crime we have to explore both objective and subjective dimensions of the criminal justice experience.

In the previous chapter we examined how strain theory explains crime in terms of blocked opportunities and cultural or learned behaviour. One of the hallmarks of positivist criminology, whether it be biological, psychological or sociological, is that crime is basically seen *as a given*. That is, it is assumed that crime exists 'out there' in the real world, and that all we have to do is record it, through classifying behaviour and searching for determining causes. Such criminology assumes that much criminal behaviour is due to forces beyond our control (genetic, psychological, institutional). Generally speaking, it is further assumed that there is a consensus in society regarding core values and norms, and that the role of the social scientist is to provide an objective investigation into the factors which underpin why certain people commit crime.

The labelling perspectives challenge this view of crime and criminal justice. Instead, it is argued that crime is a **social process**. As such, it involves different perceptions of what constitutes 'good' or 'bad' behaviour (or persons), and particular power relationships which ultimately determine what (or who) is deemed to be 'deviant' or an offender. Crime is not an 'objective' phenomenon, it is an outcome of specific types of human interaction.

Social Context

The development of labelling perspectives within criminology was due to a combination of the influence of certain intellectual currents, and wider changes occurring in society generally. We shall explore the intellectual foundations of labelling theory in greater depth further on in the chapter. For now, suffice it to say that a central concern of the 'new deviancy' theory was the issue of subjective meaning, and how this impinged upon objective social relationships. Or, to put it differently, the concern was with how human beings actively create their social world.

Part of the impetus to the rise of labelling perspectives lies in the changes which were taking place in the advanced capitalist countries, particularly the USA, in the 1960s and 1970s. The dominant image of the 1950s was one of shared collective interests, consensus on core values, economic prosperity for everyone, and standards of 'deviance' and 'conformity' which were clear for all to see. The social order was thus viewed as monolithic — everyone was dedicated to common goals, and had a stake in the status quo. Any problems which did arise were able to be dealt with through adequate research and application of appropriate technical responses and programmes.

By the 1960s, however, the presumed consensus was disintegrating. The phenomenal popularity of Elvis Presley in the 1950s signalled a new cultural form which was premised upon energy, separateness, novelty and rebellion. The birth of rock-and-roll music in the post-war period saw the creation of a leisure-based 'youth culture', one which generally represented a sharp break with the existing 'culture' of the parents. Music, fashion, language, appearance and activities — all were forged in manner which departed from existing conventions (and yet which in the end were linked to the creation of new youth-related and commercialised conventions). 'Deviancy' in the youth cultural revolution was consciously perpetrated and, simultaneously, hotly contested by the young themselves.

If conventional family relations involving the generations were undergoing massive change, so too they were put under pressure by the public campaigns of women, and gay men and lesbian women, to have their collective needs and human rights acknowledged in society. The Second Wave of feminism, in the form of a militant Women's Liberation Movement, actively challenged traditional, conservative notions of the female role and place in society. Similarly, conventional ideas regarding sexuality and sexual preference were subject to increasing analysis and condemnation by feminists and by gay and lesbian activists. Conflict went to the heart of mainstream society, and in particular, the basic assumptions concerning the 'American way of life'.

The idea of a uniform social consensus was further sundered by the coming to prominence of the civil rights movement. The radicalism of Malcolm X and Martin Luther King Jr, and the dream of creating a more just, equal and free society for African Americans, were crucial components in a mass social movement for fundamental social transformation. The movements for equal rights, and indigenous rights, were echoed in Australia with the establishment of the Aboriginal Tent Embassy on the lawns of Parliament House in 1970. People of colour, native people and migrant groups could no longer be easily silenced, nor could their demands be ignored. Social division was now on the political agenda.

The breakdown of convention, and the elevation of social difference to cultural and political prominence, was further entrenched through the fierce public resistance to the Vietnam War, particularly among the young, in a number of countries and especially in the USA and Australia, where conscription into the conflict was an ever-present reality for young people. The events of May 1968, in which students and then workers took to the streets of Paris and paralysed France for a period of weeks, underscored the fact that social change was unavoidable and was happening here and now.

One consequence of these great movements for change and reform was that social scientists started to rethink their conceptions of society, social order and deviancy. Society was now seen as **pluralistic** in nature, made up of a number of diverse interest groups and classes. It was not immutable, but subject to constant pressures to change.

Furthermore, what was deviant one day might not be the next. Likewise, what one group thought of as deviant might well be acceptable to another. Social reality thus is contingent — how we view the world very much depends upon where we are situated within that world.

One of the characteristics of the social movements of the time was the emphasis and stress placed upon human creativity, liberation and free will. The libertarian ethos emphasised choice and rebellion over passive acceptance and conformity. Translated into social theory terms, this broad orientation was reflected in the idea that **meaning** is part of an ongoing social process. Social life is not fixed and immutable. It is made up of constant interactions between groups. The meaning we give to events and situations depends upon how we negotiate definitions of each event or situation.

Basic Concepts

Labelling perspectives generally start from the premise that crime and criminal behaviour is a **social process** (see Chart 5.1). The focus of concern is with the nature of the interaction between 'offender', 'victim' and criminal justice 'officials'.

What counts as a 'crime' is, in essence, determined by the activities of the criminal justice system and its officials. That is, the definition of particular behaviour or an individual as criminal depends upon who

Chart 5.1 Labelling Perspectives

Definition of crime	• defined by social action and reaction • conferred by those who have power to label
Focus of analysis	• relationship between offender and those with power to label
Cause of crime	• stigmatisation and negative effects of labelling
Nature of offender	• determined (by) labelling process
Response to crime	• diversion from formal system
Crime prevention	• decriminalisation • radical non-intervention
Operation of criminal justice system	• system should not have stigmatising effect • greater tolerance and minimal intervention

does the labelling. Official designations of 'crime' are thereby conferred by those who have **the power to label.**

The measurement of crime is thus really a process in which the particular actions of certain people are defined by those in power within the criminal justice system as being 'deviant' or 'criminal'. This **institutionalist perspective on crime measurement** stresses that crime is not in fact 'objective': it is shaped by the nature of interactions and selective labelling by members of the criminal justice system in their dealings with the general public.

A key area of analysis is the relationship between the offender and those who have the power to label. The consequence of this relationship, and especially of the labelling process itself, is that **stigmatisation** can occur. Negative effects can arise from labelling, such that the person labelled takes on the role prescribed in the label. In other words, if a person is branded officially as a 'deviant', 'offender' or 'criminal', then this may result in the person acting in a manner which fits the label.

In effect, the labelling perspective points to the impact of labelling on the psychological and social development of offenders. The self-concept and social opportunities of the offender are determined or influenced by the labelling process. The stigma sticks to the offender, and it affects how others see them, as well as how they perceive themselves.

One result of stigmatisation is that some persons who have been negatively labelled not only engage in further criminal, offending or deviant activity, but they also seek out or find comfort in the company of others who have likewise been cast as outsiders. Another consequence of the labelling process, therefore, is that it creates an impetus for similarly labelled people to associate with each other — generally in the form of delinquent or **criminal subcultures.**

From a labelling perspective, the potentially negative outcomes of the labelling process are seen to outweigh the necessity to intervene in the first place. That is, for young people in particular, the stigmatisation of official criminal justice intervention may well **propel them into a criminal career** for activity which, for most people, is generally transitory in nature.

The response of the criminal justice system to offending behaviour therefore should be based upon a policy of **diversion** from the more stigmatising aspects of the criminal justice system. The idea is that every attempt must be made to divert certain offenders from contact with the more formal elements of the system, and thus to reduce the chances of stigmatising them.

Less serious offences, for example, should not warrant arrest, court appearance and incarceration. Rather, the response should be based upon the principle of (radical) non-intervention, or at the least minimal intervention. In a similar vein, in order to reduce the possibility of unwarranted or unnecessary stigmatisation there may be calls to decriminalise certain 'victimless' or 'non-predatory' activities.

Overall, there is a general demand that many different types of behaviour and activity should be tolerated by criminal justice officials. The power to label is substantial, and has lasting impacts. Therefore, it should be used judiciously and only where absolutely necessary.

Historical Development

Labelling perspectives have a wide range of intellectual influences. These include social psychology, phenomenology and ethnomethodology (see Muncie and Fitzgerald, 1981; Taylor, Walton and Young, 1973).

Broadly speaking, labelling perspectives have strong links to the 'symbolic interactionist' perspective in sociology. This perspective employs concepts such as 'self' and 'symbol' in order to explain social behaviour and social action. The logic of such a perspective revolves around the diversity of individual responses to social situations (see, for example, Berger and Luckmann, 1971).

A symbol can be said to be anything that stands for something else (e.g., a badge, a gesture, a word). All human beings have to learn how to respond to different situations by accurately 'reading' the symbols around them.

The self is not a psychological concept (like personality), but refers to how people see themselves. This in turn is built through social interaction. In this sense we can talk about the 'looking-glass self', that is, that your image of yourself is simply what you see of yourself reflected in those around you (see discussion of the work of Cooley, and Mead, in Coser, 1977).

Part of human interaction involves **role-playing**. For role-playing to occur, each individual has to be able to 'take the role of the Other' — to see things as others see them. In other words, interaction can occur only because each person is able to attribute appropriate meaning to the symbols — words, gestures and so on — of the other.

But the 'self' does not simply passively respond to events and people around it. It also plays an active part in selecting how it responds. How we respond to other people in our social interactions depends upon how we **define the situation**. The symbolic nature of behaviour means that the first stage of any interaction is one of definition. When people share the same definitions, communication is likely to be straightforward and clear, and we can now interpret the significance of the interaction itself.

The taken-for-granted world may appear to us as the 'real world' which exists outside us as hard, concrete objective fact. However, in actual fact we are collectively involved in constructing reality through the use of signs and symbols which each of us generally interpret the same way. The basis of our interaction with other people is the use of **typifications** which are drawn upon as part of our recipe knowledge that we use in order to make sense of the world (Berger and Luckmann, 1971).

The first step in communication therefore is one of defining situations in a process of interaction. Sometimes situations are misinterpreted if we define them incorrectly. For example, if we see two men embracing and kissing each other, a variety of explanations may suggest themselves: it could be a greeting (at an airport), a congratulatory gesture (on a sportsground) or a love affair (in a club). What is important in terms of our behaviour is not the circumstances, but whether we have defined the situation in the same way — that is, whether we share the same definition of a situation.

From these types of propositions it is concluded that, at one level, it does not matter what the actual situation is: what matters is how we define it. For instance, a blazing light in the sky could be seen as a comet, or as a sign from a supernatural being. In either case, how we collectively define the situation will still have real consequences for our behaviour and actions.

While human beings are not passive, nevertheless how we are perceived by other people does have real and immediate effects on how we see ourselves and how we behave. This social process can be negative or positive. This has been demonstrated in work that has been done in the study of hospitals, asylums, schools and prisons.

An important concept here is that of the **self-fulfilling prophecy**. The idea behind this is that who I am is determined by who defines my reality and how this is done. People who are labelled 'stupid', 'bright', 'dumb', 'genius' and so on, will respond accordingly.

For example, in the so-called Pygmalion experiment, a group of school students was divided into two. One half of the group was publicly labelled 'slow and stupid', while the other half was told they were 'brilliant'. After a while, the school grades of the two groups began to deteriorate and to improve respectively. The argument was put forward that each group had internalised the self-concepts framed for them, and had responded to the public labels by playing the role of 'stupid' or 'brilliant' (Rosenthal and Jacobson, 1968).

It is further suggested that once a person has been labelled a particular kind of person, they are liable to be treated in a different kind of way from others who may engage in the same kind of behaviour, but who have not been so labelled. This general process can be represented as follows:

1   negative labelling
2   stigmatisation
3   new identity formed in response to negative labelling
4   commitment to new identity based on available roles and relationships.

Labelling perspectives in general are based upon this kind of processual model (see Rubington and Weinberg, 1978). In essence, this says that in association with labelling, stigmatisation occurs. A person who is stigmatised is seen by others predominantly in terms of one particular character trait or behavioural pattern, based upon the content of the initial negative labelling.

For example, the negative label may be 'juvenile delinquent' because the person was alleged to have stolen an item from a shop. The person becomes subject to stigmatisation when the negative 'juvenile delinquent' label becomes a master public definition of 'what they are like'. Everyone then responds to the person according to the terms of the label, regardless of what the person may now actually be doing with their life, and with little regard for the other positive qualities they possess. Over time, if the stigma attaches, then you may commit yourself to the new label and hence change your identity to fit the label. Within labelling perspectives, labelling is usually seen to produce negative consequences.

The broad interactionist perspective thus focuses on how people typify one another (e.g., as 'mentally ill' or 'young offender'), how people relate to one another on the basis of these typifications, and what the consequences are of these social processes (Rubington and Weinberg, 1978).

From the point of view of criminology, the influence of perspectives which wish to examine the 'social construction of reality' is manifest in two major questions:

- How do individuals come to be labelled deviant or criminal?
- How do individuals come to be committed to a deviant or criminal label, and ultimately, career?

Deviance or criminality is not something which is simply objectively given (as in the positivist framework); it is subjectively problematic (Plummer, 1979). Thus, for example, it can be argued that deviancy itself can be the result of the interactive process involving individuals and the criminal justice system.

In early versions of the labelling perspective, it was asserted that deviancy is not an inherent property of behaviour. Rather, deviancy is something which is conferred upon an individual by society. According to Becker (1963: 9), the impact of **social reaction** to certain types of behaviour or particular categories of people is crucial to explaining the criminalisation process:

> social groups create deviance by making the rules whose infraction constitutes deviance, and by applying those rules to particular people and labeling them as outsiders. From this point of view, deviance is not a quality of the act the person commits, but rather a consequence of the application by others of rules and sanctions to an 'offender'. The deviant is one to whom the label has successfully been applied; deviant behaviour is behaviour that people so label.

The focus of his research was people considered to be on the margins of society, and on the margins of conformity (e.g., the homeless, 'alcoholics', prostitutes). According to Becker, the key reason why these people are placed on the 'outside' is because their particular behaviour has been labelled deviant by more powerful interest groups in society. There is nothing in the behaviour itself which is necessarily 'deviant' or 'conformative': it only becomes so in the actual process of labelling.

The importance of this view was twofold: first, it called into question the social nature of the definitions of crime by alerting us to the variability in human behaviour; and second, it showed us that 'crime' is as much as anything a matter of who has the power to officially label behaviour or persons as criminal (see Cicourel, 1976). According to labelling theorists, the use of self-report and victim surveys indicates that crime and victimisation are ubiquitous — that is, that these are found in all social classes and across gender and ethnic boundaries. Hence, the crucial issues are who gets labelled by whom, and what are the consequences of this labelling.

One explanation of the importance of labelling on people's future behaviour was provided by Lemert (1969). In this case, the main concern is with the social-psychological level of analysis. That is, we want to know the reasons why a person engages in a deviant act to begin with, and furthermore, what maintains their commitment to deviant activity. According to Lemert, in order to describe the process of labelling we can distinguish between primary deviation and secondary deviation.

Primary deviation refers to initial deviant behaviour. The proposition here is that most of us at some stage in our development engage in activities regarded as deviant (e.g., underage drinking, smoking cannabis, petty shopstealing), but we do so because of a wide variety of social, cultural and psychological reasons. Little is said about the primary causes of deviant behaviour, except that these are wide-ranging and involve a multitude of individual factors. However, the important point is that at this initial stage of deviation, when people engage in deviant activity they do not fundamentally change their self-concept. That is, the individual's psyche does not undergo a symbolic reorientation or transformation (e.g., we do not see ourselves as a drunk, a pothead or a thief). There is no change in identity, and deviance is seen as nothing more than a passing event.

The main focus of labelling perspectives is with **secondary deviation**. This occurs when the individual engages in some kind of primary deviation (e.g., shopstealing) and there is an official reaction to that behaviour (e.g., the police are called in). If a person is apprehended by the police, they may be officially labelled as 'deviant' (e.g., 'young offender'). The individual may begin to employ a deviant behaviour or role based upon this new status, which has been conferred upon them by state officials, as a means of defence or adjustment to the overt and covert problems created by the public social reaction to their original behaviour. For example, the person may start to 'act tough' to counter ridicule from peers, taunts from neighbours and persistent surveillance by police when they go out. Secondary deviation is said to occur when, because of the social reaction to primary deviation, the person experiences a fundamental reorientation of their self-concept, and thus their behaviour.

Labelling perspectives were to have most application in the area of juvenile justice. It was argued that young people are particularly vulnerable to the labelling process, and thus more likely to respond, for good or bad, to official social reaction. Matza (1964), for example, found that juveniles generally 'drift' between the two poles of conventional and unconventional behaviour (including crime), without being fully committed to either. In the end, most young people drift towards conventional lifestyles and behaviours as their permanent pattern. However, if during the teenage years of drift there is official intervention and social reaction to specific kinds of unconventional behaviour, this may well precipitate the movement of the juvenile into a more permanent state of delinquency.

The idea that young people who are subjected to public labelling may be propelled into criminal activity or careers also features in the work of Schur. The solution, according to Schur (1973), is to adopt a policy of **radical non-intervention**. This means that we should take a hands-off attitude to juvenile offending as far as possible. Young people should be free from official intervention and they should be diverted from the formal systems of juvenile justice in order to avoid stigmatisation.

Contemporary Examples

Labelling perspectives have become an ingrained part of how we think about juvenile justice institutions and processes (see Cunneen and White, 1995). As will be explored in more detail later on, many of the core ideas of labelling perspectives have spurred further conceptual development in the areas of 'restorative justice' and 'reintegrative shaming' which are at the heart of the republican theory of criminal justice (Chapter 10).

In addition to having a major influence on perspectives such as Marxist, feminist, critical and republican criminology, the labelling approach has had a marked impact at the level of policy development. This is particularly the case with respect to young people and children. For example, diversion programmes operate in a number of Australian states and territories. These take the form of pre-court programmes, such as police cautioning schemes and Children's Aid Panels, and alternatives to court, such as Family Group Conferences, Community Aid Panels and Juvenile Justice Panels. The emphasis here is to divert the young person away from the more formal aspects of the criminal justice system, and therefore to reduce the likelihood of stigma and negative labelling.

Another example of the system response to labelling perspectives is the way in which a number of jurisdictions attempt to protect the young person from being stigmatised and penalised for the rest of their life for offences committed when they are young. This can take the form of the destroying official records once a juvenile has reached a certain age and has not reoffended. Limitations on publicity in cases heard before the Children's Court, and restrictions on the taking of bodily samples and fingerprints from children and young people, are similarly designed to keep the young person at arm's length from the official criminal justice system.

One of the more unusual applications of labelling theory is the Tattoo Removal Scheme. This was part of a young offender programme in the State of Victoria in which attempts were made to reshape the public image of certain young people. The presence of tattoos was seen as part of the problem for these young people. They were too easily branded as 'crims' or 'toughs', and this fed into a long-term scenario of heightened police intervention, offending activity and criminal careers. In order to reduce the stigma attached to these young people, the detention centres introduced a scheme whereby they could have their tattoos removed (Ross, 1985). Again, the idea here is that how 'others' respond to a person is an integral part of how people see themselves and how they behave.

Critique

One of the first criticisms that spring to the mind of the student is the fact that the labelling perspectives do not provide any explanation as to why primary deviation occurred in the first place. The theory concentrates on social reaction to deviant behaviour. While this is true, those using the labelling perspective argue that they did not in fact set out to explain why primary deviation occurred. They do not see labelling theory as a discrete theory, but rather as a **perspective**, a part of the overall picture which is able to explain the negative consequences of criminal justice intervention.

Some would argue, however, that there is a problem with focusing exclusively on crime as defined by social reaction. There are a number of crimes which are characterised by high social agreement concerning both their harmfulness and their criminality. Crimes such as rape and murder are seen to possess intrinsic qualities which make them a part of criminal law across cultures (Hagan, 1987). Focusing exclusively on social reaction with respect to such crimes would seem to distort the reality of such criminal behaviour.

So, while labelling theory seems plausible in explaining minor delinquency, there are some crimes, such as rape and murder, where the labelling perspective is less useful. It is hard to conceive of these crimes as purely defined on a subjective basis, or as simply a by-product of the confirmation of a 'criminal identity' by the state. While some serious offences, such as murder, are committed by those with an extensive history within the criminal justice system, and could be seen as a result of secondary deviation, for others murder is a first offence. It is hard in these cases to conceive of these as resulting entirely from secondary deviance.

Nonetheless, even under the terms of the labelling perspective itself, it is not always clear what gives people the capacity to reject particular labels. While some seem to succumb to labels and easily slip into deviant identities, others reject the labelling process even after repeated contexts where 'labelling' has taken place. There is extreme variability in how people respond to labels in practice. This has many implications for labelling theory, and republican theory, which we shall consider in Chapter 10. Fundamentally, labelling is unable to explain what gives one person the capacity, or the will, to reject the label, while another lacks such a capacity.

There is, then, considerable variability in how people respond to a labelling process. For example, an individual may persist in shopstealing in the absence of overt or immediate social reaction. This same individual, when caught, may cease shopstealing precisely because of the stigma of being caught (and possibly not even because they think that what they were doing was 'wrong'). Others, such as political activists, may be arrested several times for their activities, yet continue to protest. This is because they see official policy — the destruction of the rainforest or bias against homosexual lifestyle — as the deviance, not their behaviour. They actively reject the labelling of the criminal justice system. Finally, for some people the act of going through the criminal justice system and its labelling processes may be seen as an important rite of passage, as has been suggested is the case with some indigenous young people in northern Australia (see Johnston, 1991). The labelling perspective cannot explain this phenomenon on its own, since it is bound up with broader issues such as colonial relationships, and in particular the relationship of Aboriginal people to the police.

However, it is important not to oversimplify the labelling process, for example, by suggesting that it only takes one event and a person is labelled for life. The process of acquiring labels is far more subtle, and as Plummer (1979) points out labels are used by a wide range of institutions, such as family and school, which extend far beyond the reaches of the criminal justice system. By the time someone reaches the criminal justice system they may well have an entrenched set of negative labels. It may be this labelling process, not that which occurs in the criminal justice system, which determines the fate of a young person. Labelling by the criminal justice system remains important, however, since as Polk (1993, 1994) points out, it can wield only negative labels — 'graduating' from a criminal justice institution has very different connotations in mainstream society to graduating from high school.

For this reason there has been much discussion of the concept of 'net-widening' in the literature. Those with concerns about the policies which emanate from labelling theory argue that diversion, rather than turning people away from formal involvement in the criminal justice system, actually draws more people into its purview. Thus the negative labels wielded by the system reach further into the juvenile population. This is particularly the case where diversion results in greater intrusion into individuals' lives, for example, through the use of Family Group Conferences in cases of minor offending (see Alder and Wundersitz, 1994; Cunneen and White, 1995). 'Failure' in the context of such diversionary programmes can mean re-entry into the justice system, possibly with harsher penalties involved. Alternatively, this possibility is minimised where diversion involves no further action, such as in the police cautioning programme in Victoria.

The concept of diversion then needs critical evaluation. Stan Cohen (1985) argues that analysis of diversionary programmes reveals several recurrent problems. First, diversionary programmes can be more intrusive of individual lives (denser nets). Second, people may be brought into the criminal justice system where previously they would have had no contact (broader nets). Finally, while the institution of social control may change, the nature of social control may remain — that is, control which marginalises and alienates the person (different nets). For example the criminal justice agencies may be replaced by some form of medical or psychiatric control.

Ultimately, however, to explain criminality it is necessary to go beyond interaction at the level of individuals and social groups. Explanation of how power is wielded within the labelling perspective is limited to the immediate institutional level (e.g., the individual police officer), which begs analysis of the wider distributions of power in society. The analytical gaze of the labelling perspective is on the 'underdogs' and their reaction to their position, not on how they are positioned in and by the more powerful in society.

Conclusion

The labelling perspective can be seen as a radical break from earlier positivist and classical explanations of criminality and criminal behaviour. It was the first time that the notion of a consensus in society was challenged by criminologists and sociologists. With this challenge came the understanding that 'crime' and 'criminal' were themselves subjective, and depended as much on context and social reaction to give them meaning, as on the nature of the actual behaviour.

Labelling theorists were ultimately concerned with the nature of action and reaction that resulted in an individual taking on a deviant identity, and pursuing a deviant lifestyle. The central problems which inform the labelling perspectives have been usefully summarised by Plummer (1979:88) and include:

- What are the **characteristics** of labels, and their variations and forms?
- What the are **sources** of labels, both societally and personally?
- How, and under what **conditions** do labels get applied?
- What are the **consequences** of labelling?

Through these questions, crime is seen as a process. Becoming successfully labelled as 'criminal' involves taking on a negative label which is primarily applied by the criminal (or juvenile) justice system. This system is full of symbols, or cues which denote who is criminal (the one in the dock) and who sits in judgement on them (those on a raised platform, the judge or magistrate). The consequences of this process include an individual taking on a criminal identity and then acting according to the expectations of that label, i.e., committing more offences. Labelling theory has important issues to raise about the social reaction process, and how best to intervene or not to intervene.

Finally, the labelling perspective raises the importance of power and competing interests in society. This combination of the power differential and conflict of interest between some groups in society often results in the powerless being labelled as deviant. Those without power are thus more vulnerable to the labelling process. It is this issue of the power differential in society which is taken up in radical and feminist theories.

Further Reading

Becker, H. (1963) *Outsiders: Studies in the Sociology of Deviance*, Free Press, New York.

Cicourel, A. (1976) *The Social Organisation of Juvenile Justice*, Heinemann, London.

Lemert, E. (1969) 'Primary and Secondary Deviation', in D. Cressy and D. Ward (eds) *Delinquency, Crime and Social Process*, Harper and Row, New York.

Matza, D. (1964) *Delinquency and Drift*, John Wiley and Sons, New York.

Plummer, K. (1979) 'Misunderstanding Labelling Perspectives', in D. Downes and P. Rock (eds) *Deviant Interpretations*, Martin Robertson, Oxford.

CHAPTER 6

Marxist Criminology

Introduction

The labelling perspective represented a major challenge to existing orthodoxies of crime, particularly positivist assumptions regarding the straightforward existence of crime as fact. Labelling perspectives instead saw the creation of crime as an active social process. When such notions were first mooted in the 1950s and 1960s, a number of significant questions were raised which created further critical waves within criminology. For instance, why are some groups in society labelled more than others, and why are some groups more vulnerable than others to the labelling process? One answer to such questions was provided by perspectives which analysed the structure of society itself as a major source of inequality and differential treatment. These were the Marxist and broad conflict perspectives in criminology.

This chapter will focus predominantly on the **Marxist perspective** in criminology. The key aspect of this approach is that it views crime as an outcome and reflection of basic class divisions in society. The focus of analysis therefore is on power and inequality, especially insofar as these embody class-related processes associated with the overall distribution of social wealth.

The chapter begins with a brief discussion of the differences and similarities between a Marxist and a broad conflict perspective within criminology. This is followed by a review of the core concerns of Marxist writers, and the particular attention they pay to crimes of the powerful as well as crimes of the less powerful. The relationship between economic, political and criminal processes is a central theme of the chapter.

Social Context

Terms such as 'critical', 'conflict', and 'radical' have all been applied interchangeably to theories which acknowledge the importance of power and social inequality in the construction of criminality. However, the terminology can be misleading. Regardless of the label, there exist important conceptual boundaries between liberal-conflict theories and Marxist analyses of crime.

The work of social scientists in the 1950s was largely conservative in nature. Writers of the period had either overtly bought into the Cold War ideology, which defended the 'American way of life' (based upon defence of capitalism), or were afraid to voice a critical response to such ideology. Their fear was created by state-sponsored attempts to stifle social criticism which bore any resemblance at all to communist ideas, e.g., the House Un-American Activities Committee in the USA. This situation was similarly reflected in the criminological writings of the time, many of which were premised upon the idea that there was a consensual social order and a core set of societal values. Deviance meant deviation from consensus and the presumed accepted core values and norms.

This **consensus perspective** adopted a functionalist approach in which everything was conceived as operating to sustain society as a whole. We all have shared values and shared interests in society. If an individual deviates from the social norm, then we bring them back into line, thus restoring the equilibrium. In this fashion, individuals are socialised into the core set of values and common interests. This view of society characterised most of the criminological perspectives until the 1960s.

The 1960s was a period which saw sustained critique of many of the dominant social institutions. There arose a general rebellion against the norms, values and activities of mainstream society. This took the form of resistance to the Vietnam War in Australia and elsewhere, of student militancy, the rise of the Women's Liberation Movement, demands for civil rights by Black and indigenous minorities, and so on. By this stage as well, the anti-communist fervour had died down, thus permitting a more open and critical analysis of society. The readiness to adopt a conflict perspective of society is reflected in the literature of the time. It is essential to note here that a conflict perspective is not necessarily radical; it does not necessarily have to question the status quo, including the processes and institutions of society.

In the 1960s labelling theory emerged as the precursor to more profound critiques of the existing orthodoxies; it questioned the prevailing worldviews, and emphasised that not all was as it appeared to be. Indeed, some of the writers who had subscribed to the consensus view of society, such as Lemert, changed their views and began conceiving of society in **pluralistic** terms (see Pearce, 1976). Society was no longer seen as a homogenous, unitary whole, but one made up of various competing interest groups. One could identify diverse ethnic, class and religious groupings, divergent economic and political interest groups, conflicting lifestyle approaches and subcultural values.

The recognition of social difference was translated at the level of theory into several conceptions of the relationship between social interests and power. Some theories suggested that competing groups are more or less even in power, and that power is more or less evenly distributed throughout the social structure. Other theories suggested that conflict exists between different elite groups in society. These theories were based on the assumption that there will always be minority powerful groups, and the less powerful majority. The question then was, what is the nature and composition of those elites in society who are able to move up or down the power hierarchy?

Whilst these **conflict perspectives** acknowledged the competitive nature of society, they were not necessarily radical. In many cases, for example, they still assumed a basic consensus in society in relation to the appropriate means of dispute resolution. That is, a 'consensus' still existed, but this related to the **methods of resolving disagreements**, rather than to a commonality of values and interests. The basic institutions of society therefore were not challenged. The state is seen as essentially neutral and detached from the competing interest groups. An appropriate forum for change, for example, would be the existing parliamentary procedures. At any time, there is conceived to be a plurality of opportunities to move in and out of parliament. The balance of power is therefore in a constant state of flux.

Radical pluralists held a different view of competing interest groups in society. Becker, for instance, observed that there is not a constant movement up and down the power ladder. Instead, it is always the same composition of people on the bottom; it is always the poor, the black and the disadvantaged. A key concept here is that of the 'underdog' (see Pearce, 1976). According to this view, the solution to the problem was to **assist the disadvantaged** who were locked out of the process of acquiring wealth in society via piecemeal management programmes. This strategy does not challenge society's basic institutions, however: it merely tries to ameliorate the more blatant negative aspects and inequalities of the system.

Marxist conceptions of society are rooted in the analysis of **social power**. A crucial aspect of the theory is the notion that power is concentrated increasingly into fewer and fewer hands; there is a ruling or capitalist class. There is therefore not a plurality of power. Those who ultimately wield power are said to be those who own the means of production, the factory owners, land owners and media owners; it is these individuals who will dictate the nature and shape of society.

A liberal-conflict conception of the state sees it as a coordinating body within society. It recognises that conflict exists within society between competing groups, but sees the state as acting in the capacity of a neutral arbiter or umpire, independent of and not aligned to any particular class interest. Marxist theory disagrees with this view. From the more radical perspective, power is concentrated in a capitalist society and the state and its personnel are not neutral. The argument here is that if one conducts a class analysis of the state's personnel and analyses critically the state's policies, including economic and military ones, it becomes apparent that the state is far from neutral and impartial.

Ultimately, the state apparatuses (the courts, judiciary, police, prisons and community programmes) operate in the interests of capitalism. Questions were therefore raised in relation to the criminalisation process; structurally, if the state reflects the interests of capitalism and the capitalist class, then who is subject to what kind of state sanctions, and why?

Basic Concepts

Marxist conceptions of society are based upon an analysis of structural power in society (see Chart 6.1). As mentioned, those who wield decisive power in a society are those who **own and control the means of production** — the factory owners, the land owners, the media owners, the owners of information technology. An individual in class society is defined not so much by personal attributes or by reference to universalising statements regarding 'choice' and 'determinism', but by their position and opportunities in society as dictated by class forces.

To understand crime, we need to examine the actions of the powerful in **defining and enforcing a particular kind of social order,** and the activities of the less powerful in the context of a social structure within which they have fewer resources and less decision-making power than the owners of the means of production. Power is concentrated in a capitalist society, and the activities of the state reflect the interests of capital-in-general in fostering the accumulation of capital, in maintaining the legitimacy of unequal social relations, and in controlling the actions of those who threaten private property relations and the public order. The general tendency of state institutions (such as the police, the judiciary, the prisons and community programmes) is to concentrate on specific kinds of behaviour (usually associated with working-class crime) as being more 'deviant' and 'harmful' than other kinds of destructive or exploitive behaviour (usually associated with crimes of the powerful) which is deemed to be less worthy of state intervention.

The initial difficulty in determining what is 'crime' is that, if the laws reflect the interests of the ruling class, then many types of social harm may not be incorporated into the criminal law if they go against capitalist interests. In such circumstances there is a need to establish wider criteria relating to the nature of offences. Thus, for example, crime has been redefined in a broader sense to encompass any activity which interferes with **basic human rights** and causes **social injury.**

Chart 6.1 Marxist Criminology

Definition of crime	◆ human rights conception ◆ class interests
Focus of analysis	◆ economic and state crimes of the powerful ◆ economic and socio-cultural crimes of the less powerful
Cause of crime	◆ institutionalised inequality, exploitation and alienation ◆ marginalisation and criminalisation of working class
Nature of offender	◆ choices of offender dictated by structural imperative to maximise profit, or by subsistence pressures ◆ alienation
Response to crime	◆ challenge state repression of working class ◆ expose extent and nature of social harm by the powerful
Crime prevention	◆ radical democracy ◆ collective ownership and control over means of production ◆ redistribution of societal resources according to need
Operation of criminal justice system	◆ democratisation of institutions ◆ public accountability ◆ upholding of human rights ◆ law reform to reflect working-class interests

Marxist criminology directs attention away from an exclusive focus on 'street crimes' or working-class crime, toward the social harms perpetrated by the powerful within society. It attempts to demonstrate how **class situation is linked to specific types of criminality.**

According to the Marxist view, a broad distinction can be made between the crimes of the powerful and the crimes of the less powerful.

- **Crimes of the powerful** are linked to both a personal desire to augment one's wealth, and a structural imperative to get an edge in the overall capitalist economic competition. They include economic crimes (e.g., fraud, violation of labour laws, environmental destruction) and state crimes (e.g., misuse of public funds, violation of civil rights, corruption).

- **Crimes of the less powerful** stem from a combination of economic and social motivations. In the first instance, they are related to efforts to bolster or supplement one's income relative to subsistence levels; in the second, they may represent anti-social behaviour linked to varying types of socio-cultural alienation. They include subsistence-related crimes (e.g., shopstealing, work-place theft, welfare fraud) and socio-cultural crimes (e.g., vandalism, assault, public order disturbances).

The cause of crime is found in the **structure of unequal class relations** in a society. It is institutionalised inequality, the intrinsic economic exploitation of workers by the capitalist class, and the alienations associated with consumer capitalism which form the context for criminality under capitalism. In essence, where you are located in the class structure will influence the kinds of criminal activity you engage in, the propensity for you to engage in such activity, and the intensity of that involvement.

The pressures and limits of circumstance — and thus **offender choice** — vary according to class position. For example, economic forms of criminality involve different motivations, propensities, and characteristics, depending upon class background and circumstance. Crimes perpetuated by the working class are largely the result of a need to ensure economic subsistence; that is, a need to live. This situation can be contrasted with motivations based on accumulation rather than subsistence. Hence, the choices open to an offender are dictated by wider structural imperatives to maximise profit, or by immediate subsistence pressures. In addition, both individuals who are powerful and those who are less powerful in society can be deeply alienated from other members of the human community.

For a Marxist, to respond to crime is to expose the extent and nature of the social harm perpetrated by the powerful in society. It is argued that crimes of the powerful have a much greater economic and social impact than 'street crime' and working-class crimes generally, and that if coercion is to be used it should be directed at those doing the **most harm**.

Simultaneously, effort is put into challenging the manner in which the state apparatus is used to **repress the working class**. This extends to such issues as public order policing, especially of the unemployed, poor and minority groups, and the policing of class conflict in the form of union strikes and industrial disputes.

In ideal terms, the operation of the criminal justice system should be based upon full **public accountability** of each apparatus of the state (e.g., the police, courts, prisons); a genuine upholding of human rights; law reform which is designed to protect the interests of the working class (e.g., enshrining the right to strike); and a **democratisation of institutions** (e.g., by a combination of participatory involvement of citizens and election to decision-making positions within the criminal justice system).

The best form of crime prevention is one which addresses the basic problem of a concentration of wealth and power into a small number of hands in society. Crime is seen to flourish in a context of inequality and structural pressures toward capitalist accumulation and profit. Alternatively, it is felt that much crime can be eliminated or reduced through the extension of radical democracy throughout society and its institutions, the **collective ownership and control over the means of production** (e.g., various forms of nationalised industry), and a redistribution of societal resources according to **human need.**

Historical Development

Within the Marxist framework it is argued that history can be seen in terms of a succession of different 'modes of production' (see, for example, Cornforth, 1987). Each mode of production encompasses particular forces of production (tools, techniques), relations of production (lord–serf, capitalist–proletariat) and social institutions (monarchy, parliamentary democracy). Thus as we move from, for example, feudalism to capitalism, we see a shift in the mode of production across these areas: from agriculture to industry; from power concentrated among the aristocracy to power concentrated among the bourgeoisie or capitalist class; from institutions built upon the notion of the divine right of monarchs to those based upon rule of law which binds the ruler as well as the ruled.

The emergence of different modes of production has been associated with the rise of different kinds of class societies, where the central dynamic of each society is that of the expropriation of surplus from the direct producers and into the hands of those who own and control the overall means of production. For instance, in a slave-based economy (as in ancient Greece or Rome) the slave owner appropriates the surplus product of slave labour; in a feudal society the lord appropriates the surplus product of the serf; and in capitalist society the factory owner appropriates the surplus labour of the worker. Hence, the concept of economic exploitation and class struggle are central to the Marxist view.

In order to place the rise of conflict approaches and Marxist criminology into perspective, we need to acknowledge the impact of recent historical developments. In the last century and a half, for example, we have witnessed the birth and growth of a new class — the working class or proletariat — and with this the rise of distinctively working-class political organisations (e.g., trade unions) and theories (e.g., social democracy, socialism). In particular, the philosophies and analyses provided by Marxism and anarchism voiced the concerns of working people to forge a new kind of social order in which the working class, rather than the capitalist class, was in power. Revolutionary ideas were in a number of instances accompanied by actual revolutions. Some of these were successful (as in the overthrow of the Tsar in Russia in 1917), and some were not (as in France in 1871 and Germany in 1918–19).

As the twentieth century unfolded, rebellion and revolution were to be features of many peasant and working-class revolts around the world. Class conflict was an ingrained part of life for many people. Class conflict was manifest in the form of periodic economic recessions which disproportionately affected the working class (e.g., in Australia in the mid-1800s, the 1890s, the 1930s, the mid-1970s), and in the form of struggles over industrial issues (e.g., strikes and lock-outs) and political activism (e.g., with the formation of the Labor Party and later the Communist Party of Australia). It was a time of conflict, revolution and change.

Early Marxist writings on crime in the first few decades of this century discussed the ways in which crime is an outcome of the precipitating economic and social conditions of capitalism. Bonger (see Taylor, Walton and Young, 1973), for example, argued that 'criminal thought' is generated by the conditions of want and misery foisted upon sections of the working class, and is also the result of the greed which underpins the capitalist competitive process. In Australia, the work of Wood on convict history provided an important stepping stone for later radical historians who likewise saw crime as stemming from the twin evils of poverty and a savage and unjust criminal code (see Garton, 1991). However, generally speaking, these writings went against the mainstream of criminology of the time. It was not until the 1970s that Marxist criminology was incorporated into the field as a significant and popular perspective in its own right.

During the 1960s and 1970s American criminologists such as Quinney and Chambliss directly challenged the prevailing approaches in criminology. Clear distinctions were drawn between a conservative ('functionalist') and a radical ('conflict') perspective on the nature of crime and law enforcement. It was argued that where there are class divisions in a society, there you will find different capacities to determine the content of the laws of that society. The powerful ruling class will be able to shape the criminalisation process in such as way as to protect its own collective interests, which reflect the interconnection between this class and a particular state form (see Chambliss, 1975b; Chambliss and Mankoff, 1976; Quinney, 1970, 1974).

How issues are constructed, how crime is defined and how crime is responded to relates directly to one's position in the class structure. If social power is concentrated in the hands of those who own the means of production, then they will influence and generally dictate what behaviour will be defined as criminal and what will not. For example, shopstealing may be considered theft, but false advertising may be viewed as only a trade practices violation. Similarly, those with power are capable of influencing the nature of societal reaction to behaviours deemed to be socially harmful, for example, to prosecute industrial homicide as murder or simply to see it as accidental or a product of negligence.

In developing a new typology of crime, one which dealt with both crimes of the powerful and crimes of the less powerful, Quinney (1977) argued that analysis of the relationship between class, state and crime is essential. It was put forward that on the one hand, there are **crimes of domination**. These are crimes committed by the capitalist class, the state and the agents of the capitalist class and the state.

They include crimes of control (e.g., police brutality, violation of civil liberties), crimes of government (e.g., warfare, political assassination), and crimes of economic domination (e.g., pollution, price-fixing). On the other hand, there are **crimes of accommodation and resistance**, which are associated with the working class. These include predatory crimes (e.g., burglary, robbery), personal crimes (e.g., murder, assault, rape) and crimes of resistance (e.g., workplace sabotage, protests).

Criminality is intimately tied to class position, and the logic of a system which is geared toward capital accumulation rather than the meeting of social need (see Greenberg, 1993). According to Quinney (1977: 60) crime must be understood from the point of view of the political economy of capitalism:

> Those who own and control the means of production, the capitalist class, attempt to secure the existing order through various forms of domination, especially crime control by the capitalist state. Those who do not own and control the means of production, especially the working class, accommodate and resist in various ways to capitalist domination.

A crucial concept within the Marxist framework is that of **surplus population**, in that much of the existing forms of criminalisation and public concern with 'street crime' are seen to be targeted at those layers or sections of the population which are surplus to the labour market and the requirements of capitalism generally (Spitzer, 1975). A broad political economic analysis of capitalism set the scene for research and writing on more specific aspects of class conflict and class processes relating to crime.

For example, arising from concerns with class and class analysis of society, attention was drawn to the specific ways in which the activities of working-class juveniles have been subject to particular processes of criminalisation. The research of the Birmingham Centre for Contemporary Cultural Studies in England, for instance, re-examined the issue of youth subcultures from the point of view of the unequal material circumstances of working-class boys and girls (Hall and Jefferson, 1976). It was argued that class was central to any explanation of the experience of 'growing up', and that the relationship between young people and social institutions such as the school, work and legal system is characterised by different forms of class-based resistance to the dominant relations of power and domination. Certain youth subcultural forms were seen to 'solve', in an imaginary way, problems experienced by working-class young people (e.g., unemployment, educational disadvantage) which at the material level remained unresolved (Clarke et al., 1976; Brake, 1985).

From the point of view of social control and policing, various studies pointed to the ways in which the media portrayed certain types of youth subcultures, which in turn led to a form of 'deviancy amplification' (Cohen, 1973; Young, 1971). That is, the sort of public labelling which pertained to some groups of young people actually generated further 'deviant' behaviour in the group so labelled. More generally, the link was made between the actual experiences of working-class young people, culturally, socially and economically, and the manner in which the state, particularly the police, intervened in their lives both coercively (e.g., arrest rates) and ideologically (e.g., through the promulgation of 'moral panics' over their behaviour and attitudes).

By providing a structural perspective on social institutions, social processes and social outcomes, Marxist approaches argued that revolutionary or profound social transformation is needed if 'crime' is to be addressed in a socially just manner.

Contemporary Examples

In Marxist criminology the concern is to highlight the inequalities of a class society (e.g., wealth and poverty; business profits and low wages), and to show how these impact upon the criminalisation process. The powerful are seen as designing the laws in their own collective interests, while having greater capacity to defend themselves individually if they do break and bend the existing rules and regulations. The less powerful in society are propelled to commit crime by economic need and social alienation. They are also the main targets of law enforcement and wider criminal justice agencies. This is reflected in statistics which show an overrepresentation of the unemployed and poor in prisons, in police lock-ups and in the courts.

Due to a range of academic institutional factors (e.g., the rise of post-modernism as a perspective) and external political changes (e.g., the collapse of Stalinism, the demise of large Marxist-oriented political parties in the West) the Marxist perspective waned within criminological circles in the 1980s. In its stead, there developed a broader and more inclusive radical approach which we describe in Chapter 11 as critical criminology, and various liberal strands of criminology such as Left Realism and republican theory. Nevertheless, there are ongoing attempts to restate and make applicable the basic propositions of Marxist criminology today, especially in the light of the increasing polarisation of wealth and poverty on a world scale, and the further concentration and monopolisation of production.

A recent article by White and van der Velden (1995), for example, discusses the relationship between class and criminality. It is argued that there are typical patterns of crime associated with specific classes. This is because class position embodies diverse material circumstances and capacities of people to marshal economic and political resources, and this in turn depends upon one's relationship to the means of production. To put it differently, the wealth and power one has determine the kind of crime in which one might engage. Thus, the crimes of the capitalist class are linked both to augmentation of personal wealth and to attempts to secure an advantage in the process of 'doing business'. This translates into various types of criminal fraud and illegal business transactions. By way of contrast, working-class criminality is seen as based on subsistence, designed to supplement income or in some cases to be of a survival nature (e.g., theft, shopstealing). Further, working-class crime also includes a range of activities which reflect the various alienations experienced by workers, such as vandalism, rape, racist attacks and so on.

The impact of the crimes of the powerful is often diffuse, yet they affect a large number of people directly or indirectly simply because of the capacity of the capitalist to do harm on a large scale. For example, tax avoidance or environmental destruction may have a considerable social cost, but not be 'visible' in the public domain in the same way as 'street crime'. In defending themselves against prosecution, the powerful have greater social resources at their disposal with which to protect their interests. Furthermore, the sheer costs associated with investigation and prosecution of white-collar and corporate crime often make it prohibitive for the state to proceed or to cast a wide net to catch other violations similar to the exceptional few which are prosecuted. Crimes of the powerful may have significant structural effects in terms of lives lost and financial impacts. Because such crimes are usually directed in the first instance against other capitalists or against the rules governing the marketplace, they are rarely perceived by the general public as being of special interest to them personally (except in the case of events such as industrial homicide).

By way of contrast, the crimes of the less powerful tend to be highly visible and to be subjected to wide-scale state intervention involving police, welfare workers, social security officials, tax department officials, the courts, prisons and so on. A feature of relative powerlessness is that the crimes committed tend to be individualised and thus to have a discrete impact. There is usually one victim (or a few), whether personal or business or household, and the impact of the offence is limited to the actual household or person violated. The response of the major institutions in society is largely oriented toward stopping these kinds of crimes, regardless of the comparatively greater amount of damage caused by crimes of the powerful. The lack of access to resources, such as control of the media and legal experts, means that working-class people are more vulnerable to apprehension, prosecution and punishment at the hands of the capitalist state. They are exposed to societal control mechanisms in such a way that they feel the full force of the state for any transgression they might commit.

In this analysis, issues of the regulation of an 'underclass' and the policing of working-class communities is bound up with the cyclical and long-term deterioration of the social and economic conditions of life for the majority in capitalist society (see White and van der Velden, 1995). The structural conditions producing working-class crime (e.g., unemployment, cutbacks in welfare spending) are seen to have implications as well for the capacity of the state to respond other than coercively to 'street crime'. Because the state is undergoing a fiscal crisis, it cannot use welfare-type measures as a means to deal with the social fall-out arising from capitalist restructuring. Harsher 'law-and-order' strategies will thus only make worse the political isolation, socio-cultural alienation and economic immiseration of the marginalised layers of the working class, thus causally feeding the very criminality which the campaign for enhanced social control is designed to overcome.

Most criminological theories focus their attention on those crimes perpetrated by the working class. Marxist theory, however, redirects our attention away from 'street crimes' and compels us to examine crimes of the powerful. The question then arises how are we to do this, given the concentration of power and the ability of the powerful to define crime in their interests. For example, within capitalist society there are contested definitions concerning criminal behaviour (what ought to be criminalised), and instances where criminal offences exist but are not enforced (what is actually criminalised). In other words, the criminality of this behaviour is perceived as ambivalent within the capitalist system — there is uncertainty whether or not an activity is *really* criminal — and whether or not the powerful in some instances should be labelled as criminal (e.g., industrial homicide).

Alternatively, Marxists argue that there is a need to broaden the definition of crime. This entails establishing wider criteria relating to the nature of offences (see Schwendinger and Schwendinger, 1975). The definition of crime would accordingly extend to encompass any activity which interferes with one's human rights, including things such as racism, sexism and so on. Ultimately, Marxists argue that wherever economic exploitation exists, a crime has occurred.

Critique

Despite the overview given above, it is clear that Marxist criminology like many other strands of criminology has variations on a particular theme. The theme here is that capitalist exploitation leads to criminal behaviour and criminalisation of one group (the workers) to a greater extent than the powerful in society. While there are considerable areas of agreement between Marxist criminologists, there are also considerable areas of disagreement.

One concern of some Marxist criminologists relates to the use of the term 'criminal'. For example, Steinart (1985) argues that the term 'crime' has lost any useful meaning it might once have held. It is too imbued with the capitalist ethos, so that the symbolic emotive aspect of the label cannot be separated from its capitalist connotation. For this reason the term is of no use to Marxists. Rather, he argues that the term should not be used; instead, the aim of Marxist criminology should be to highlight those who are harmed the most (the proletariat) and devise policies which have the sole aim of reducing harm, without recourse to criminal law or criminal process. Such a position is labelled as 'left idealist' by those advocating Left Realism, a theory discussed in Chapter 9.

While some would see this position as extreme (including many Marxists), it does overcome a central problem in Marxist criminology, namely how to define crime. Is there a qualitative difference between the harm which is labelled 'criminal' and other sorts of harm? Traditional perspectives in criminology insist that crime consists of both 'the harm' and 'the guilty mind'. One of the problems with this definition is that 'the guilty mind' takes actions out of context, in particular a context where the powerful dictate the conditions under which the powerless act. Furthermore, harm in the white-collar area results in many cases from, not one guilty mind, but many negligent minds. For these reasons Marxist criminologists have moved away from the notion of *mens rea*, and focused on the degree of harm.

The problem then becomes what harm to define as criminal. This has led, as we have seen, to very broad definitions of what constitutes criminal activity: for example, 'any activity which interferes with one's basic human rights', or 'wherever economic exploitation exists', a crime has occurred. Some would argue such definitions are so broad that they lose any useful meaning (Cohen, 1993), and alienate wide sectors of society which may be sympathetic to the general thrust of Marxist criminology. This raises big issues for criminology generally. That is, the terms crime/non-crime are dichotomous, whereas in reality degrees of harm can be considered along a scale. Definitions of crime which are broad (or narrow) do not solve this problem of trying to squeeze a variable which exists on a continuum (such as harm) into dichotomous categories, such as criminal/not criminal.

Furthermore, Cohen (1988) argues that there is a tendency for those who argue for greater use of the criminal law against white-collar crime, such as the Marxists, to forget the problems associated with using the criminal law to curb harmful behaviour. Earlier research has mapped out a multitude of problems associated with processing people through the criminal justice system, such as the problems associated with stigmatisation and the costs involved in criminal prosecutions. There is also the issue of the politics of criminalisation. Any push to criminalise behaviour is subject to political contingencies that result in unintended consequences of reform: instead of ameliorating the harm, it may indeed exacerbate it.

Marxists have been subjected to further criticism as well. It has been argued that aspects of Marxist writing in criminology have a romantic image of the criminal as 'primitive class rebel'. These conceptualisations understate the real harm caused by such 'rebels'. Those who are the victims of anti-social behaviour, often poor themselves, suffer considerable hardship at the hands of those who commit 'street crime'.

Some Marxists have been criticised for conspiratorial overtones in their analyses regarding, for example, the direct involvement of members of the ruling class in dictating the operational activities of the police (Hall and Scraton, 1981). Critics argue that there are many examples where laws are enacted to fetter the activities of specific capitalists (e.g., insider trading). There are many laws in existence that restrain the activities of individual capitalists, which would seem to refute the Marxist argument of the criminal law always defining the activities of the powerless as criminal and never those of the powerful.

This criticism, however, highlights a debate within Marxism itself concerning the precise nature of the state. Some, such as Miliband (1969) argued that the state is an instrument of oppression controlled by members of the ruling class. Others such as Poulantzas (1972) have argued that the state exists to promote the interests of **capital-in-general**, not individual capitalists. In the end, both Miliband and Poulantzas would be unfazed by the criticism above that laws impact negatively on individual capitalists. They would see that the state exists to maintain conditions for capital accumulation, and defend those conditions, whether threatened by individuals of the ruling class or the proletariat. However, the state, by defending the conditions of capital accumulation, ultimately enhances the prospects of the ruling class *as a whole*.

In terms of crime, it is clear that one cannot reduce crime to a simple equation with poverty or alienation. If this were so, then we would need to explain why it is that not every person living in poverty commits crime, and why some people who appear to be well-off do engage in crimes such as vandalism, homicide, etc.. This does occur. However, Marxists are more interested in general trends and broad predictions, based upon the notion that social context shapes the choices or options actually available to a person. The choices for the poor concerning whether to steal or not are categorically different to the choices for the rich; furthermore, these conditions are structurally determined.

Not all criminal laws can be defined as 'class' laws, however, in that some deal with class-neutral questions such as rape. This suggests that power may not be totally encapsulated or explainable in class terms. Power and powerlessness can exist in a sense outside the class structure, such as the power of men over women. Similar concerns have been expressed in relation to issues of racism and the relative position of different ethnic groups in society. In either case, however, there are usually strong class factors which shape the contours of the power relationship between men and women, and different ethnic and 'race' groups.

There are many diverse interpretations and explanations for crime from within the broadly Marxist framework. Some of them offer rather simplistic formulations (e.g., the ruling class directly defines what is criminal or not) and some of them provide detailed, sophisticated accounts as to how class power is exercised via the state to enforce basic class rule (e.g., through analysis of personnel, decision-making processes, limits to reform). Overall, however, it can be said that the strength of such approaches is that they attempt to locate social action within the wider structural context of a class-divided society. In doing so they elevate the issue of power and control to the foreground of criminological analysis, and they stress the ways in which social background and social processes give rise to certain propensities (on the part of the powerful and on the part of the less powerful) to engage in criminal activity.

Conclusion

Marxists argue that within contemporary capitalist societies, the capitalist mode of production operates at many levels, both national and global, and this has an impact economically, socially and politically. There is a concentration of wealth and power into the hands of transnational corporations, which control both material and cultural production. The penetration of capitalist relations and enterprises (e.g., in Russia), and the concentration of economic power into fewer hands (e.g., Murdoch), is apparent on a world scale. Internationally and at the national level, the number of poor is growing and the rich are getting richer.

Marxist criminology argues that the concentration of wealth and power into the hands of a small capitalist class has ramifications for the definition of and responses to crime. If power is concentrated in the hands of those who own the means of production, they will influence, and to a certain extent dictate, what behaviour will be defined as crime and what will not. Those with power are likewise capable of influencing the nature of societal reaction to behaviours deemed to be criminal. There is thus an ability here to influence how the state will intervene, for example, on issues relating to environmental destruction.

According to a Marxist perspective, if we wish to examine crime and class in the global context, we must determine who it is that controls the finances (e.g., the banks, the International Monetary Fund); we must evaluate trade agreements which define how the benefits of trade are to be distributed, and the conditions of trade which will be adhered to; and we must consider the impact of mass production and technology (including new information technology) on the lives of workers. Class divisions exist both within and between countries. The existence of the rich and the poor, the divide between the North and the South, are symptomatic of processes of polarisation which fundamentally determine the distribution and definition of crime. For a Marxist, the fundamental questions revolve around the implications of such divisions for the nature and causes of crime, and for the manner of state intervention into people's lives.

Further Reading

Greenberg, D. (1993) *Crime and Capitalism: Readings in Marxist Criminology*, Temple University Press, Philadelphia.

Quinney, R. (1977) *Class, State and Crime: On the Theory and Practice of Criminal Justice*, David McKay Company, New York.

Schwendinger, H. and Schwendinger, J. (1975) 'Defenders of Order or Guardians of Human Rights', in I. Taylor, P. Walton and J. Young (eds) *Critical Criminology*, Routledge and Kegan Paul, London.

Spitzer, S. (1975) 'Toward a Marxian Theory of Deviance', *Social Problems*, 22: 638–51.

White, R., and van der Velden, J. (1995) 'Class and Criminality', *Social Justice*, 22(1): 51–74.

CHAPTER 7

Feminist Perspectives

Introduction

The intention of this chapter is to discuss and review issues pertaining to **feminist perspectives** in criminology. To do this adequately, we need to know something about the position of women and girls generally within the broad criminological discipline, and how gender differences or similarities have been theorised within the field.

The previous chapter outlined the impact of class structure on the construction of criminality. Fundamental motivational distinctions were drawn between crimes of the powerful and those of the powerless. Generally, crimes of the powerful are said to be committed in order to enhance competitive advantage or to augment personal wealth. Additionally, these individuals are said to possess or have access to social resources which enable them to resist detection or prosecution attempts. By contrast, working-class crimes are tied to issues of economic subsistence and alienation — be it economic, social, political or cultural. Furthermore, it is the activities of this class that are excessively regulated; given the lack of access to social resources, they are in the most vulnerable position.

This chapter shares some themes in common with Marxist criminology. Namely, feminist criminology has been centrally concerned with issues of power, the distribution of economic and social resources, and the differential position of selected groups in society which has implications for their activities as either 'offenders' or 'victims'. According to feminist criminology, the sexist nature of the criminal justice system is an ingrained part of that system, and is long overdue for reform.

Social Context

Marxist criminology put questions of power on the agenda in a forceful way during the 1970s. Feminist criminology also looks at who holds and wields power in society, and questions how this impacts on women. Feminist criminology developed in the late 1960s and into the 1970s, and was closely associated with the emergence of the Second Wave of feminism at this time. History reveals that women have long been oppressed as a group, denied rights and subjected to violence. The new movement was called the Second Wave of feminism, in recognition that towards the end of last century the First Wave of feminism had surfaced in the form of the suffragette movement. This movement had been expressly concerned with attaining political power through gaining the vote for women.

The advent of the Second Wave of feminism in the 1970s saw the formation of a dynamic social movement which projected many issues into the public domain, highlighting both the structural oppression of women and the general abuses and crimes directed at them. In its radical phase, the Second Wave of feminism was called the **women's liberation movement**. The social agenda was radical social transformation. The key demands were:

- equal pay
- equal education and job opportunities
- free contraception and abortion on demand
- free 24-hour nurseries, under community control
- legal and financial independence
- an end to discrimination against lesbians
- freedom from intimidation by the threat or use of violence or sexual coercion, regardless of marital status
- an end to the laws, assumptions and institutions that perpetuate male dominance and men's aggression towards women. (Feminist Anthology Collective, 1981).

In any discussion of feminism, there is a fundamental distinction to be made between sex and gender. This distinction is likewise at the nub of explanations of male and female offending and victimisation. **Sex** (male/female) is a biological classification indicated primarily by genital characteristics. **Gender** (masculine/feminine) is a social construct, not a biological given. Concepts of masculinity and femininity are part of the learned culture of the actor indicated by dress, gestures, language, occupation, and so on.

Notions of masculinity and femininity — that is, the experiences and interpretations of gender — are not universal; they are culturally specific. Social constructions of masculinity/femininity vary historically and culturally. For example, in some societies men exhibit what could be considered feminine traits, such as caring and sharing, and this is viewed as positive. Child-rearing in such societies is a responsibility assigned to males, which indicates that femininity is a culturally specified concept not a biologically determined one. Conversely, in some societies both men and women are considered to possess masculine traits. For example, in ancient Sparta, men and women were viewed as equally tough and aggressive. Since women were equally fierce fighters, they therefore exhibited traits stereotypically viewed as masculine.

Sexuality is likewise socially constructed. In some societies homosexuality is viewed as part of the normal continuum of behaviour, not as behaviour discrete from and opposed to heterosexuality. For example, in some ancient warrior cultures, boys would customarily serve as sexual partners until such time as they became functional warriors.

In some societies, the construction of gender encompasses recognition of a third gender role; there is social recognition and acceptance of cross-gender actors. A biological male hence becomes a social female. For example, the movie *Little Big Man* portrays the life of a group of native Americans living on the prairie. In the movie, the male person who is endowed with feminine qualities (sensitivity) is viewed as special and as sustaining a legitimate role in the society.

Feminism says a lot in relation to both biological and social constructions of the female (see, for example, Eisenstein, 1984). Early feminist works looked at sex roles and distinguished the differences between males and females in a biological and social sense; they essentially sought to explore whether sex roles are biological or social.

This questioning was followed by a period in which feminists looked not at the polarisations between men and women, but rather a: the similarities. The focus of analysis here was on androgyny. Males and females were said to exhibit characteristics which were similar as a whole. For example, rock stars such David Bowie and Michael Jackson at times have presented an androgynous image which combined elements of 'femininity' and 'masculinity'.

Another approach adopted a women-centred analysis, which explores the specifically different characteristics of women stemming from their biology or physiology. The emphasis here is on the fundamental, special divisions that separate men and women. For instance, the ability of women to give birth — to perpetuate the human race — is viewed as rendering women essentially superior to men in regard to aspects of caring, sharing and loving another person.

Regardless of specific orientation, feminism deals with the structural position of women in society. For example, there is a call for greater autonomy and the advocacy of rights for women in social, political and economic spheres. Feminist movements were initially motivated for change because of a perceived inequality of autonomy and rights. This can be generalised to all women in society or can be applied to specific categories of women. Aboriginal women, for instance, tend to be overrepresented in the criminal justice system. Some groups of women therefore experience specific concerns related to or stemming from their ethnicity, class position and national background.

Feminism itself has many different strands, and this has implications for how we view the world and respond to it. There are a number of competing explanatory frameworks focusing specifically on the place of women in society which need to be acknowledged (see Eisenstein, 1984; Tong, 1989; Segal, 1987).

Conservatism

This is a traditional view of women which holds many basic assumptions. Essentially, this approach accepts tradition and the way things are. It is contended that the different sexes in society perform different functions and these are necessary and based upon complementary differences. Issues of nature are often emphasised over nurture here.

The role of women is tied in with the family and this is seen as biologically natural. Biological essentialism therefore is seen to render women with a female nature that is naturally inferior to men. It is regarded necessary for the good of society that women be wives, mothers, nurturers and domestics. Whereas men are viewed as complete persons with rights, women are defined in relation to men, not in relation to themselves. This perspective acknowledges the existence and legitimacy of clearly defined social roles for male and female.

On the other hand, the various feminist strands are primarily concerned with autonomy, rights and power. The different perspectives within feminism broadly include the following types of approaches.

Liberal feminism

This views the individual as the most important part of society. There is talk here about rights, dignities and freedoms of the individual. The hallmark of this perspective is the need to value reason, not to discriminate against anyone. In the view of liberal feminists, the question of rights is paramount in the context of competitive views of the individual. Hence, the laws should be changed to ensure that women have equal rights. For example, it is seen as necessary to change legislation in order to provide equal opportunities in the sphere of paid work. There was a recent example of the assertion of such rights in a Western Australian case of female construction workers. The argument was that sexist violence existed in many forms on the worksite, and that female workers should not be exposed to this; for example, pornography and abusive language. The Equal Opportunities Board decided in this instance that the women were being denied the right to participate in the workforce.

Marxist feminism

This perspective is not so much concerned with traditional rights, but instead analyses the structural position of women in society in terms of paid and unpaid labour. The key category of employment for women is seen to be that of domestic labour, which is unpaid. This situation is viewed as exploitative. Even in those instances where women participate in the paid workforce, they tend to be lowly paid relative to their position and their male counterparts, and to be concentrated in insecure positions such as part-time and casual work. The argument advanced here is that if we want to deal with gender inequality then we need to do something to fundamentally transform class societies such as capitalism which are organised around the exploitation of female (and male working-class) labour.

Radical feminism

This stresses the common experiences of women; it is basically involved in collective consciousness-raising about the oppressions shared by all women. The assertion here is that all aspects of women's lives (both personal and political) are touched and shaped by patriarchal relations. The personal is viewed as inherently political. Women are viewed as an oppressed class, and all women are said to be subject to the oppressive structures of male domination. At the same time, all men share in some way in the benefits of that oppression. This approach examines the historical exclusion of women from political, social and economic spheres. The social institutions of home, the law, the workforce, the courts, etc. are examined in order to expose the victimisation of women across all spheres and institutions of life. The issue of male violence — physical, verbal and psychological — is of major significance.

Socialist feminism

This agrees that in both the public and private spheres women have been and are exploited and oppressed, but this is viewed within the framework of capitalist society. There is an emphasis here on the necessity of examining the commodification of women's bodies as a capitalist enterprise; for example, the pornography industry. It is contended that the nature of a class-divided society and the issue of male domination need to be considered in tandem. Women as a broad social category are subject to oppressive images and practices, but the specific nature of concrete instances of exploitation and inequality needs to be examined from the point of view of capitalist accumulation. In essence, the social and economic needs of women have been subordinated to the requirements of profit-making institutions, a process which directly affects many men as well. It is possible, therefore, to think of alliances with certain sections of the male population on some issues as a means to institute social change to the benefit of women.

Cultural feminism

This adopts a women-centred analysis which is often not tied to any specific economic or political programme. It concentrates instead on the development of a separate women's culture and the special nature of women's relationships to each other, society, etc. This perspective manifests itself philosophically in the appeal of New Age religion, magic, and mysticism. Women are seen as intrinsically and fundamentally different from men. They are seen to exhibit a number of gender-specific traits (such as caring and sharing attitudes) which are positive feminine features which make them somehow superior morally to their male counterparts. Alternatively, male traits such as violence and egoism are constant dangers to women individually and collectively. Hence, for many women, the solution is to separate themselves from male society, and thus domination, as far as they can. As part of this, it is also important to develop and expand a 'female discourse' or construction of the social world which sees things in specifically female gender terms.

Female crime

Each of the above perspectives has implications for how we view female crime and respond to it. We must further understand that how we respond to 'crime issues' is determined by the way in which the law positions women in society. It is essential here to note that the language adopted within the law is generally male-gendered language, which clearly advances the rights of 'man' but makes little if any mention of the rights of women.

Criminological theorising did not escape this gender-based critique (see, for example, Allen, 1990). A couple of important observations in that regard can be made:

- There has been sheer neglect of women in criminological thought and inquiry, in part due to the male domination of academic criminology both historically and in the present. This is an important point, since what results is necessarily a male perspective of the world and selection of issues perceived to be important by males.

- The criminal justice system is also dominated by male personnel — judges, barristers, solicitors, prison officers, and police. Again, it can be argued that the composition of institutional workforces can have a significant impact on how that workforce pursues its tasks in practice.

Hence, in terms of theory and research and at the level of the practitioner, the system is dominated by men; there is obvious male structural domination. This is not to say that there have not been periods where individual men have challenged overt sexist practices. Judges, magistrates, and barristers have indeed done so, but this has not necessarily produced changes in the overall structural domination (i.e., the way institutional practices themselves are systematically biased against women). Similarly, individual women are directly involved in policing and other justice agency practices, but in doing so may simply serve to reinforce the conservative views of ideal female sexual behaviour. For example, the policing of morality and behaviour of female children during the period of the 'child savers' movement at the turn of the century was both conservative *and* spearheaded by women (Platt, 1977). Such practices did not challenge the position of women in society in any way.

The neglect of women within the discipline of criminology is a reflection not only of the composition of the criminal justice system, but also of the picture portrayed by criminal statistics. Women do not appear to be as statistically significant a problem as men. They generally appear to commit fewer crimes and the crimes they do commit appear to be less serious than those committed by men; they are less violent. Furthermore, in examining victimisation statistics, although there are female-specific categories of victimisation such as rape and domestic violence in which women appear overrepresented, females do not appear to be victims of homicide to the same extent as males. As a consequence of such observations, investigators within the criminological field have often regarded it as unimportant to look at female offending or female victimisation.

When seeking to examine female offending, there has been the additional problem of applying male correlates. Theories of offending have generally been conducted within a male framework and constructed in male terms. Since mainstream criminological theories reflected a male experience, it was difficult to apply them to females; for example, strain theory's concept of opportunity structures and cultural goals (see Naffine, 1987). The limitations of mainstream criminology are discussed further below. For now it is important to acknowledge the need for, and significance of, a perspective which argued that female crime was tied to wider structures of gender and power in society.

Basic Concepts

The feminist perspectives are based on the premise that women are structurally disadvantaged in the present society (see Chart 7.1). That is, male domination and female subordination are an entrenched part of **patriarchy** which expresses fundamental inequalities between the sexes. Sexual inequality and the disempowerment of women are embodied, as well, in the legal and criminal justice systems.

Feminist criminology defines crime in terms of gender-based and gender-related types of activities. Specifically, a major concern is with the nature of **male violence** as this impacts upon both female offenders and female victims, and the ways in which forms of **gendered inequality and discrimination** are institutionalised throughout society. A substantial part of feminist criminology has been directed at exposing the 'hidden' levels of violence against women, and the structural oppressions which they have had to face over long periods of time.

The main focus of analysis, therefore, is the unequal position of women in society, the specific kinds of crimes committed against women *as women*, and the status of female offenders in the context of wider social inequalities and gender-based oppressions. Crime against and involving women is seen to be the result of **social oppression** and **economic dependency** upon men or the welfare apparatus of the state.

The way in which women, as victims and offenders, are processed by the criminal justice system is described in terms of the **sexualisation thesis**. This refers to the notion that when the criminal justice system and its agents deal with women (in whatever capacity) they do so on the basis of certain gender-related criteria. That is, the behaviour, marital status and appearance of women are constantly

Chart 7.1 Feminist Perspectives

Definition of crime	◆ male violence ◆ institutionalised inequality and discrimination
Focus of analysis	◆ unequal position of women in society ◆ victimisation of women ◆ victim status of female offenders
Cause of crime	◆ criminality is a function of patriarchy ◆ result of social oppression and economic dependency on men/state
Nature of offender	◆ sexualisation of offences and victimisation according to gender criteria (e.g., 'femininity')
Response to crime	◆ social empowerment of women ◆ confront institutions of male domination
Crime prevention	◆ economic, social, political power and equality ◆ anti-sexist training programmes for judiciary and other sections of criminal justice system
Operation of criminal justice system	◆ provision of gender-specific services and support systems within criminal justice (e.g., gaols) and welfare spheres (e.g., refuges)

linked to particular ideas regarding the preferred forms of 'femininity'. In this way, what is labelled 'criminal' or an act of 'victimisation' depends to a large extent upon the perceived sexual behaviour and social status of the woman in question.

It is argued that there is a **double standard of morality and power** with respect to women in the criminal justice system. Men and women are treated differently on the basis of gendered stereotypes. Furthermore, in many cases this leads to inequitable and unfair treatment of women who present themselves as offenders or victims before the system. One manifestation of this double standard is the fact that the senior members of the police, judiciary and correctional apparatus are men, and that generally speaking they reflect existing prejudices regarding women's roles, status and position in society.

From the point of view of feminist criminology, there need to be major changes to the existing criminal justice system and to society as a whole. The problem is ultimately seen as one of **social empowerment** of women as a broad category, and of confronting the negative and restricting nature of male domination as this is evident in the present institutional set-up.

To prevent crimes against women, and to forestall many of the crimes committed by women, it is necessary to have greater economic, social and political equality. Institutional reforms could include affirmative action policies to advance the position of women within the criminal justice and judicial systems; anti-sexist training for lawyers and judges; and law reforms which recognise and acknowledge the gendered nature of the social world. The criminal justice system needs an overhaul with respect to the provision of gender-specific services and support systems in areas such as detention (e.g., trauma counselling, skills training), and more resources are needed in the wider 'welfare' domain (e.g., rape crisis centres, refuges).

Historical Development

In the historical development of feminist criminology there are two points to note at the outset. The first is that, while female offenders were generally ignored in mainstream analysis, there were instances when they were specifically examined. However, this was a rather small and neglected area of criminological theorising. Second, the critique offered by feminists was that such theories as did exist were either overtly sexist in nature, or extremely limited in what they could say about the nature of female involvement in the criminal justice system.

When attempting to explain female crime as a distinct and specific social phenomenon, the mainstream theories accepted the narrow, conservative view regarding the place and position of women in society, and more often than not did so on the basis of a form of **biological reductionism**. This refers to instances where female experiences and behaviour are reduced to the imperatives of biology — the (biological) sex of a person is seen to dictate or determine appropriate social roles and practices in terms of one's gender (social constructions of femininity).

A key contribution of feminist criminology has been to critique one-sided, distorted views of women in the traditional literature that did exist on female offending. The basis of the critique had to do with the conflation of sex and gender (failure to distinguish the biological and the social) in much of the analysis on offer, and the misogynous (women-hating) character of some of the writing. Here we can point to several different theories which have ultimately based their conclusions upon the idea of innate female social characteristics linked to female biology.

Biological explanations

These explanations view female crime as stemming from biological causes (see, especially, Smart, 1976; Naffine, 1987). Most focus on sex-specific biological differences as the standards by which to compare men and women, and as explanations for particular kinds of activity. They vary in substantive emphasis, but the overall message of biological determinism remains the same:

- Early theories argued that the true, biologically determined nature of women was antithetical to crime. Such views were based upon stereotypical notions of women as being passive, non-aggressive creatures. Criminality was linked to 'maleness' and 'masculine' traits such as aggression and physicality. Therefore the female offender, who was seen as exhibiting male traits, was considered doubly deviant, both socially and biologically: she was an exception to the usual sex of the offender; and as a woman, she went against her biological nature and thus was not fully female.

- Some theories discussed female criminality in terms of the physiological differences between the sexes. In this case, women conceal their offending behaviour (and thus have lower rates of report and detection than males) and use their sexuality to attain (presumed) greater leniency by the police and the courts; they do this because their nature is inherently deceitful and manipulative. This in turn is linked to their physiological make-up, in that women are capable of concealing their sexual arousal (unlike men) and thus in the most intimate human acts they have the opportunity and ability to manipulate those around them.

- In some recent theories, research on hormonal disturbances and social behaviour has tried to establish a link between pre- and post-menstrual activity and the propensity of women to engage in criminal activity. In a similar vein, it is sometimes argued that post-natal depression is responsible in some instances for infanticide. In other words, as the female body fluctuates in terms of hormonal activity, the woman may engage in a wide variety of anti-social and criminal activity.

Socialisation theories

A common way to explain female crime is to point to differences in the ways in which men and women are, or should be, socialised (Smart, 1976). These types of explanations are generally closely tied to specific notions of appropriate sex roles. The problem is usually seen as inadequate socialisation, leading to a violation of the behaviour appropriate for members of the female sex. Again, very often the approaches reduce crime causation to essentially biological factors.

- Some theories see deviancy or delinquency as a form of 'acting out' on the part of young women. It is stated that women have traditionally been socialised to be passive and need affection, and that this explains their lower crime rates. However, if they have been abnormally or poorly socialised, then they may be susceptible to manipulation by men, and this manipulation can result in sex-related deviancy such as prostitution.

- A variation of this theory argues that the key issue is the under-socialisation of individual female offenders. The maladjustment of the offender to mainstream social norms manifests itself in the form of sexually inappropriate conduct, such as promiscuous sexual relations. The desire of girls and women for acceptance and approval may result in gratuitous sexual relationships because this is seen as the only way in which the young women can assert themselves (i.e., through their sexuality).

- Some theories begin by arguing that crime is due to the disconnection felt by some women. The psychological absence of love produces instability in these females and this in turn leads to various 'acting out' behaviours of an anti-social or deviant nature. The argument assumes that emotionality is an inherent biological feature of the female sex. Women are said to have a need for dependencies because they are primarily emotional creatures — again a biological reductionist argument.

Feminist responses

The response of feminist writers to these kinds of biological explanations and socialisation arguments is that they represent a 'double standard' in terms of morality and power. Underpinning this double standard is a blurring of the distinction between 'sex' and 'gender'.

Females are presumed to have a fixed biological nature which is indistinguishable from their fixed social role. Any maladjustment to this stereotypical femininity is said to be the consequence of biological defect or inherent biological weaknesses of the female sex. Women's social nature is thus thought to be given naturally by her biological being.

The crucial issue from a feminist perspective is that of relative social power and access to community resources (Alder, 1994). The criminalisation process itself is heavily laden with sexist assumptions which reinforce and reproduce structural inequalities of gender in society (Gelsthorpe and Morris, 1990). Sexist assumptions determine how offending behaviour is constructed, and how victims are portrayed (see Chart 7.2). The central proposition of much feminist analysis is that women are treated differently in and by the criminal justice system because of the persistence of traditional gender-role expectations regarding 'appropriate' and 'feminine' behaviour for women (and men).

Underpinning this gendered division of the sexes is the question of *power*. That is, society is male-dominated, and this is reflected in a myriad of social institutions, including the law and the criminal justice system. Thus, feminist jurisprudence has been concerned to demonstrate the gender biases built into the very processes of the law (for example, the 'reasonable man' argument in legal reasoning), as well as specific overt instances of gender inequality (for example, laws which allowed rape in marriage). The status of women as 'property' and as 'rights holders' has been examined historically and as part of an ongoing struggle to assert women's place and position in a patriarchal system and society (Scutt, 1990; Graycar and Morgan, 1990; Naffine, 1990).

The nature of **female offending** is placed into a wider social, economic and political context, rather than one which reduces female experience to biological or psychological determinants. Women who commit homicide, for instance, have very often been victims of violence themselves. Similarly, women who commit social security or other minor forms of fraud and theft usually do so, not for themselves, but to support children and dependants. Hence, the generalised violence against women as a social category, and the relative

Chart 7.2 Women and Crime

	Women as offenders	Women as victims
Nature of crimes	◆ Sex-specific offences, e.g., prostitution, infanticide ◆ Sex-related offences, e.g., shopstealing, fraud	◆ Sex-specific offences, e.g., rape, sexual assault ◆ Sex-related offences, e.g., consumer rip-offs
Mainstream explanations	◆ Related to issues of female sexuality, e.g., biological drives and hormonal activity ◆ Related to notions of gender, e.g., constructions of 'feminine' behaviour, and socialisation into these ◆ Categories of 'mad' and 'bad' based upon essentially passive and/or deceitful nature of women	◆ Categories of 'deserving' and 'undeserving' victims based upon sexuality and relationship to men, e.g., married ◆ Related to notion of 'weaker' sex and dominant sex roles and social functions, e.g., housewife ◆ Sex-specific victimisation explained in terms of male biological drives, e.g., rape and 'provocation'
Feminist explanations	◆ Double standard of morality, e.g., sexualisation of offences for women but not men ◆ Prior status of women as victims, e.g., of persistent abuse, of economic dependency ◆ Attempts to control and regulate female behaviour by criminalising certain offences as sex-specific ◆ Different social opportunities linked to male-dominated institutions and cultures	◆ Emphasis on women as victims of male violence generally ◆ Sex-specific victimisation linked to patriarchal cultures and institutions ◆ Relative powerlessness of some women to protect themselves from personal and property crime ◆ Traditional gender-role expectations shape victimisation process

disadvantages they suffer economically, are explored as vital preconditions to any personal or individual offending behaviour.

In the case of **victimisation,** much attention is paid to the ways in which crimes against women have historically either not been considered as crimes (e.g., domestic violence) or are subject to trivialisation and sexual bias (e.g., rape trials involving sex workers). It has been argued in some cases that a woman who has been victimised is herself judged in relation to a man, rather than a specific offensive action. For example, a married woman subjected to injury may be seen in terms of a 'serious crime' insofar as it affects her status as her spouse's 'sexual property' or 'homemaker'. An unmarried woman who has a sexual history of multiple partners may be treated by the courts as having actually provoked a criminal assault. Questions of what is an 'offence' and who is a 'victim' are thus often intertwined with gender stereotypes and biases which reflect a general inequality between the sexes in society.

A fundamental question assessed by feminist criminology is how the **sex variable** has been dealt with by the various perspectives.

- There are theories which ignore the sex variable altogether; the vast majority of traditional criminology appears to do this, since it deals only with male criminality and ignores the specific conditions under which women exist in society; that is, the female experience.
- There are then theories which conflate or blur the distinctions between sex and gender. Females are presumed to have a fixed biological nature and/or role(s), and any maladjustment to this stereotypical femininity is said to be the consequence of biological defect. Women's nature is hence thought here to be given naturally by her genitals.
- There are theories which ignore the impact of gender relationships. There is a discussion here of women, but the male/female experience is presented as androgynous. These theories neglect the impact of sex relationships on people.

Feminist criminology wanted to explore issues relating to women and looked initially at sex-role differences. Smart (1976) stated that there was a double standard operating in society in relation to morality and power. This was particularly indicated in the nature of offences with which women were charged — they were primarily **sex-specific** offences such as infanticide and prostitution (women's crime). The legal framework — both historically, and as revealed by the official statistics — has similarly treated the category of prostitution as relating to women. We know male prostitutes exist, but prostitution is not constructed as a male-specific offence.

There are also **sex-related** offences such as shopstealing — of the total number of crimes reported by the official statistics, a proportionately higher incidence of shopstealing offences are committed by females. The content of the goods stolen also appears to be sex-related — perfume, lipstick, tampons. These goods are sex-related in character in that they are tied to the gendered identity of women.

In terms of activities pertaining to young offenders, historically men have been picked up for certain 'conventional' violations of the law, whilst young women were seen as delinquent because of their presumed immorality or promiscuity (see Alder, 1985; Cunneen and White, 1995; Chesney-Lind and Sheldon, 1990). It is thus presumed that men are in court because of their criminal offending, while females are there because they have slept around: clearly there are double standards operating. Gender is also tied to other offences. For example, passing fraudulent cheques and social security fraud tend to be female offences.

Contemporary Examples

If we examine contemporary female offending, some interesting pictures emerge:

- A significant proportion of offenders are single parents, of low educational standing, unemployed; many have been victimised through male violence, such as rape, sexual abuse, incest, etc. There is also an overrepresentation of indigenous women in the system.

- Feminist theorists state that there are obvious double standards operating in terms of how women and men are treated, both as victims and offenders. This can be highlighted once again by referring to the example of prostitution. Why is it that the female service providers are charged with solicitation and offences associated with prostitution, whilst the male service recipients are not? While there is a dual relationship between servicer and servicee, rarely is the male patron implicated.

- With respect to the offence of rape, again for many years and still today, there are many myths relating to the nature of rapists. The stereotypical rapist has customarily been portrayed as a violent sexual psychopath and serial offender. Thus the individual is disturbed, and/or the victim has been seen to act to arouse the uncontrollable desires of the male attacker, by wearing inappropriate clothing for example. This image reduces rape to an individualistic biological problem, disregarding societal explanations which view rape as relating to social power.

• Likewise, in terms of victims, there has been a league table established in relation to the worthiness or otherwise of the victim status; distinctions are made as to who is or is not to be believed. As conveyed in a judge's comments in Victoria, claims of rape made by a nun or married woman are to be believed, while those made by a prostitute are to be treated as dubious. Such distinctions misconstrue the nature of the issue — the exertion of violence and power, and actual evidence of harm.

Such double standards of power and morality are represented as the **sexualisation thesis** by feminists; that is, women who deviate from what is construed to be the norms of sexuality and morality are seen to be offenders (see Chesney-Lind, 1974; Smart, 1976).

In particular, when such offenders are young, they are viewed as being immoral or in moral danger. This has been a traditional way of bringing young women into the system, that is, through a category of welfare provision (what are called 'status offences' in the USA) rather than criminal offence. Hence, they did not necessarily have to have done anything illegal to warrant state intervention. Young women who were considered to be sexually promiscuous (thus 'exposed to moral danger') were incarcerated in juvenile institutions 'for their own welfare'. Historically, intervention was often followed by physical examination and subjection to 'treatment' regimes. Institutionalisation aimed to impart necessary instruction in domesticity; adolescent girls were taught to play their 'natural' subservient role as the servers of men. They were released when considered to be 'of a marriageable age'. Men have not been classified, diagnosed and treated in the same way. Their sexuality has been encouraged, because it is viewed as a 'natural' part of manhood.

The clause in child welfare provisions concerned with 'moral danger' has historically resulted in long periods of incarceration for considerable numbers of young women in Australia (Jaggs, 1986). It is important to recognise that in Australia such provision were not part of the criminal law as such, but were part of the child protection legislation. In reality such treatment regimes translated into harsher penalties than those given for offending behaviour. Such provisions, it should be added, no longer exist, but they form an indelible part of the history of women's involvement with the criminal justice system.

It should be noted that not only the justice system, but psychiatric, welfare and other relevant establishments all tried to reinforce these conventional boundaries and distinctions. Women who transgressed the boundaries of dominant conceptions of femininity were seen as falling within one of two categories — they were either **mad** or **bad**. The policing of female behaviour occurs not only in the legal and medical arena, but also in the wider social community. This is evident, for example, in the examination of the nature of the interactions between men and women in youth centres (Nava, 1984). The policing of females is widespread, with the objective of preserving the good sexual reputations of the women. Derogatory language, such as 'slut', 'slag', etc., is commonly used as a tool to regulate female behaviour.

In recent times, there has been a critique of the sexualisation thesis. Carrington (1993) criticises the sexualisation thesis on the grounds that from the mid-1970s there have been equal proportions of males and females appearing before the courts. She discusses the notion of the sexualisation of offending, but looks also at the nature of penalties imposed. She examines the notion that young women are prosecuted primarily on the grounds of their immorality and are dealt harsher sentences because of this. She argues instead, however, that when welfare intervention occurs, irrespective of whether the offender is male or female, harsher sentences are received, *because the actions are initiated by the welfare/helping professions.*

Carrington also challenges the sexualisation thesis on another ground. If the sustenance of male patriarchy is the objective of the legal system, then one would expect the system to be dominated by men. She claims we should instead look at the composition of all those seeking to control women's behaviour — welfare workers, youth and community workers, social workers, and so on. If we do, we see that a large proportion of those who are the gatekeepers and custodians of female behaviour are women. And among those who wield derogatory and negative labels are young women themselves. Research by Lees (1989), for example, found a liberal use of such terms by adolescent girls within the schoolground setting, as well as stereotyped labelling by women teachers of their students.

The impact of 'race' or ethnicity on female offenders is also raised by Carrington as part of the critique of the sexualisation thesis. In particular, concern is expressed regarding why working-class and Aboriginal young people are overrepresented in the crime statistics. These are the types of questions asked by a number of contemporary feminist criminologists (see Gelsthorpe and Morris, 1990). A more sophisticated and complicated analysis is obviously required: it should focus not just on sex differences, but also on differences of class and ethnicity.

Carrington's rejection of the sexualisation thesis has not been entirely convincing, however. In a recent review of Australian feminist criminology, Alder (1996) argues that the sexualisation thesis itself should not be oversimplified. While acknowledging differences between women's experiences, Alder argues that the power of the sexualisation thesis lies in linking the similarities of women's experiences. Women's offending behaviour, and their subsequent involvement in the criminal justice system, form but one part of their lives. If we were to examine the totality of women's lives, in all their complexities and diversities, both the similarities as argued by the sexualisation thesis, and the differences as argued by Carrington, can be supported. Alder goes on to argue that contemporary feminism cannot be oversimplified and parodied any longer as somehow merely advocating a simple relationship between gender and experience. Nonetheless, exploration of the diversity of women's lives reveals consistent themes of surviving, coping and thriving within patriarchal structures, all of which demand further attention and analysis.

Feminist criminology is diverse, particularly when reviewing the contemporary debate. Feminists focus on the creation and construction of female offending via the sexualisation thesis, but they also seek to explore the area of victimology, particularly in relation to the victimisation of women. Feminists have long been associated with activism, as well as theoretical debate. In particular, feminist criminologists are concerned to change the law to promote a recognition of issues of violence directed against women. This has led many to argue for the harsher enforcement of laws against perpetrators at the operational level, and a call for greater sensitivity of police to these crimes. However, others see limitations to this, arguing that calling for greater use of the criminal law in a patriarchal system to defend and protect women is fraught with problems (Edwards, 1990).

Critique

Various issues have been the subject of intense discussion and debate within feminist criminology. For example, it has been noted that some feminist approaches do not deal adequately with questions relating to class, ethnicity and 'race' in discussions of the female offender and the female victim. Yet as various recent studies show (e.g., Carrington, 1993), the 'race' of a person is a crucial factor in terms of overall representation of some groups within the criminal justice system. Likewise, the class background of the offender or victim has significant consequences with regard to the actual nature of the criminalisation and the victimisation process.

A second area which is generating more attention is the notion that feminist criminology needs to do more than provide a woman-centred analysis: it needs to foster a non-sexist criminology which focuses more broadly on gender relations in their entirety. Specifically, it has been suggested that issues of female and male criminality need to be examined in terms of the social constructions of both 'femininity' and 'masculinity', and with regard to the relationship between each of these social constructions (Gelsthorpe and Morris, 1990; Cunneen and White, 1995).

A greater concern has been expressed in relation to victimology. There is the argument that victims should not be viewed merely as passive, but need to be empowered, by extending to them the alternative term of 'survivors'. This term is said to imply active response. Hence, debate within the feminist movement has served to push the boundaries as they relate to women, both as victims and as offenders.

More generally, the issue of power, and how this is manifested institutionally, remains an area where more research and discussion are also required. This is particularly so with respect to feminist conceptualisations of the state. Meanwhile, an immediate problem confronting feminist writers and activists is that of the conservative backlash against many of the concepts and issues raised by feminists generally. The profile of female victims, and the dilemmas and inequities surrounding the processing of female offenders, have been actively raised by feminist criminologists. But in the light of contemporary calls for greater 'law and order', there is a fear that such work will be subverted and/or swamped by the simplistic moralising, and simplistic answers, of the New Right.

Conclusion

In summary, the feminist perspectives within criminology challenge the male biases and neglects of mainstream criminology. It is identifiably part of Second Wave feminism, which has been part of the social landscape since the 1960s. Within criminology, criticism is levelled at historical and contemporary examples of the double standards applied to women and men in the criminal justice system. As well, active intervention has been called for in areas such as inappropriate responses to female offenders (e.g., imprisonment); law reform which prevents discrimination against women (e.g., equal employment opportunity); the legal recognition of certain crimes against women (e.g., sexual harassment); and active enforcement of laws to protect women from male violence (e.g., domestic violence, incest, rape).

Feminist criminology cannot be seen, however, as a single theoretical perspective. As outlined in this chapter there are many strands of feminism, from radical feminism and socialist feminism through to liberal and cultural feminism, each having a distinctive voice within criminology. Taken as a whole, feminist criminology has radically altered the nature of the criminological debate. Challenges highlighted by feminists have influenced debates within left-leaning perspectives such as Left Realism and critical criminology, as well as conservative and liberal theories such as New Right criminology and republican theory. Thus, as well as constituting an identifiable perspective within criminology in its own right, feminist criminology has significantly influenced the wider criminological debate.

Further Reading

Carrington, K. (1993) *Offending Girls*, Allen and Unwin, Sydney.

Naffine, N. (1987) *Female Crime: The Construction of Women in Criminology*, Allen and Unwin, Sydney.

Scutt, J. (1990) *Women and the Law*, Law Book Company, Sydney.

Smart, C. (1976) *Women, Crime and Criminology: A Feminist Critique*, Routledge and Kegan Paul, London.

Tong, R. (1989) *Feminist Thought: A Comprehensive Introduction*, Unwin Hyman, London.

CHAPTER 8

New Right Criminology

Introduction

The 1960s and 1970s were broadly characterised by rapid social change and heightened political conflict, which manifested themselves in the rise of radical theories about society in the social sciences, including criminology. By the 1980s, however, a major change in thinking had occurred in society at large. Conservative politicians and political ideologies dominated the electoral landscape across many countries, and 'law and order' emerged as a predominant issue along with that of high levels of unemployment.

The aim of this chapter is to outline the main currents of **New Right criminology**. This particular approach or perception of crime has both a populist dimension (related to the political process) and an academic dimension (related to the work of criminologists). The fundamental ideas of New Right criminology are based on two themes: placing responsibility for crime squarely on the individual, and reasserting the importance of punishment in responding to crime.

The chapter makes a broad distinction between 'right-wing libertarian' views and those of 'conservatism'. These describe essential differences in the political perspectives contained under the New Right criminology umbrella. The chapter also discusses those traditional academic approaches within criminology itself which reflect and are reflected in the general New Right perspective. In particular, the ideas of 'social control theory' and of 'opportunity-rationality theory' will be discussed.

Social Context

The phrase 'New Right' refers to a particular political orientation, rather than to a systematic, coherent theory in its own right. A conservative perspective in criminology, directly opposed to the liberalism of strain theory and labelling perspectives in particular, arose at a time when the long boom of economic prosperity in the advanced capitalist countries was coming to an end. The mid-1970s saw a world economic recession, followed over the next two decades by periodic, and in some instances devastating, economic slumps.

In these new times there was likely to be an increase in property and personal crime at both corporate and street level. The alienation and marginalisation of a significant layer of the population, many of them young people, was associated with a range of anti-social and deviant behaviour. For example, 1977 saw the rise of punk rock music and the overt rebellion of many young people against both the commercial music industry for its insipid conformity and slick production values, and the power-brokers and 'respectable' members of society who had done so little to stem the tide of youth unemployment and yet condemned the ripped shirts of the poor.

Politically, by the 1980s there had been a swing to the right at the level of policy formulation and development, regardless of the political party in power. The economic ideas of Margaret Thatcher in the UK and Ronald Reagan in the USA, the advent of 'Rogernomics' (named after the Treasurer) in New Zealand, and the approach adopted by Hawke and Keating in Australia all signalled an **economic rationalist** platform for dealing with contemporary issues. This emphasised the notion of 'economic efficiency' above all else in policy development, and in each case led to tax cuts for both individuals and corporations, while at the same time universal provision in the allocation of the welfare services and benefits was curtailed. According to the economic rationalists, the wealth created by these measures would benefit both rich and poor. Many argue, however, that the net effect was to exacerbate the growing distance between the rich and the poor in society.

Simultaneously, efforts were made to neutralise any resistance to the economic restructuring that aimed to increase competitiveness and efficiency. Conservative parties in particular made concerted attempts to drastically reduce trade union power. For example, Reagan smashed the air traffic controllers' strike in the USA, while Thatcher took on the miners' union in the UK. In Australia, union power was curbed more subtly and, some would argue, more effectively. The Prices and Incomes Accord between the Australian Labor Party and the Australian Council of Trade Unions was used to defuse any possible union militancy. Nonetheless, strong-arm tactics were also used against 'recalcitrant' elements; notably the army was used to break the airline pilots' strike, and the police and courts were used to deregister the Builders Labourers Federation.

The 1980s saw an emphasis on controlling union power and enhancing wealth creation. In the 'decade of greed', much media prominence was given to business entrepreneurs, many of whom gained near folk-hero status. Labour and financial markets were deregulated, and the idea of a 'free economy and a strong state' (Gamble, 1988) was entrenched in places like the UK through the rhetoric of defending the 'people's capitalism'. Market structures were opened up in order to stimulate greater economic activity. In reality, in most cases it was the strong who stood to benefit most, while the rest would have to work that much harder to gain a share of the societal wealth. State agencies which were seen to impede economic growth were more closely scrutinised. Welfare provisions were often downgraded or targeted at a minority of the most impoverished in society; those institutions which maintained public order and protected private property, such as the police, were strengthened.

In the context of increasing economic hardship and an ideological swing to the Right, supported largely by an economic rationalist mentality, there was a rise in 'law-and-order' politics, both domestically and internationally. For example, internationally, the former concern with the preservation of 'human rights' propounded by world leaders was quickly transformed into an emphasis on terrorism and the drug trade, and the necessity to combat these 'by any means necessary'.

Domestically, the law-and-order push assumed the tone of a 'war on crime' and an attack on the disorder of society. This translated into a call during the 1980s for increased police personnel, powers and resources, for longer gaol sentences, the provision of more prisons, stronger discipline within families and schools, and a return to more traditional values generally. For young people there was the demand for 'greater responsibility', which translated into more punitive attitudes in the area of juvenile justice.

New Right criminology tends to revolve around the individual in society, and to provide a moralistic and punitive approach to issues of crime and criminality (Young, 1981). While recent academic work has provided sophisticated defences of these ideas (Tame, 1991; Buchanan and Hartley, 1992), in the public domain the get-tough approach has generally been associated with populist appeals to the public at large. This has proved to be electorally expedient and attractive, even if the consequences of the adoption of such measures leave something to be desired.

Populism is not a political ideology as such, but is a loosely defined mood. It appeals to people on the basis of 'us' versus 'them'. The 'us' is always viewed as virtuous. The 'them', whoever they are, are viewed as being parasites and destructive to the social body. In terms of crime, the essence of **populism** exaggerates the dangerousness of crime, and the foreign or alien nature of the criminal. The criminal is seen to be outside the society — its networks, institutions, communities, mores, values, methods of income, ways of life. Insofar as the criminal is not seen to be bound by normal social rules of conduct, so too it is argued that normal rules of order should not necessarily be adhered to if criminals are to be brought to book for their offensive activities.

The rhetoric of populism is one which reduces all crime problems to simple solutions. Offenders are made entirely responsible for their actions, particularly since they exist outside the mainstream institutions of society. They are not seen as members of the 'community', and indeed are sometimes presented as not being members of the human race (e.g., they are described as 'animals' or 'savages'). Insofar as this social distancing occurs at the level of rhetoric and policy development, it is not a far step to encourage ever more draconian solutions to the crime problem. If the problem is constructed as being one of 'us' against 'them', as a 'war' which implies violence and destruction, then redemption of the situation is seen to lie in enhanced state power.

The 1980s saw populist rhetoric about crime used actively as a major electoral tool, particularly in the UK. **Authoritarian populism** refers to a process in which crime is ideologically conveyed in a series of moral panics about 'law-and-order' issues (Taylor, 1981; Hall, 1980; Hall et al., 1978). The extent and seriousness of crime is highlighted (but not necessarily backed up by statistical or other research findings), and this, in turn, is used to justify harsher penalties, and the assertion of state authority in more and more spheres of everyday social life. As part of this process, specific groups or categories of people are singled out for special attention: young people, Aborigines, welfare recipients, striking workers, sole parents. Thus, 'we' are protected by having ever greater state intervention into the affairs of 'them', the most likely candidates for membership of the criminal class. Again, the rationale behind such intrusion is usually a combination of protection of private property, and the differential treatment that should be meted out to the moral and immoral in society.

The broad appeal of authoritarian populism is due in part to the pervasive influence of the print and electronic media in conveying particular types of images regarding crime in society (see Grabosky and Wilson, 1989). The flooding of the media with stories of 'street crime' has real and pertinent effects: heightening the fear of crime, feeding the stereotypes regarding the 'typical offender', exaggerating the extent of extremely violent and serious crimes, and fostering acceptance for policies which appear to 'get something done' about the crime problem. The politically important role of New Right criminology is thus related to the basic electoral appeal of authoritarian populist rhetoric. Unfortunately, the trend toward such 'law-and-order' politics was readily apparent in recent (1995) elections in Queensland and New South Wales, signalling its continued and growing appeal as a political vote-catcher in Australia.

Basic Concepts

The main elements of New Right criminology include a combination of conservative moralising and free-market competitive ethos. These sometimes contradict each other at the level of specific policies. However, the overriding message is that there is a need to 'get tough on criminals', to hold them responsible for their actions, and to punish the wrongdoer in a consistent manner.

New Right criminology is opposed to perspectives that emphasise 'treatment' and 'reform' rather than punishment. It opposes the views of orthodox positivist criminology which have a deterministic view or model of the causes of crime; rather, it asserts that **people do make choices**, and that they therefore must pay for these choices. In a nutshell, the argument is that if you 'do the crime', then you must 'do the time'.

The New Right criminological perspective includes several strands: some deal with more philosophical views regarding the nature of human activity, and some with specific areas of interest such as retributivist concerns with sentencing; the range extends to economic analyses of the causes and social responses to crime. For present purposes, however, we will illustrate the broad orientation of these kinds of perspectives by examining two general views on the nature of crime and crime control. Each is concerned with the **punishment and disciplining of offenders**, but the overall analysis of crime in society does nevertheless differ.

Right-wing libertarian

The **right-wing libertarian** perspective harks back to the days of classical liberalism, characterised by competitive free-market capitalism and minimal state intervention, including welfare provision (see Chart 8.1). In this approach, human beings are conceived of as rational entities with **free will**. It is based upon a moral philosophy of egoism (selfishness), in which the only constraints on behaviour are that there should be a duty not to initiate force over others.

The notion of a **competitive ethos** pervades this perspective. This is usually tied to the idea of rights to private property as being the first virtue of the legal and criminal justice system. Accordingly, crime is defined in terms of the infringement of private property, including infringements of one's physical self. Generally this approach defines crime in restrictive terms, as only those acts which violate the 'natural rights' of others.

Since human nature is conceived of as being possessive and individualistic, and since crime is conceived mainly in terms of private prop-

Chart 8.1 Right-wing Libertarianism

Definition of crime	◆ (restrictive) only those acts which violate the 'natural rights' of others
Focus of analysis	◆ individual liberty and protection of private property rights
Cause of crime	◆ matter of rational choices involving incentives and disincentives
Nature of offender	◆ fully responsible for their own actions
Response to crime	◆ retribution, deterrence, incapacitation and punishment insofar as individual held responsible
Crime prevention	◆ decriminalisation, minimal state intervention, moral call for taking of personal responsibility and self-control
Operation of criminal justice system	◆ reduction in number of laws relating to 'victimless crime' ◆ greater use of incarceration and detention ◆ use of restitution to compensate victims ◆ support for privatisation of security, law enforcement, prisons

erty, then the role of the state should be restricted to those instances where other people actually come to harm by one's social actions. In other words, there should be **minimal state intervention** in one's life. What intervention there is should be tightly focused on enhancing and protecting individual liberty and protecting private property.

The cause of crime is seen to lie with the individual. In reinforcing notions of individual selfishness, rights and individuality, this perspective simultaneously asserts that criminological theorising of the recent past has made excuses for individuals, by taking away people's **responsibilities for their actions**. It is argued, for example, that to speak of biological drives or social determinants such as poverty takes away any notion of choice in the selection of behaviour and activity.

Individuals should be held fully responsible for their actions. Crime is seen fundamentally as a matter of **rational choice**, involving various incentives and disincentives. Since individual liberty is highly valued, however, the perspective believes that so-called 'victimless crimes' should be **decriminalised** insofar as they do not directly affect those beyond oneself. In other words, anything goes — people should have complete liberty to do as they want, as long as they do not infringe upon the property or person of others in an illegal way.

Where harm to another individual does occur, as in the case of the commission of an offence, then the offender should be **punished**. The perspective generally favours the promotion of retribution, deterrence, incapacitation and punishment in its response to crime. It is informed by a **just deserts** philosophy, whereby punishment should be proportional to the crime. Furthermore, it favours the enforcement of **restitutive measures** with respect to the victims of crime. That is, compensation should be paid by the offender to the victim for any harm which they may have caused in the course of the offence.

In response to perspectives which see behaviour mainly in terms of psychological or social influences, this approach calls for a **moralising** of society. Morality is seen in this context to be rooted in the individualistic ethos of personal responsibility and self-control. In return for minimal state intervention, it is essential that people use their liberty in accordance with the law. Where this is not so, then they should have to shoulder the penalty themselves.

In line with a general libertarian philosophy which de-emphasises the state, this approach also supports the idea that security, law enforcement and prisons should be **private** rather than public institutions. This reflects a broad ideological commitment to the so-called free market as the best and most efficient avenue for the provision of social services.

Traditionalist conservative

The **traditionalist conservative** perspective takes a broader view than the right-wing libertarian of what constitutes a crime (see Chart 8.2). The conservative view of crime includes not only that activity which endangers property or the person, but also that which **offends morality**. Hence, attacks on certain traditional values and people's general respect for authority may be viewed as criminal.

From this point of view, crime is not only a matter of 'free choice'; it is linked to certain intrinsic aspects of humanity. In particular, people are seen to possess certain 'natural urges' which go against the more civilised or divine purposes of society. Whether it be a concept of 'original sin' or a secular theory of human nature which sees

Chart 8.2 Conservatism

Definition of crime	• (expansive) violations of law, and acts which offend morality as well
Focus of analysis	• personal discipline and self-control
Cause of crime	• lack of self-discipline, undermining of traditional loyalties, lack of respect for authority
Nature of offender	• inherently 'evil' or flawed
Response to crime	• need for strong coercion, general deterrence strategies, assertion of authority
Crime prevention	• importance of traditional morality in maintenance of social authority, emphasis on self-discipline and submission to authority
Operation of criminal justice system	• expansion of laws relating to 'moral' issues such as pornography • harsher penalties to enforce the legal and moral code • order to take priority over justice • emphasis on conformity to established traditions and social roles

people in a negative light, the idea is that all people are somehow **inherently evil or flawed.**

In order to constrain the 'natural' urges to do bad or wrong, it is necessary to establish a strong order based upon personal sacrifice, self-discipline and submission to authority. **Order** must take precedence over all else, including justice. Crime is said to be caused by the unwillingness of people to accept discipline, the undermining of traditional loyalties — such as to the (patriarchal) family — and the pursuit of immediate individual gratification without appropriate hard work.

According to this approach, punishment is an essential part of deterrence. This is so not only because it establishes personal responsibility for one's actions, but also because it has an important **symbolic impact** on society as a whole. That is, punishment has to be seen in terms of its effect on the establishment of moral solidarity through stigmatisation. Punishment is, in effect, a form of social **retribution,** and may thus represent a response which is not proportional to the offence (in fact it may be much greater) due to the important symbolic role of punishment in bonding community members together.

Strong emphasis is placed upon the importance of **morality** in the maintenance of social authority. Thus, if someone does something deemed to be wrong or harmful, then they must be punished swiftly and appropriately in order to set the moral standard. Simultaneously, it is important to set clear moral standards and guidelines to conduct.

The traditionalist conservatives generally possess anti-libertarian views with respect to pornography, sexual behaviour, drug use and abortion; that is, they favour intervention in areas regarded as victimless crimes. Indeed, the conservative point of view often favours **increased state intervention** in everyday social life because it is felt that only strong coercive measures will ultimately keep people in line and teach them the discipline they require to live as members of a civilised community.

Historical Development

The New Right perspective has historical links with several different traditions within criminology. The right-wing libertarian approach is clearly identified with a **classical** criminological perspective. The emphasis on individual choice and responsibility, punishment and proportionality, and protection of liberty and property all have their echoes in the previous discussions of the social contract.

The traditionalist conservative approach has also been reflected in some criminological theorising. Its emphasis on discipline, coercion and self-control are mirrored in the concerns of **control theory**. Whether it emphasises bio-social processes (as in Eysenck's work) or socialisation processes (see Nettler, 1984), a social control perspective argues that the nature of crime is intertwined with the connection between individual and society.

Control theory as formulated by Hirschi (1969), for example, is premised upon the idea that it is an individual's bond to society which makes the difference in terms of whether or not they abide by society's general rules and values. From this perspective, all people are inherently antisocial, and thus all people would commit crime if they so dared. It is the nature of the bond that children have with their society which ultimately determines their behaviour (Empey, 1982; Nettler, 1984).

Hirschi (1969) theorised that the social bond is made up of four major elements:

- **Attachment:** the ties of affection and respect to significant others in one's life, and more generally a sensitivity to the opinion of others.
- **Commitment:** the investment of time and energy to activities such as school and various conventional and unconventional means and goals.
- **Involvement:** the patterns of living which shape immediate and long-term opportunities, for example, the idea that keeping busy doing conventional things will reduce the exposure of young people to illegal opportunities.
- **Belief:** the degree to which young people agree with the rightness of legal rules, which are seen to reflect a general moral consensus in society.

It is the combination of attachment, commitment, involvement and belief which shapes the life world of the young person, and which essentially dictates whether or not they will take advantage of conventional means and goals of social advancement, or whether they will pursue illegal pathways to self-gratification.

It is up to society, and its agents, to step in and ensure that its younger members are imbued with the right bonds. In other words, there is a high degree of intervention necessary if children and young people are to be guided the right way, and if they are to follow paths which uphold social values, but which ultimately go against their essential antisocial nature. Without adequate socialisation — a strong social control presence of some kind — criminal behaviour would be common.

Contemporary Examples

In related and more recent work, Gottfredson and Hirschi (1990) argue that the central issue in explaining crime is that of **self-control**, that is, people differ in the extent to which they are restrained from criminal acts. This in turn is linked to the question of social bonding, and especially the problem of ineffective child-rearing. The theory incorporates elements of other theories and perspectives: classical theory, in its acceptance of the idea that people are basically self-seeking; bio-social positivism, in its focus on the importance of proper 'conditioning' or training of the young; and sociological perspectives, which look to the nature of the family as a key variable in the development of self-control.

The theory does not analyse specific social divisions (e.g., class, gender, ethnicity), but rests upon a conception of human nature which sees all people as essentially driven by the same kinds of 'universal tendency to enhance their own pleasure'. Given this, the crucial issue is then one of how best to socialise all people to conform to society's values and to engage in conventional law-abiding behaviour.

In policy terms, the answer to juvenile crime lies in redressing the **defective social training** which characterise offenders who have in some way 'lost control'. In other words, the emphasis from a practitioner's perspective will be to reattach the young people to some kind of family, to recommit them to long-range conventional goals, to involve them in school and other constructive activities, and to have them acquire beliefs in the morality of law (Empey, 1982: 269).

Importantly, the control perspective is premised upon the idea that 'deviancy' stems from lack of self-control, and that this is fundamentally a matter related to the processes of socialisation. Whereas Gottfredson and Hirschi emphasised the significance of relationships within the family, other contemporary criminologists have concentrated on making changes to the costs and benefits of crime.

Much work, for example, has been done in the general area of **opportunity-rationality theory**. This approach reflects the libertarian emphasis on choice and responsibility for one's actions. It is postulated that crime cannot be understood apart from the nature and distribution of opportunities for both crime and non-criminal behaviour. Thus, when people find themselves in situations in which they have opportunities to commit crime, the decision to do so or not to do so is a rational one (see Barlow, 1993).

In fact, from the point of view of rational choice theory we need to assume that most 'criminals' are rational agents who can be deterred from committing additional crimes by an increase in the punishment they might expect to receive (Buchanan and Hartley, 1992). In economic terms, the idea here is that individuals will always act in such a way as to maximise their own benefit. They are responsive to incentives and disincentives. From an economic rationalist position, therefore, the best criminal justice policy is one which prevents the commission of crime at the least financial cost. For example, according to the advocates of this approach, the most economically efficient way in which to manage the crime problem is to privatise institutions such as prisons, and to increase the probability of detection and conviction of offenders.

The broad philosophical orientation of rational choice theory is also closely related to the adoption of crime prevention techniques directed primarily at **opportunity reduction** (see Felson, 1994), rather than the structural reasons for offending behaviour or the criminalisation process itself. Analysis of particular activities and locations can form the basis of a strategy designed to change the risks and costs associated with certain behaviours. In this way, the potential offender is deterred from making the decision to commit crime in certain areas, against certain targets.

Whatever the specific theories which have been developed over the years, the fact remains that many have adopted a New Right criminology position simply due to the fact that 'nothing else has worked'. The so-called new realists, for example, have observed the deficiencies of a system partly built upon 'treatment' and positivistic assumptions, and concluded that it is time to reassert order and authority across our social institutions (see Tame, 1991).

Given the trends toward social and economic polarisation outlined at the beginning of this chapter, and given the apparent electoral appeal of 'law-and-order' scapegoating, it is also the case that New Right criminology dovetails nicely with New Right politics generally. The academic work which has supported the turn toward more coercive and punitive forms of state intervention has largely flourished under the political patronage of government leaders and right-wing think-tanks keen to capitalise on the adoption of such an approach.

One result of this has been the generalised escalation in the punishment ethos. This is apparent at a policy level in the establishment of a 'boot camp' in Western Australia, which promises to instil self-discipline and respect for authority in young offenders (see Indemaur and White, 1994; see also Parent, 1994). It was also apparent in the 1995 election campaign in New South Wales, where each main party outbid the other in terms of who was going to be the toughest on crime. In response to publicity surrounding a 'three strikes and you're in' policy (wherein an offender committing a third serious offence would be put in prison for life), the other party simply offered the policy of 'one strike and you're in' (in instances of very serious crimes against the person). For all the criminological talk about 'rationality', the politics of the New Right criminology has been marked by sensationalist hyperbole and a high degree of irrationality.

Critique

A critique of New Right criminology stems from the way in which theories within this perspective ignore issues of power in their assertion of choice and free will. In this way the critique of New Right criminology mirrors, to some extent at least, criticisms of classical criminology. On 'rational' criteria, there is much to criticise in New Right criminology, particularly in its populist political guise.

On a theoretical level New Right criminology does not analyse the nature of choice within a society that is characterised by inequality, as opposed to equality. It does not address concerns about the ethnic and 'racial' divisions in society, and the way in which certain groups, such as indigenous people, are systematically overrepresented in the criminal justice system. The explanation that such overrepresentation can be explained purely by a 'choice' to offend does not seem to take us very far. Much New Right criminology simply ignores issues of 'race', ethnicity, gender and class by prioritising the individual, along with individual choice and individual values.

Where levels of analysis other than that of the individual are evident, it is clear that they rest on a particular set of values which do not include significant sectors of society. For example, control theory talks unproblematically about inculcating majority values, expressed through belief in the rightness of legal rules which are seen to reflect a general moral consensus in society. The interdependence of individuals which prevents criminal behaviour is premised upon adherence to the moral consensus. Non-adherence predisposes an individual to criminal offending. Within a multicultural society such as Australia, there are major problems if the notion of consensus is defined in the narrow terms that traditional conservatives tend to use.

Many of the policies proposed by New Right theories have themselves been discredited. In particular, the capacity of harsh, or even proportional, punishment to deter individuals from re-offending has been the subject of long debate. There is substantial evidence that imprisonment in particular is counterproductive, and serves only to exacerbate, not diminish, rates of offending. Prison, and the 'big stick' in general, are both ineffective and expensive.

Furthermore, the debate concerning the need for harsher penalties has negative consequences in and of itself. For example, it engenders a fear of crime, which, in Australia at least, is out of all proportion to the realistic possibility of victimisation. The problem of how to deal with the fear of crime, independent of how to deal with crime *per se*, is an urgent issue facing Australian states.

Finally, crime itself is defined narrowly. For the majority of New Right theorists, the major concern is with 'street crime'. Crimes of the powerful and crimes of the state are hardly mentioned. Where they are mentioned, the state is seen as able to deal adequately with the problem, since there is no conception that the state itself may favour the powerful over the powerless.

The popularity of the law-and-order debate, and with it the popularity of New Right criminology in general, cannot be accounted for adequately by reference to a rational 'scientific' debate. It is best explained by the need of societies for symbolic assurances of certainty in the face of growing economic uncertainty. The symbolic and political nature of the crime debate is well evidenced through the popularity of New Right criminology. It provides government with a justification to capture the emotional needs of an electorate within a capitalist democracy. The potency of the symbol of 'law and order' is not lost on governments increasingly at the mercy of unpleasant financial and employment trends in the economic sphere.

Despite the negative aspects of New Right criminology, there are elements which are of importance to the criminological debate. While it asserts issues of individual responsibility, it also highlights individual rights and, in particular, the right to feel safe and secure. The rights of victims, which had been ignored by the majority of criminologists, are brought to the fore within this perspective. Victims' rights and needs can no longer be ignored within criminological theory. Finally, the phenomenon of New Right criminology is a timely reminder of the political nature of crime and crime policy. Criminological theory has to come to grips with political realities if its policy proposals and strategic plans of action are to go beyond mere conjecture.

Conclusion

New Right criminology refers to a particular political orientation, rather than to a systematic, coherent theory in its own right. For this reason there is a broad range of theoretical perspectives which are brought together in this chapter, from authoritarian populism and right-wing libertarian perspectives through to traditionalist conservatism and control theory. Despite the differences of these approaches, all can be characterised by a focus on the rights, responsibilities and free will of the individual who offends. Each has a particular moral stance which upholds the status quo of society and the right of those with power to dictate what constitutes the moral consensus.

Each strand of New Right thinking also tends to see human nature as ultimately depraved. Without sufficient deterrent measures put in place by the state, or strong social bonds as defined by control theory, human nature would automatically lead to antisocial and criminal behaviour. Overlaid on this perspective of human nature is the need for society to clearly define right from wrong, to reward the right and, more importantly, to punish the wrong. Without such an approach, a general breakdown in law and order will result.

Like many criminological theories, the popularity of New Right criminology cannot be divorced from the broader political environment. The political popularity of the law-and-order debate and calls for tougher punishment on a political level are legitimised through many of the perspectives outlined above. The prominence of the law-and-order debate, as fostered by New Right ideas, led directly to the emergence of a new theoretical perspective on the left, namely Left Realism. It was the success of the New Right at a popular level which led sections of the Left to 'take crime seriously'. To do so they recognised that issues such as victims' rights and the popularity of a strong response to criminal behaviour resonated with community concerns, and were thus important.

Further Reading

Braithwaite, J. and Pettit, P. (1990) *Not Just Deserts: A Republican Theory of Criminal Justice*, Clarendon, Oxford.

Buchanan, C. and Hartley, P. (1992) *Criminal Choice: The Economic Theory of Crime and Its Implications for Crime Control*, Centre for Independent Studies, Sydney.

Gottfredson, M. and Hirschi, T. (1990) *A General Theory of Crime*, Stanford University Press, Stanford.

Nettler, G. (1984) *Explaining Crime*, McGraw-Hill, New York.

Tame, C. (1991) 'Freedom, Responsibility and Justice: The Criminology of the "New Right"', in K. Stenson and D. Cowell (eds) *The Politics of Crime Control*, Sage, London.

CHAPTER 9

Left Realism

Introduction

Left Realism is best seen as a response to two conflicting perspectives on crime which emerged strongly in the mid-1980s, New Right criminology and Marxist criminology. The last chapter outlined the political popularity of the conservative political perspective with its strong emphasis on 'law and order'. Left Realism was concerned that the political debate was being dominated by the right wing, which had a destructive impact on the lives of the working class. It attempted to capture the political debate by focusing, like the conservatives, on the victims of so-called street crime. However, Left Realists wanted to highlight the fact that the majority of victims of street crimes were from the working class, not the middle and upper classes. In doing so, Left Realism wanted to reorient the law-and-order debate — away from the middle-class fear of the working class, and towards a consideration of how the working class itself suffers from crime.

Left Realism saw radical criminology as unable or unwilling to ameliorate this suffering of the working class because it failed to take crime seriously. This failure further meant that such criminological analysis was unable to provide the antidote to the conservative 'law-and-order' politics which dominated crime policy. Left Realists contrasted the political popularity of the conservative Thatcher government in Britain with the political marginalisation of the radical perspective, or 'left idealist' view (as it was labelled by the Left Realists). The reason for such marginalisation, they suggested, was the lack of practical suggestions put forward by Marxist criminology to deal with crime in the inner city.

This chapter will outline the origins of Left Realism and the nature of the response it made to 'law-and-order' politics from a left perspective. It has received considerable criticism, mainly from the left, and has undergone considerable revision. The major revisions within Left Realism will also be outlined in this chapter. What is central to the Left Realist endeavour, and common to all permutations of the theory, is its pragmatic core. Left Realism sees itself as both a reasonable and practical response to the problem of crime in inner city communities.

Social Context

In terms of social context, Left Realism can be seen as a concern within (initially) British criminology with the policies of neo-conservatism in general and the Thatcher government in particular. It was avowedly political in that it saw itself as a political response to the law-and-order agenda of the right. It was this response to the law-and-order debates of the early 1980s which galvanised the thinking of Left Realists. Prior to this time they had been writing as predominantly Marxist or radical criminologists debating with other radical criminologists from within the same essential paradigm.

In attempting to enter into the political discussions of law and order, the Left Realists joined in the conservative debate about crime control, which was less concerned about the causes of crime. In doing so, they confirmed that conservative politics had successfully defined the crime problem as one where there were clear distinctions between those who were criminal and those who were not. In this conception, crime was a unitary phenomenon defined by common sense. With this in mind, crime policy was properly concerned with controlling crime, not with reducing conditions which might give rise to criminal behaviour, such as inequality and unemployment.

This emphasis on controlling crime, rather than on dealing with the causes of crime, could be clearly seen in the contribution Left Realist writers made in response to the **riots** experienced in Britain in 1981. These riots occurred in places such as Brixton, areas of poverty and high levels of unemployment, but it was not this unemployment and deprivation *per se* which captured the imagination of the Left Realists. These theorists argued that while poverty and deprivation were a precondition of riots, and more generally of increases in crime, they were not a sufficient cause. Poverty and unemployment could be associated with quiescent fatalism and the acceptance of adversity, as much as with rebellion and violence (Lea and Young, 1982). Left Realists argued that the riots had their genesis in three factors: West Indian counterculture; the political marginalisation of the inner city; and, crucially, the police methods of dealing with people who lived in deprived neighbourhoods.

The explanations by the realists for the existence of a violent and aggressive counterculture are similar to the explanations of the strain theorists, which were outlined in Chapter 4. Left Realists argued that countercultures thrive where the expectations of material rewards engendered by the education system and the mass media are manifestly not available to certain sectors of society. In particular, successive generations of West Indian immigrants in the UK saw themselves as discriminated against and alienated from the mainstream culture. In the face of this lack of opportunity, a counterculture developed — based on a 'hustling' mentality and street culture — which was competitive, disorganised and antisocial. Along with poverty and unemployment, the existence of this counterculture produced extremely high rates of inner-city crime. In opposition to Marxist criminologists, who downplayed or denied the existence of rising rates of street crime, Left Realists argued that street crime was much higher than police figures suggested.

Those who lived in the decaying inner city lacked access an effective voice within the political process; this exacerbated the alienation that people in those neighbourhoods experienced, and spawned the counterculture. Those marginalised within the inner city had no access to traditional centres of power within society, such as those controlling capital or the trade unions. Such people were locked out of the world of production, and with this, access to the political system was also denied. Left Realism suggested that the return to violence, epitomised by the riots, was the politics of last resort. Economic marginalisation exacerbated political marginalisation.

The marginalisation felt by people in these neighbourhoods was not addressed by government or state agencies. Rather, the arm of the state which had the greatest impact in the area, namely the **police**, was disastrous. Left Realists argued that in deprived neighbourhoods police deliberately shifted away from 'consensus' policing (policing for the community), which might have at least gone some way to reducing alienation in these communities. Instead, police used military tactics, 'swamp' procedures and 'stop and search' provisions which allowed on-the-street searching of any suspicious-looking person. These tactics had the effect of blurring the distinction between offender and non-offender to a point where, Left Realists argued, any action by police became perceived as a symbolic attack on the community as a whole. At this point any consensual relationship which existed between the police and the public breaks down, and actions by police can trigger rioting (Lea and Young, 1982).

The analysis of the riots in the UK set the scene for the early formulations of Left Realism, and defined the theory as one primarily concerned with the control of crime, rather than amelioration of the preconditions of crime. Relief of the preconditions of the counterculture, for example, was not the primary policy goal of the theorists. Rather they took as central planks the second and third strands of analysis outlined above — political marginalisation and policing reform. The political dimension was seen as addressed by alignment with the British Labour Party and producing policies with which the left could intervene effectively in the law-and-order debate (Lea and Young, 1984). The substance of the policies provided by Left Realism predominantly addressed the third strand of analysis, that of policing reform, and the creation of consensus-style policing within inner urban areas.

The focus on policing was seen as justified because of perceived omissions by Marxist criminology concerning the reality of crime in working-class areas. The theory argues that the major concern of the working class and marginalised poor in the city was not the crimes of the powerful, as suggested by Marxist criminology, but the property offences, robbery and domestic violence that were experienced as an everyday reality. The victims of such crimes, as well as the perpetrators, were predominantly the poor and vulnerable sections of society. The radical criminological focus on crimes of the powerful and crimes of the state 'missed the point' and failed to accurately represent the needs of the working class. Furthermore, when 'street crime' was mentioned by radical criminology it was too often romanticised: street criminals were characterised as 'latter-day Robin Hoods' rather than as perpetrators of criminal behaviour that was seriously antisocial and destructive. It was the street crime of inner-city neighbourhoods which should form the predominant focus of criminology.

Basic Concepts

Left Realist criminology is characterised by its pragmatic focus on crime control (see Chart 9.1). Because of this it is not concerned with lengthy analyses of what crime actually is. Rather, it is content to define crime as that contained in the legal code. This can be seen as partly a result of the major means of data collection used by the Left Realists, namely local crime victim surveys (see for example Jones, MacLean and Young, 1986). **Local crime victim surveys** target specific inner-city locations, and ask residents about their victimisation from criminal activity, and what residents would like done about it. As a result, the definition of crime is driven by the definitions of crime which are reported on the survey. Local residents are more likely to see crime as defined in traditional terms, and so Left Realism itself defines crime in traditional terms.

The local crime victim survey is the major tool of analysis of Left Realists. Because the emphasis is on addressing the concerns expressed by inner-city populations, analysis is directed towards concerns raised about crime in local areas as expressed through the crime surveys. In particular, this perspective is noted for concern about **intra-class crim**e, namely criminal behaviour by the working class against the working class.

More recent analysis has focused on the 'square of crime'. This consists of two dyads. One is concerned with the **criminal act**, which comprises offender and victim. The other is concerned with **social control**, which comprises social action (e.g., the actions of police and 'multi-agencies') and social reaction (e.g., the reaction of the public). A complete analysis of crime, according to Left Realists, should focus on both dyads (Young, 1991).

Chart 9.1 Left Realist Perspectives

Definition of crime	◆ as contained in legal code, with main focus on street crime
Focus of analysis	◆ crime by and against working class, with working class as both offender and victim ◆ use of crime victim surveys
Cause of crime	◆ relative deprivation ◆ ineffective methods of policing
Nature of offender	◆ most crime is intra-class ◆ offenders must be held responsible to a degree for their own actions
Response to crime	◆ develop more effective policing, and greater community control over criminal justice agencies
Crime prevention	◆ reduce alienation of community from the criminal justice system ◆ adopt problem-solving approaches ◆ take crime seriously
Operation of criminal justice system	◆ active co-operation between police and community members ◆ meeting of victim needs ◆ crime prevention programmes

The causes of crime as perceived by the Left Realists span both the conditions endemic to inner-city working-class areas, such as poor facilities and lack of jobs, and the response by the criminal justice agencies, notably the police, which exacerbate the problem of crime by their heavy-handed response. The cause of crime, according to Left Realism, results from the amalgamation of three aspects: the relative **deprivation** of those in working-class areas which gave rise to countercultures; the lack of access to the political sphere which spawned **feelings of powerlessness**; and **dissent and police responses** which antagonise local populations and cause further breakdown in these communities. This leads to rising crime rates in these areas. The level of crime, according to Left Realists, is higher than that in official figures, and is rising in areas of high social breakdown (Young, 1991).

Concern with the suffering of the victims of crime has led Left Realism to adopt a less than sympathetic view of the offender. Offenders are **responsible for their behaviour**, which is antisocial and destructive and causes great hardship within already impoverished areas of society. However, unlike New Right criminology, Left Realists do not see offenders or offending totally as a result of free will. The motivation to offend springs from the relative deprivation in these areas. Young people and ethnic minorities are led by the broader culture to expect material reward, yet their situation within the social order prevents them achieving that reward. Further to this, social cohesion in these areas has broken down. Left Realists argue that in other times of great hardship, such as the depression of the 1930s, there was a working-class solidarity and working-class culture which saw people pull together. Today inner-city areas with a high crime rate **lack social solidarity** which could insulate against feelings of deprivation. The result is anger and frustration, particularly in young people.

How do Left Realists see effective responses to these problems? The primary response has been in the area of **police and policing**. Crime can be controlled by a police force which is responsive to the needs of the local community (Kinsey, Lea and Young, 1986). Furthermore, the community needs to be in control of the police force: police should respond to local city councils rather than a distant bureaucracy at the state or national level. Local communities need effective political responses to their concerns which can be brought about by giving greater power to local councils to control criminal justice agencies. More recent writing in the area of Left Realism has dealt with what to do once offenders are apprehended. However, in areas such as penology (the study of corrections), Left Realism has largely 'borrowed' from the liberal analysis which emphasises the need for **community-based corrections.**

Crime prevention then, will be achieved by reducing the alienation of the community from the criminal justice system. This will not be achieved, though, by the agencies themselves deciding which is in the best interests of these high-crime areas. What is needed is policies which will reduce the alienation of the community from the criminal justice system. These policies will **give the local communities an active voice** in how the police in particular go about dealing with people in local areas. Local communities should be able to decide what the problems are that the police should tackle, and then should be able to work co-operatively with police to solve these problems.

The criminal justice system under a Left Realist policy agenda would involve active co-operation between community members and police, in particular. The system would be geared towards the concerns of **local communities** rather than driven by a broader, and more partisan, political agenda. The law-and-order debate would then be immune from capture by political concerns aimed at providing 'quick fix' , such as military-style policing, which is ultimately a symbolic and destructive solution.

Historical Development

The historical development of Left Realism can be seen as two 'waves': the first came out of the analysis of the Thatcher years by Left Realists in the mid-1980s; the second, more comprehensive, theory arose in response to a critique of early formulations of the theory, mainly from the so-called left idealists. Before describing these two waves, it is important to describe the way data is gathered for analysis and theorising under a Left Realist perspective. Left Realism prides itself not only on development of a paradigm with which to understand the problem of crime and criminality, but also on development of the research instrument which underpins this theorising, namely the local crime victim surveys.

The local crime victim surveys can be differentiated from broad-based crime victim surveys undertaken at state or national levels. The aim of these local surveys is to understand the problem of crime and victimisation within specific locations. These locations are the poorest and most marginalised. In Britain, for example, the first survey was undertaken in Islington, a predominantly black working-class area in London. The aim of the surveys is to monitor people's needs concerning crime, and then develop policies which accurately reflect those needs. Questions in the surveys concern themselves broadly with issues of victimisation and relationship with criminal justice agencies. The surveys purported to measure some 550 variables (MacLean, 1993).

Importantly, the surveys are seen as a complete method in themselves of obtaining the necessary information on which to base theory and policy. This can be contrasted with the traditional methods of radical research, namely case studies and ethnographies (interview and participant observation). Left Realists claim that the victim surveys generate better empirical data, which is then more authoritative in the public sphere.

There are, however significant shortcomings in victim survey data. Among these shortcomings is the problem of reporting only on those crimes which are included on the survey; white-collar crimes, for example, were omitted from early studies. Furthermore, other crimes, such as domestic violence, pose problems for those using a survey format due to the sensitivity of the material. In addition, the surveys were not used to explore the various meanings of the label 'criminal', and terms such as 'violence', 'vandalism' and 'sexual assault'. While there may be consensus regarding their seriousness, there may be little agreement concerning what these terms actually mean (Hogg, 1988). Finally, asking about what people want done about crime may not elicit the most useful response. Organised burglaries may result from the influence of the receiver of stolen goods, not the actual burglar. Arresting one burglar is unlikely to stop burglaries from happening if it is the receiver of stolen goods who provides the primary influence for the offending (Hogg, 1988).

Left Realism has attempted to deal with some of these criticisms, primarily through redesigning the survey instrument. Successive waves of victim surveys have resulted in successive refining of the theory itself. It is to the major developments that we now turn.

Early versions of Left Realism

The first formulation of Left Realism was well summarised by Russell Hogg (1988), and is substantially reproduced here. The main points are outlined below, in each case pointing to the similarities and differences to mainstream radical criminology.

- Crime is a major problem, especially personal violence and property crime, and is a problem of growing proportions.

By denoting 'crime' as the major focus, Left Realists were reasserting the centrality of 'crime' as a unifying focus for criminology. While Marxist criminology, as well as labelling theory, had gone to great lengths to highlight the contextual nature of labelling an event 'criminal', Left Realists saw crime as a unitary concept, something 'out there' and measurable. Furthermore, unlike Marxist criminology,

Left Realism emphasised 'street crime' and played down white-collar and state offences. Finally, this differed from Marxist criminology in that it saw crime as increasing. Some Marxist criminologists are less convinced of an increase, and see the rise shown by statistics as more likely a result of a 'law-and-order' panic, than any real increase in the rate of offending.

- Official crime statistics considerably underestimate the problem due to the levels of unreported crime, which is in large part a result of public alienation and frustration with the ineffectiveness of criminal justice agencies, particularly the police.

Here Left Realism is somewhat similar to mainstream radical theory in that it asserts that the community is alienated from the criminal justice system (in this case the police). However, unlike radical criminology, Left Realism argues that there is even more crime, defined in traditional terms, than suggested by police statistics.

- Most personal crime (robbery, assault, burglary etc.) is intra-class and disproportionately afflicts the poor and their neighbourhoods, thus compounding the inequalities and exploitations they already suffer.

The similarity with mainstream radical theory here is that it is the working class which primarily suffers exploitation and hardship. However, unlike some Marxists, Left Realists argue that the victimisation is primarily **intra-class**: that is, the working class preys on the working class. This is a marked diversion from traditional Marxist criminology, which emphasises that the ruling class preys on the working class.

- The police are both extremely inefficient at dealing with inner-city crime and are endemically hostile and discriminatory with regard to the inner-city populace (especially youth and ethnic minorities).

Much of this resonates with a traditional radical view with respect to the endemic hostility between police and the working class. Unlike traditional Marxists, who see police as an instrument of class control and maintenance of the status quo, Left Realism sees possible positive roles for police. Police might well be useful, if only they were more effective.

- The mutual antagonism between police and local communities sets in train a vicious circle of non co-operation whereby the alienated community does not report crime to the police, and the police respond by heavier pro-active and discriminatory police strategies, which alienates the community further.

This elaborates on why the police are ineffective, and underscores the futility of current policing methods in attempting effective control of crime. Marxist criminologists would argue, however, that the purpose of discriminatory policing is not crime control, but control of the working class. For Marxists, then, such discriminatory policing is fulfilling its purpose if it is effective in 'quieting the masses'.

- Inner-city working-class communities are deeply concerned about local crime, want effective policies to control it, and see the police as central to crime control.

This is crucial to the Left Realist position. Left Realism takes the working-class communities' opinion at face value and reasserts the position that the communities themselves see police and police response as key elements of crime control in inner-city areas. Left Realists argue that these sentiments must be listened to and acted on if radicals are to claim any credibility in attempting to help these communities. If the communities say police are potentially useful, the task for criminology is to assist in making police more responsive to the communities' needs, not to decry the police existence.

- Effective policing requires that police concentrate on those crimes that the public see as most serious, that they cease alienating the public by heavy-handed intrusive strategies, that they be brought under local democratic control through elected police authorities.

This is the last major argument of the early formulations of Left Realism. It argues that crime can be controlled within working-class communities to some extent. This must be achieved through active co-operation between the police and the policed. This differs from the general thrust of Marxist criminology, since it places prime emphasis on the possibility of reform within the capitalist system which would benefit the working class in the long term, and also argues that reform of police is possible.

This early version of Left Realism caused much debate. It became clear that the theory was too narrow, and too fixed on issues of policing. The key criticisms of this first attempt hinged around four major areas, and sprung in part from weaknesses in the research instrument, the local crime victim survey.

The first criticism concerned the problem of using 'crime' as the unifying focus. While Left Realists asserted the need to 'take crime seriously', critics asked which crime should be the major focus, and more importantly what was meant by the term crime. Critics argued that the theory treated definitions of crime as if they had common meanings that were universally accepted. Such an assumption is anathema to many on the left who assert that the term 'crime' has no common meaning. Further, popular definitions of crime are too heavily influenced by the state to be of constructive use. Terms such as 'vandalism' and 'graffiti' are used in the political sphere for political ends. The theory failed to take account of the political dimension of terms concerned with crime and criminality.

Furthermore, the use of politically tainted terms allows popular misconceptions of crime and criminality to continue. In particular it exacerbates the problem of stereotypic impressions of who 'we' are (the goodies), as opposed to 'them' (the baddies). Critics argued that Left Realism tended to treat the results of the victim surveys as if they represented a true picture of crime, and what crime is. Public concern must be understood as the result of a political process, and in particular a result of the active influence of the police and the media in shaping popular conceptions of crime and criminality.

Besides the problems of the definition and meaning of the term 'crime', critics also pointed to the narrow scope of victimisation covered by Left Realism. Concern was expressed that only certain forms of victimisation were considered as important. The most notable omissions were in the area of white-collar crime. Certain forms of white-collar crime also disproportionately affect the working class, most notably industrial pollution and negligence, loan sharking and false advertising.

Great criticism was also levelled at the narrowness concerning effective responses, notably the almost exclusive focus on policing. This partly resulted from the emphasis of the surveys themselves. Early surveys placed a great weight on what the victims felt should be done about crime. Critics argued that this allowed the assumption to remain unchallenged that in order to reduce crime one must necessarily focus on police action. Effective reduction strategies may mean something else entirely: in particular, solutions may lie outside the criminal justice system. A good example of this arises within Australia. Aboriginal communities recognise that the problem of violence within their communities results in part from the availability of alcohol. Some of these communities have taken action to limit the availability of alcohol, in some cases restricting sales in multiracial towns, such as Tenant Creek. This is seen to be far more effective than direct police action. Police action, however well-intentioned, may simply exacerbate the violence, since the cause lies outside police control.

Critics also argue for greater attention to the possible consequences of greater co-operation between the public and the police. Police responding to complaints may be ineffective in solving burglary, as mentioned above, if the primary problem is one of receiving stolen goods. Left Realists argue that changes in policing style, so that it is reactive, co-operative and accountable, will increase the flow of information to police and dramatically improve clear-up rates. However, the opposite might occur if clear-up rates were substantially boosted by verballing (i.e., untrue police testimony), for example.

If policing strategies did lead to greater numbers of arrests, Left Realism had also left open the question of what to do with offenders once they had been apprehended. They had not considered what was appropriate in dealing with offenders in terms of a humane penal policy. Furthermore, penal policy, in particular greater use of gaols, is very expensive, and Left Realism had not come to terms with methods of funding an increase in the size of the system. There were fears that this vacuum in theorising would result in the familiar conservative plea for harsher penalties.

The second wave of Left Realism

Left Realism has made attempts to come to terms with the criticisms levelled at the theory as it was initially expressed. In collection of data, analysis and policy-making there has been considerable revision of the original theory.

In terms of data collection, Left Realists have undertaken a second wave of surveys. They argue that the notion of 'victim surveys' is now a misnomer, since they now attempt to deal with a far broader range of issues. Among the new questions considered are those concerning self-report data, public evaluation of police service deliveries, police public encounters, public attitudes to adequate punishment and avoidance behaviour with respect to some crimes. Left Realists have also retreated from seeing the survey as the sole focus of data collection. They now argue that, while these surveys are important, it is necessary to supplement the data gathered in this manner with other forms of empirical inquiry. Positivist methods of data collection (such as psychological testing, for example) are seen as relevant, along with traditional radical research methods such as case studies and ethnography.

In theory at least, Left Realism has widened the focus beyond exclusive concentration on the offender, towards a broader emphasis which they conceptualise as the **square of crime**. The square of crime, as we have seen, involves two dyads. The first concerns social control and comprises police and other agencies of social control on the one hand, and the public on the other. The second concerns the criminal act and comprises the offender and the victim. The current aim of Left Realism is to address all parts of the square, in that all aspects need to addressed in theory, research and policy. Further to this, each aspect should not be taken as a separate entity, as the interaction between each element is crucial to understanding crime and crime control. Crime rates are, according to Left Realists, a product of the four aspects of the square of crime (Young 1991).

What is being argued by Left Realists in this proposal of the 'square of crime' is that in order to deal in a comprehensive manner with crime, all four aspects — the police, the public, the victim and the offender — need to be addressed. There needs to be analysis of the state and the problems of defining crime within a political system, as the left argues *but* there also needs to be realistic account taken of the 'reality' of crime and the offender–victim dyad. This means researching appropriate responses which can address the needs of victims, as well as supporting programmes and policies which both reduce offending before it occurs (crime prevention), and respond effectively when offences do occur.

Left Realism has also broadened its focus in terms of the crimes which are considered of major concern. Recent volumes contain analyses of white-collar offending and issues of gender which are more explicitly brought into the Left Realist fold (Lowman and

MacLean, 1992). Importantly, Left Realism has also acknowledged the need to discuss penal reform.

However, much of this writing has not come from the Left Realists themselves, but from authors with particular research interests which are used to 'fill the gaps' of earlier versions of the theory. In addition, when theorising is undertaken by those readily identified with Left Realism, such as Roger Matthews (1989) in the case of penal reform, the suggestions which are mooted do not differ significantly from liberal suggestions in the same area.

Left Realism has then shifted ground from identifying with radical or Marxist criminology to a position which is more easily described as social democratic or liberal. That is, it is more concerned with a reform agenda that deals with the issues of crime and crime control within the current social system, than with suggesting that the system itself is the root of the problem and should be changed. In doing so, it borrows heavily from theories and research which are characteristic of the middle ground, such as strain theory, labelling, and certain strands of radical criminology. By shifting ground in this way, Left Realism loses some of its identity and at times becomes indistinguishable from the theories it replaces, or purports to supersede.

Contemporary Examples

This section looks at Left Realism in Australia. It is important to point out that Left Realism *per se* does not exist as an independent entity within Australia. Nonetheless, a group of academics, working primarily out of Sydney, have taken up many of the Left Realist ideas. It is interesting to note that a Left Realist perspective was taken up in New South Wales at a time when that state was experiencing a strong political emphasis on law and order by the (then) Liberal (conservative) government in the late 1980s. The government of that period promoted a law-and-order policy which purported to take crime seriously by increasing police powers and increasing the use of prison as a sentencing option, as well as increasing the time spent in detention.

A group known as the Campaign for Criminal Justice (CCJ) challenged the 'law-and-order' rhetoric of the Liberal government and proposed a new direction for crime policy. The group comprises not only academics but youth workers, left lawyers and those working in the criminal justice system in that state. Like Left Realists in the UK the CCJ argued that crime was rising, and that those who were the victims were the most vulnerable, in this case old people, women, children and the Aboriginal population. Furthermore, the group also advocated the use of the local crime victim survey, undertaking a survey in inner Sydney. This survey was concerned with the fear of crime and its connection to the local social and economic organisation of particular communities.

It is important to note that the expression of Left Realism within Australia is much broader that the predominant focus on policing which characterised Left Realism, at least in the early stages in the UK. 'Left Realism' within Australia is not seen as a radical break from critical criminology generally.

However, like Left Realists in the UK, the CCJ sought to influence the political process directly. In particular it worked with the Labor opposition in the formulation of policy which could neutralise the conservative 'law-and-order' rhetoric. Both the nature of that influence, and its eventual effectiveness, deserve comment. In terms of policies, the CCJ proposed such measures as:

- a requirement that all new government policy be accompanied by a crime impact statement
- crime related social impact be a factor built into urban planning
- development of local safety strategies
- maintaining staffing on public transport
- development of strategies be built around community participation, using local action groups like tenants groups, refuges resident and action groups.

These measures seek to place 'crime' on the political and academic agenda in a way that recognises the social and political motives of crime and crime policy. It seeks to engage government in dialogue about reforms to reduce the victimisation of vulnerable groups.

The fate of this policy was considerably undermined, if not abandoned, in the 1995 New South Wales elections. Instead of promoting a broadly Left Realist agenda, the Labor party was in the forefront of a renewed conservative law-and-order debate, promoting tough new crime policies aimed at increasing imprisonment, especially for 'serious' offences. Left Realists still have a way to go if they are to capture the political debate.

Critique

An adequate critique of Left Realism has to encompass both early and later versions in order to get a clear picture of the strengths and weaknesses of the theory as a whole.

It will be remembered that the criticisms of early versions of Left Realism were as follows:

- **The definition of crime.** In particular, the theory treated definitions of crime as if they had factual uncontested meanings.
- **The scope of victimisation covered by Left Realism was very narrow.** It omitted certain offences, most notably white-collar offences, and then presented the results as if this gave a total picture of crime.
- **The focus of response was very narrow.** The theory was almost exclusively concerned with issues of police and policing style.
- **There was a lack of any realistic penal policy.** The theory had not considered to any degree how to deal with offenders once they were apprehended.
- Finally there were concerns, mainly expressed by radical criminologists, that **Left Realists accepted the notion that the criminal law could be liberating.** Critics argued that the problem in working-class areas was not crime, but community breakdown. This being the case, the criminal law could only exacerbate problems, not ameliorate them.

As stated, Left Realists made a concerted effort to ameliorate these problems. In particular, they broadened the scope of their analysis to include white-collar offences in their victim surveys. They also began to look at the issues surrounding an adequate penal policy. Rather than being a narrow, single-issue theory, Left Realism now attempts to look at what it calls the 'square of crime' concerned with both social control and the criminal act, as outlined above. How successful has this been?

In broadening its focus Left Realism could be said to have lost its defining parameters, and with them any claims for being a separate theoretical entity. Many elements of Left Realism appear in similar form elsewhere: for example, elements of strain theory deal with the formation of anti-social cultures; and liberal forms of criminology also seek to redress the inequities of the system here and now. Left Realism is an eclectic mix of criminological theory of a generally liberal nature, which sees society as based on conflicting, but ultimately not irreconcilable, differences.

There is nothing wrong with an eclectic theory or one based on 'multifactorial explanations'. However, when a theoretical perspective draws together theoretical insights from diverse traditions, the question of compatibility of ideas arises. Left Realism identifies itself with a Marxist tradition; however, this tradition sees attempts to democratise sections of the state apparatus, such as the police, as being linked to wider political strategies which go directly to the heart of who controls production and government in a capitalist society. Indeed, attempts to democratise the police through local councils in the UK kindled the ire of the conservative national government; it responded by substantially reducing the power of local government in that country, effectively neutralising police reforms. The point is that eclecticism is acceptable if the theory links diverse traditions in a way which is ultimately productive and without irretrievable conflict.

Some would argue that Left Realism has failed to do this. It retains a notion of consensus concerning crime which many would argue is not sustainable. Furthermore, the aims of the theory itself may be incompatible. For example, to enlist the co-operation of police in 'fighting crime' while at the same time attempting an adequate critique of the role of the state in perpetuating crime would be seen by many as a contradiction in terms.

Nonetheless, Left Realism has contributed positively to the criminological debate. It has reasserted the need to take account of those most affected by crime, the marginalised and the working class. It has sought to take the views of these people seriously and to translate their views into a workable policy agenda. This has been particularly important at a time when 'law-and-order' policies dominate the political debate.

Conclusion

Left Realism can be seen as a left-wing response to the law-and-order debate dominated predominantly by the right in politics. As such, it sees itself in contrast to that criminology which sees the discipline as a value-free and neutral exercise. Left Realism identifies itself as part of a socialist strategy to democratise the state apparatus and other areas of social and economic life. Responding to crime is a political process, not a neutral research exercise. However, Left Realists argue that doing something practical in the current environment means much more than simply raising class-consciousness or working for 'the revolution' some time in the future.

Left Realism has stimulated much debate, most of it from other radical traditions. The response to the criticisms has been for Left Realism to broaden its focus, use a wide range of empirical research, and borrow from other theoretical perspectives in order to 'fill the gaps' of its initially narrow focus. There have been some successes in this attempt, and it has spawned useful debate in the Australian context with the work of the Campaign for Criminal Justice.

In the next chapter we focus on another recent theory which is generally eclectic in nature. In this case, however, the theory starts from a very different philosophical base, that of republicanism.

Further Reading

Hogg, R. (1988) 'Taking Crime Seriously: Left Realism and Australian Criminology', in M. Findlay and R. Hogg (eds), *Understanding Crime and Criminal Justice*, Law Book Company, Sydney.

Lea, J. and Young, J. (1984) *What is to be Done about Law and Order?*, Penguin, London.

Young, J. (1986) 'The Failure of Criminology: The Need for a Radical Realism', in R. Matthews and J. Young (eds) *Confronting Crime*, Sage, London.

Young, J. (1992) 'Realist Research as a Basis for Local Criminal Justice Policy', in J. Lowman and B. MacLean (eds) *Realist*

Criminology: Crime Control and Policing in the 1990s, University of Toronto Press, Toronto.

Young, J. (1991) 'Left Realism and the Priorities of Crime Control', in K. Stenson and D. Cowell (eds) *The Politics of Crime Control,* Sage, London.

CHAPTER 10

Republican Theory

Introduction

This chapter discusses the **republican theory** of criminal justice. As a relatively new theoretical perspective, republican theory draws upon a wide range of concepts and trends which we have previously examined. The hallmark of the republican approach is its stress on the need for a restorative form of justice, rather than a punitive one.

The strength of republican theory is that it provides a wholistic view of crime and society. In moving toward a general theory of crime, republicanism offers a **normative** theory of crime, based on the premise of how to make a good society by outlining the values that should underpin the ideal operation of the criminal justice system. With respect to this, the theory seeks to reform or reshape our major institutions in accordance to the ideals of republican liberalism. The theory thus stands as a systematic critique of authoritarian populism, which it views as wrong and dangerous, in that it claims we can use reason and justice to inform institutional practices rather than refer to base emotions such as hatred and fear.

The theory also offers an analysis and outline of how the criminal justice system could be reorganised **in practice** to reflect restorative justice. It is here that the theory has gained much prominence, insofar as the notion of 'reintegrative shaming' has received much international attention. The theory argues that we need to emphasise positive ways in which to deal with offenders, and victims, and that a punitive response to crime will lead only to negative social consequences.

Social Context

Some criminological theories commence with a broad conception of the society we live in and what the society as a whole should be striving to achieve. Such theories usually begin with a theory of society, and a vision of 'the good'. Within the radical framework (Marxist and feminist theory), for example, society is characterised by profound inequalities, such as poverty, racism, sexism and other exploitative situations created by imbalances of power. The solution sought is for a revolutionary change in the core structures and nature of society generally, requiring collective mobilisation for change. There is an attempt to raise the consciousness of those most affected by the discriminatory actions of the capitalist state, to expose the evils and injustices built into the system, and to expand democratic participation and economic redistribution.

Conservative theories (New Right and other populist versions of this) also start with a conception of society as a whole. Here society is characterised as being comprised of self-interested individuals, some of whom are particularly evil or bad. This perspective asserts that crime results as a consequence of the disorder in society. It therefore seeks to re-establish discipline, order and authority. The aim is to restore society to the way things used to be. In this sense, it often appeals to a mythical 'golden age'. The theories argue that the society requires a strong state which will assert its authority in a moral way, in order to maintain the free economy. In this system, law and order must take precedence over justice. The focus is on 'street crime' and crimes committed by the less powerful, for example social security fraud etc. Crime is seen to result from a breakdown in the societal moral fibre, hence the stress on morality, liberty and authority.

As we saw, Left Realism emerged as a response to the conservative backlash of the 1980s. This perspective has tended, however, to move away from a theory of society *per se* (i.e., based upon socialist principles) to focus specifically on crime, which is viewed as a problem that needs to be taken seriously. There has been a consequent shift away from the big picture, that is, structural causes, to focus on specific issues, such as the victims of crime and the effects of crime on the less powerful — the working class, the poor, blacks, females, etc. It is argued that the community is concerned about crime, hence the focus should be on fighting crime at the local level, and the main concern is with developing an effective form of policing which is responsible, responsive and democratic.

The conservative push to get tough on offenders through concerted law-and-order campaigns spurred the particular response adopted by the Left Realists. Republican theory likewise is a response to the conservative push of the last two decades (see Braithwaite and Pettit, 1990). Many conservatives were critical of the crime prevention strategies of treatment and rehabilitation being pursued by the positivists in dealing with offenders. The **retributivists** claimed treatment, rehabilitation and preventive measures had not worked and had in some instances been grossly unjust. They pointed to cases where indeterminate sentences had been wrongly applied (e.g., in the USA, a juvenile offender making obscene phone calls was put into detention for six years). They highlighted the injustice and futility of strategies adopted by the **preventivists**, who sought to rehabilitate and deter offenders through incapacitation. The retributivists called for punishment of the offender in accordance with their 'just deserts' — that is, offenders should get what they deserve in proportion to the gravity of the offence and the culpability of the offender.

Retributivists have tended to focus on sentencing. The notion is that we must change the way in which we sentence people, because treatment is not working. Braithwaite and Pettit (1990) challenged the retributivist perspective on a variety of levels. They argued that:

- The criminal justice system should be organised so as to promote the goal of republican liberty, which is construed as personal dominion; and
- A theory of criminal justice needs to cover a broad range of issues. A comprehensive theory is required to cover such things as what should be criminalised; what guidelines should cover police surveillance; what initiatives should be possible in the pursuit of offenders; and what procedures should be followed in prosecution and adjudication and the sentences to be imposed for given offences.

Braithwaite and Pettit (1990) argued that the retributivist theory does not address these questions adequately and instead focuses solely on sub-questions. They argue that if a theory deals only with questions of sentencing, as the retributivist theory does, then any initiatives taken in respect to this area of the justice system are likely to flow on and affect other parts of the system. Hence they argue that we cannot simply tinker with only one part of the system: we need to look at the system as a whole.

They are critical as well of other goal-oriented approaches such as **utilitarianism** — a system that suggests we should promote the greatest good for the greatest number, because injustices can lead to good for the greatest number. They are also critical of the sole goal of the criminal justice system being that of crime prevention, because this can lead to increased intrusiveness, such as holding parents totally responsible for their children's actions.

The alternative theory proposed by Pettit and Braithwaite is the **republican theory** (Braithwaite and Pettit, 1990; Pettit and Braithwaite, 1993). This theory seeks to link up with older republican traditions of thinking that sought to promote the notion of liberty. These theories extend from Roman times, through the philosophies of republicanism developed in the northern Italian republics, to those apparent in the course of the English Civil War and in the American Revolution in the eighteenth century. In this historical thinking about liberty, freedom was perceived as the social status enjoyed by someone other than a slave, someone so protected by the law and culture of their community that they did not have to depend upon the grace of another for the enjoyment of independent choice. Liberty was conceptualised as the negative good of not being interfered with by others.

This republican notion of negative liberty was displaced in the nineteenth century by a new, different sense of liberalism. Here the main objective is to avoid interference by the state and the law altogether, and thus, as well, to exclude the enjoyment of being protected against possible interference. This right-wing libertarian perspective promoted the notion of the free market and sought to remove government constraints on trade, the labour market, and so on. The enjoyment of non-interference in our lives was thus at the mercy of those who chose to interfere. Based upon a competitive 'law of the jungle' notion, this perspective is premised on the belief that we are all free and should be able to do what we want without any interference whatsoever.

The republican conception of liberty differs from this nineteenth-century conception. It involves the concept of personal liberty constituted by **protection of liberty by the law**. Non-interference should not be enjoyed only as a matter of contingent luck; instead, it should be extended to all by the law and its related institutions. The non-interference involved is to be of a resilient or secure nature. That is, the person who enjoys non-interference is thereby protected from the predations of the potential interferer. Should someone choose to interfere, then the law or other protective institutions would move to block that interference and provide whatever compensation is necessary in order to restore the person to their former status.

The law and its related institutions are seen to play a central role in maintaining republican liberty. There has to be equal knowledge that we collectively enjoy that status of being guarded from interference.

Basic Concepts

In the republican view, crime is seen as the **denial of personal dominion** — evil is always represented by this denial (see Chart 10.1). Three characteristics of these denials are identified.

- The first is a negative challenge to the **dominion status** of the victim. A threat to, or disregard for, the dominion of an individual is an attack on the status of that individual as someone who holds a protected dominion status in society. If someone commits a crime against an individual then the criminal act asserts the vulnerability of the victim to the will of the criminal, nullifying the protected status of the victim.
- Second, if successful, the criminal attempt not only disregards the victim's dominion, but also undermines, **diminishes** and perhaps even **destroys the individual's dominion**. For example, kidnapping or murdering someone will destroy their dominion, while stealing a person's property will diminish their dominion, by undermining certain exercises of dominion they might otherwise have pursued (e.g., it diminishes their liberty to use that property).
- Third, every crime also represents **communal evil**; it does an evil to the community as a whole. A crime not only affects the dominion status of the individual victim, but also endangers the commu-

Chart 10.1 Republican Theory

Definition of crime	◆ denial of dominion, largely reflected in legal code
Focus of analysis	◆ victim, community and offender dominion, particularly in areas where shaming may be appropriate (drink-driving, white-collar crime, juvenile justice)
Cause of crime	◆ lack of self-sanctioning conscience and appropriate social connections (lack of inter-dependency) ◆ broader society characterised by mobility and a focus on individualism (lack of communit-arianism)
Nature of offender	◆ partly voluntary, partly determined, responsi-bility and opportunity
Response to crime	◆ reintegrative shaming, least restrictive measures
Crime prevention	◆ promotion of valued norms, fostering of communitarianism
Operation of criminal justice system	◆ expansion of reintegrative shaming into social life of community through family group conferences, victim–offender meetings

nity's notion of resilient status. Every act of crime represents a challenge to the dominion of people in society generally who will begin to doubt that they really do have resilient status.

If every act of crime represents damage to dominion, then the system's task is to promote dominion, by rectifying or remedying the damage caused by the crime. What should the courts do in response to the convicted offender, for example?

Theoretically, in sentencing the convicted offender the courts need to consider certain elements: First, the offender must **recognise** the personal liberty of the victim in order to restore the victim's status. In order to do this, the offender must withdraw the implicit claim that the victim did not enjoy the dominion which was challenged by the crime. Second, in order to restore the victim's former dominion — which may not only have been disregarded, but may also have been diminished or destroyed — there must be some form of **recompense** for the damage done to the individual's personal dominion. And third, there must be a general **reassurance** given to the community in general of a kind that may undo the negative impact of crime on their enjoyment of dominion.

The republican theory thus assumes an equilibrium model of criminal justice, because it seeks to **restore the dominion status of the victim,** by reintegrating the victim back into society so that they can once again exercise their personal dominion. Abstractly, the recognition of dominion of the victim by the offender requires a mix of measures, both symbolic and substantive.

From a republican point of view the causes of crime lie in a combination of social and psychological factors. Part of the problem is the lack of a **self-sanctioning conscience.** This is where an individual has not learned adequately the interpretation and acceptance of societal norms as being right and just. One of the results of a punitive and stigmatising system is that it propels people into associating with other similarly ostracised individuals (for instance, in a criminal subculture) who individually and collectively do not develop this conscience.

The lack of adequate and appropriate social connections is expressed in the concept of **communitarianism.** This describes interdependency at a societal level involving relationships of loyalty, trust and concern. Interdependency is itself reflected in a person's relationship to school, work, marriage, stable residence and so on. The issue of social opportunity is important insofar as it affects the interdependencies and eventually the moral development of an individual.

The response to crime in a specific sense is to utilise the least restrictive measures possible, and to undo the wrong that has been committed. The republican theory of criminal justice is intended to deal with the victim so they can once again exercise public dominion and the community can be reassured. The focus is on **maximising personal dominion** for the victim. However, there is also the assumption that the offender should be reintegrated so that their dominion can be reinstated also. The theory seeks minimalist response on the part of the state to the offender. A reintegrative equilibrium needs to be established, where the victim, the community and the offender are considered.

The republican response to crime therefore bases itself on the concept of **reintegrative shaming.** This involves a process in which the offender is shamed for their action, but is not 'cast out' as a person.

It describes a process whereby the offender is publicly rebuked for the harm they have caused, but is then forgiven and reintegrated into the mainstream of society. As part of the reintegrative shaming process, the victim is directly involved in proceedings and is able to be compensated in some way for the harm done.

From a crime prevention perspective, steps should be taken to **promote valued norms** (which, in turn, become the basis for the formation of a self-sanctioning conscience) and to **foster greater communitarianism** by enhancing educational, work and social opportunities. The criminal justice system ought to incorporate a broad range of informal and more formal institutional arrangements, such as conferences of the offender and victims, and be oriented toward the least intrusive kind of intervention as is possible.

Historical Development

The historical development of republican theory is undoubtedly tied to the liberal tradition, outlined earlier in the chapter. It can be traced to the concern with crime and criminality as championed by Montesquieu which aimed at 'lessening the burden of fear in the minds of ordinary citizens' (Shklar, 1987, cited in Braithwaite and Pettit, 1990: 61). Its roots can be clearly seen within the classical tradition.

Furthermore, however, republican theory can be seen as a liberal response to the changing shape of capitalism and the ensuing uncertainty and opportunities this engenders. Just as positivism was seen earlier in light of the challenges posed by the industrial revolution, with its emphasis on positive reform, so republican theory can be seen to have a similar emphasis on attempting constructive changes based on contemporary research and reflection about the current challenges posed by the fragmentation and fluidity of contemporary capitalism.

The advent of significant social and economic transformation, and the existence of a highly educated population as in Australia, means that current theories can in part be measured by their ability to provide solutions to immediate contemporary concerns. These include issues such as white-collar crime and the plight of victims of crime, particularly of family violence. In fact, republican theory has had a longstanding concern with white-collar crime. In contrast to Marxist criminology, however, with which it shares many similar concerns, republican theory is essentially optimistic about changing business practice within the current capitalist structure. Fundamentally, the principles applied to the control of 'street crime', republican theorists argue, have equal applicability in the white-collar sphere.

The concern with victims evident in republican theory can be seen as part of a much broader shift within criminology in recent years. Victimology, the study of victims of crime, is a recently established subdiscipline within criminology. It has gained considerable popularity at a theoretical level, and also in government policy. An example of its acceptance by governments is the introduction of victim impact statements (i.e., written statements by victims handed to the judge at sentencing) in some states, such as Victoria and South Australia. Republican theory shares common ground with a number of perspectives which aim to integrate the needs of both victims and offenders within the same system. The term **restorative justice** is sometimes used in association with these perspectives (Wright, 1991). The aim of such perspectives is to develop policies whereby the offender makes reparation for wrongdoing, and in doing so restores the victim's and the general population's faith in society. The popularity of this notion, combined with escalating costs of court hearings, has seen the proliferation of mediation centres as alternatives to court.

The key to republican theory, then, is that it attempts to provide a normative theory of crime and society; it comes from a particular value stance or goal of criminal justice — to maximise personal dominion, which is construed as republican liberty.

The main elements of the theory were developed in the light of differences between republican and retributivist perspectives on sentencing (Braithwaite and Pettit, 1990). Retributivists argue that in sentencing an offender, the motivation of the criminal justice system is to ensure that no crime goes unpunished. The republican theorists agree that convicted offenders need to be sentenced, but this is seen as necessary because the goal of the criminal justice system should be the promotion of dominion. This view leads to different conclusions regarding the operation of the criminal justice system.

Whilst retributionists seek some sort of repayment for the offence and argue for penalties proportional to the crime, republican theorists argue for a **rectification of the offence** — to put the harm right. Hence, while the retributivist concentrates on the offender, the republican examines the harm done to both the victim(s) and the community. In terms of the kind and degree of penalty to be imposed, the two perspectives differ once again. The retributivists look for hard treatment as the appropriate form of response on the grounds of proportionality and a guarantee of deterrence. Thus, retributivists tend to impose upper and lower limits on sentences which are available to the courts, and generally ignore circumstantial and mitigating factors.

Republican theorists seek to impose upper limits like the retributivists; however, they disagree with the imposition of lower limits, arguing that there should be a whole range of measures available at the lower levels. Furthermore, they argue against long sentences and capital punishment.

In outline, the main features of the republican theory as a response to 'just deserts' retributivist perspectives are follows (see Braithwaite and Pettit, 1990):

1   It is a comprehensive normative theory of criminal justice. It tackles questions ranging from how to define crime to how prisons should be run.
2   It is a consequentialist theory — it looks at the consequences of what we do and evaluates the criminal justice system in terms of the consequences it promotes, not the constraints of the system.
3   Republican theory sets up as the consequences of concern the republican target of maximising dominion. That is, there is an assumption that the system should ensure that the consequences promote maximisation of dominion.
4   The theory involves a restrictive rights-respecting form of consequentialism. People within the system are restricted against breaching certain rights of individuals. The emphasis is on the equal rights of republican liberty. In terms of practical policy, this translates into the notion that the system should not intrude in our lives in any major way.
5   The theory is limits-respecting. The system should intrude in our lives in a minimal way. If the goal of the system is to prevent crime, then there is no end to the extreme measures that can be

enacted, and this may see an escalation of intrusive measures and invasive techniques of investigation. As the republican theory promotes the goal of maximising dominion, it steers away from a police state which it sees as introducing measures which reduce dominion. The system should not intrude into our lives under the rubric of crime prevention.

6   The theory supports four main assumptions of systems operation:

- **Parsimony:** which assumes that the onus of proof must always rest on the side of justifying criminal justice intrusions, not on the side of justifying their removal.

- **Checking of power:** controls should be established and constraints placed upon those who have the power in the system to intervene in our individual and collective lives. In this way the required accountability can be achieved.

- **Reprobation:** the criminal justice system should be designed to expose offenders in a constructive way to community disapproval.

- **Reintegration:** the system should seek to restore to the enjoyment of full dominion those who have been deprived of it by either crime or punishment.

Republican theorists argue that the practical theory can be introduced bit by bit in a strategy of incremental implementation. Some other measures that they favour include: a codification of rights; a system supporting the right to a fair trial; a system which guarantees the right to protection of the person (i.e., against capital punishment and corporal punishment); and a presumption in favour of punishments against the property rather than the province of offenders, that is, fines, restitution and community service rather than imprisonment.

The kinds of principles which republican theorists support in practice include such things as rendering police more accountable for surveillance of suspects, and decrements to all layers of criminal justice intervention, such as less criminal law, less police surveillance, less prosecution and less punishment. Hence, republican theorists support a system that is as unintrusive as possible, where consideration is extended to victims, offenders and community alike.

Contemporary Examples

The republican theory is built upon responding to crime in a manner which is unique and, theoretically, positive for all parties. As Braithwaite and Pettit (1990: 2) see it, 'we need a theory of criminal justice which allows us to respond in the best way to harmful conduct, where responding in that way sometimes will, and more often than not, entail punishment'. In broad conceptual terms, republican responses to crime entail both **symbolic measures,** and **substantive measures** which involve material actions necessary to give credibility and sincerity to the symbolic measures. The measures adopted in practice depend upon the immediate circumstances of the players.

The substantive nature of recompense involves either restitution, compensation or reparation. **Restitution** means to return to the victim whatever it was that was lost in the commission of the offence. For example, it may involve giving back stolen property. **Compensation** occurs where restitution is not possible. This entails an attempt to make up for the loss the victim has experienced. **Reparation** is where neither restitution not compensation is possible, for example, in the case of murder. This is an offering of compensation to those close to and dependent on the victim of the offence.

At a theoretical level, the remedies and responses put forward by the republican theorists reflect their overall concerns with personal dominion and restorative justice. The actual response to crime should reflect the following concerns (Pettit and Braithwaite, 1993):

- The offender must **recognise** the personal liberty of the victim in order to restore the dominion status of the victim. In order to do this, the offender must withdraw the implicit claim that the victim did not enjoy the dominion which was challenged by the crime. This can be achieved through some type of symbolic measure (e.g., an apology on the part of the offender for their behaviour, a commitment not to re-offend, reconciliation with the victim).
- In order to restore the victim's former dominion — which may not have been simply disregarded, but may have been destroyed or diminished — there must be some form of **recompense** for the damage done to the individual's personal dominion. This can be

achieved through a range of substantive measures (e.g., restitution to the victim of whatever was lost in the commission of an offence, compensation where restitution is not possible, and reparation where restitution or compensation is not possible, as in the case of those close to or dependent upon a victim of murder).

- There must be a general **reassurance** given to the community at large of a kind that will undo the negative impact of the crime on their collective and personal enjoyment of dominion. This means that there has to be some guarantee that the community will be protected from future acts. For instance, through a process of reprobation the criminal justice system should be designed to expose offenders in a constructive way to community disapproval, and to reintegrate the victim and the offender back into community life.

An explanatory theory of republican justice is one which moves from a normative view of the criminal justice system (what ought to be) to a discussion of practical intervention measures (what can be put into place). Here the republican theory argues strongly that reintegrative shaming is the key to crime control (Braithwaite, 1989). In arguing this line, Braithwaite looks to labelling theory in order to highlight how his theory moves away from the undesirable effects of shaming.

In discussing labelling theory (Chapter 5), we saw that when an individual is termed 'bad', that label can stigmatise the individual. There is a need, however, to distinguish between stigmatisation which increases the risks of reoffending by the shamed actor, and reintegrative shaming. In terms of the preferred second approach, disapproval is extended while a relationship of respect is sustained with the offender. Stigmatisation is disrespectful — it is seen as a humiliating form of shaming, where the offender is branded an evil person and is cast out permanently. Reintegrative shaming, by contrast, seeks to **shame the evil deed** but sees the offender in a respectable light. The shaming is finite and the offender is given the opportunity to re-enter society by way of recognising the wrongdoing, apologising and being repentant. In this way, shame is seen as useful as a means of combating crime as long as it is not applied in a stigmatising fashion.

Braithwaite (1989) argues that we need a culture where we promote a self-sanctioning conscience. If we can develop in society certain norms and cultures, then individuals will not engage in certain activities because their conscience will prevent them: they will feel ashamed for doing the wrong thing. In this respect, republican theory links up with older conservative theories which look to the internalisation of controls in addition to societal imposition of controls. Thus, the theory looks to both external processes of shaming (as expressed in official institutional intervention) and also internal self-sanctioning forms of shaming (as expressed in the ideas of control theory).

The concept of reintegrative shaming has been employed in a number of different ways. The importance in the system of criminal justice of combining formal and informal processes of social control is seen to be relevant in such areas as business practices, domestic violence and juvenile justice (see Braithwaite, 1991, 1992, 1993).

The theory asserts that we need a fair degree of community shaming before the offender reaches the stage of formal institutional shaming. In this manner, we need to ensure that a 'public' conscience exists in society, along with a culture that develops this kind of conscience within each person. For example, if **domestic violence** is deemed intolerable by the community, then potential violators will stop themselves because they imagine wider community disapproval. This informal shaming process occurs outside the criminal justice system in order to prevent the crime from occurring. It is argued that formal sanctions should not be imposed until further down the track.

In terms of **business regulation**, what do we do when corporations are stepping outside of the bounds of legality? Braithwaite (1992) argues that we need to persuade rather than to jump in with legal responses. He points to consumer organisations and lobby groups and their persuasive potential to encourage corporations to refrain from, for instance, pumping toxic waste into our waterways. In other words, there are a number of informal controls that can be employed to regulate business deviance.

The approach advanced by republican theory is most evident in a practical sense in Australia, New Zealand and the USA in the area of **juvenile justice**. The theory is premised on the notion of communitarianism — a societal characteristic most critical for fostering shaming that is reintegrative. The assumption here is that people need to be connected at the local level, primarily via family relationships. The three elements of communitarianism are:

- a densely enmeshed interdependency between the people involved
- this interdependency is characterised by mutual obligations and trust
- mutual obligations and trust should be interpreted as a matter of group loyalty rather than individual convenience.

The practical implications of republican theory have been witnessed in relation to how some systems are currently attempting to deal with juvenile offending — in a non-bureaucratic way at the local level, with strong community participation. For example, the New Zealand family conference programme (Maxwell, 1993; Maxwell and Morris, 1994) and recent Australian police cautioning programmes (see Alder and Wundersitz, 1994, and Cunneen and White, 1995) revolve around programmes that bring the offender, the victim, and other members of the community together. The offender is made to apologise and provide some sort of restitution; after being shamed among their friends and family, they are then 'forgiven' and reintegrated into the community.

The practical face of reintegrative shaming is meant to reconstitute or restore the personal dominion of both the victim and the offender. However, major questions remain as to whether or not such juvenile justice programmes can actually succeed in 'reintegrating' young people in a period of profound economic downturn. Furthermore, while a sharp distinction can be drawn at a conceptual level between 'shaming' and 'stigmatisation' (see Braithwaite and Mugford, 1994), it is debatable whether this is in fact what will occur at the level of practice. This is particularly so when one considers the prominent role of the police in such programmes in several Australian jurisdictions (Cunneen and White, 1995).

Critique

A number of criticisms can be levelled at the republican theory. One weakness of the theory is that it does not really look at the causes of crime. What it does do is provide a whole range of variables which are associated with crime, at the level of both the individual (interdependency) and society (communitarianism). The theory thus provides a description of 'background' characteristics of the 'typical offender' (e.g., young, unemployed, male, transient) without really exploring how these factors interact with the given environment that leads to offending.

Furthermore, the societal-level variable 'communitarianism' needs greater analysis if it is to be a truly useful concept in analysing potential levels of criminality within a given society. It is one thing to link variables by way of association to an underlying construct; it is quite another to map out, in any given society, how each is ordered, and what the 'flow' of the variables is. It is important to do this in order to explain why some parts of society are more vulnerable to crime, and in particular to locate the individual offender within society in a way that provides a meaningful explanation for the pressures to offend. Thus far, republican theory has tended to remain at the level of description when dealing with the way the world actually is, with the theory outlined in its fullest extent with respect to some notion of an ideal society.

When dealing with a less than ideal society, further problems arise. The notion of exercising self-control and the concept of the self-sanctioning conscience raise a number of questions when they are applied to a society which has a great divide between rich and poor. The theory assumes that individuals make incorrect choices which ultimately lead to their criminal behaviour. However, if the social and economic world of the individual is falling apart, the offender is obviously in a difficult situation. The theory has little to say about the structural characteristics of the young offenders being targeted. How does the family group conference or other arenas which flow from republican theory aim to take account of these issues? The policies that have been suggested thus far appear unable to deal with real clashes of interest between wealth and poverty, issues of racism, and the wider issues of class structure. The policies emanating from the theory do not address the degree to which young people may be brought into the system because of institutional biases, such as police bias, or bias in decision-making of the courts.

These problems arise partly because the theory works on the idea of a presumed consensus within society. In particular, there is a consensus concerning the nature of criminal activity: crimes are those predatory acts which are accepted by all as criminal. From previous chapters we have seen that many would argue with this. The concern is that the definition of crime itself, and the application of criminal law, are subject to political interests; as a result, both the definition and the application are biased. The theory does not take adequate account of these biases within the system itself. Rather, it relies on a policy of minimal intervention, expressed through the underlying principles of parsimony and checking of power, as a way of attempting to deal with such problems.

The notion of reintegrative shaming also raises a number of issues. It is not clear from the model which comes first, effective shaming, or low crime rates. It may be that low crime rates are a precondition for the success of a criminal justice process which relies on shaming a transgressor so they do not re-offend. Following on from this, it is possible to argue that it may not be possible to shame successfully in a society which is low on communitarianism. Put another way, if an offender was never integrated into society in the first place, it makes no sense to 'reintegrate' that person. Reintegrative shaming loses its meaning when faced with someone who is marginalised from society and not repentant in the least.

Problems also arise with the way shaming works in practice. For example how, in practice, do we distinguish between reintegrative shaming and stigmatisation? It may be that a wider form of stigmatisation occurs because so many more people are involved in situations such as the Family Group Conference. There are further problems with the concept of shaming and compliance, in that there is a need to distinguish between compliance with what the group wants, which is not internalised, and conformity, which is internalised (Potter, 1992). Presumably the ideal is for shaming to lead to changes internal to the individual which will reduce the chance of future offending. Shaming, then, is ultimately a concept which is internal to the individual, and yet the theory does not detail how successful shaming is to be measured, so that we can avoid stigmatisation or mere external compliance, both of which may lead to future offending.

Furthermore, the notion of shaming is used with certain types of offenders, mainly young people. There is little discussion regarding the success or otherwise of reintegrative shaming as it might be applied to white-collar offenders. There are yet other crimes, state crimes for example, which do not lend themselves easily to the concept of reintegrative shaming which focuses on individual transgressions.

It can also be argued that the practical examples of republican theory, such as Family Group Conferences, involve a denial of due process. If guilt is not admitted by those who are the subject of these programmes, such programmes can be seen to be attempting to shame someone before they admit to offending, which is problematic. In practice, then, those accused of offending who participate in such programmes either need to plead guilty, or to have their guilt assumed before they participate. This can be seen as a denial of due process of the law which presumes people are innocent until *proven* guilty. Many pre-court processes come up against this difficulty. The problem is, if a given body is granted the power to punish an individual, the state has to be satisfied that the individual in question really committed the offence. The traditional way for this to happen is for the case to be tried in a court. However, these programmes try to avoid the court process, because it is seen as stigmatising and also expensive, but in doing so they deny the accused the right to having their case proved in the appropriate manner in open court.

Without the mechanism of the court ensuring those who receive punishment are really guilty, it can be argued that reintegrative shaming is potentially nothing more than a net-widening process of social control, without reducing the number of people subject to punitive sanctions of the state. If the aim of the criminal justice system is to reduce the number of people being caught up in the system, programmes set up to 'reintegratively shame' people as an alternative to court may simply make the overall system larger, without any positive effect in terms of reduction of crime. It can be argued that the programme represents an extension of power into civil society in the process of shaming. Some would argue that there needs to be a clear distinction between a process that is based in the criminal justice system, and that which properly resides within the community. The concept of reintegrative shaming blurs this distinction.

Despite these problems, republican theory has some clear strengths. First, it provides a more wholistic account of crime and crime prevention, rather than individualistic and 'bad apple' approaches. It attempts to provide an overall view of society, and then locate criminal justice policy within this broader framework. As such, it can be seen as a comprehensive theory which provides an integrated view of all parts of the criminal justice system.

The view of society posited by republican theory as a whole also has clear advantages in terms of individual liberty over those perspectives which rely heavily on punishment and deterrence, such as certain aspects of New Right criminology outlined in Chapter 8. Republican theory is based on ideas of a system that respects rights and limits, and thus clearly upholds individual liberty better than more punitive systems.

Finally, republican theory is politically attractive. It provides justification for a consensus in society and has an emphasis on restorative justice which is positive. Furthermore, the method of achieving lower crime rates is relatively inexpensive in that it is based on minimal intervention. In addition, it captures many of the political concerns of the day, such as the need to take account of the victim, and the emphasis on family as the basic unit in society.

Conclusion

The rise in popularity of republican theory, especially of Braithwaite's idea of 'reintegrative shaming' — both in Australia and America — needs to be considered. The political directions of crime in recent years have seen a concentration on individual responsibility for one's actions, with the retributivists arguing that the individual who has committed the action must be punished. Republican theory agrees that people should be responsible for their actions, but argues that our response to those actions should be constructive.

The attraction of the theory can be explained in part by the economic directions of criminal justice. The fiscal crisis being experienced in Australia has seen successive state governments severely constraining expenditure in order to curb state debt. In this climate, prisons are viewed as expensive, and the legal aid crisis is seen as a problem arising out of the lengthy, and hence costly, formal court process. Hence, from a strictly economic viewpoint it makes sense to look at alternative cost-effective and efficient measures of crime control.

Nonetheless, a minimalist approach to crime policy has severe shortcomings if conditions in the rest of society undermine the cohesiveness of that society as a whole. In the next chapter, we look at critical criminology which has attempted to address some of these issues.

Further Reading

Braithwaite, J. (1989) *Crime, Shame and Reintegration*, Cambridge University Press, Cambridge.

Braithwaite, J. (1991) 'Poverty, Power, White-Collar Crime and the Paradoxes of Criminological Theory', *Australian and New Zealand Journal of Criminology*, 24(1): 40–58.

Braithwaite, J. (1992) 'Reducing the Crime Problem: A Not So Dismal Criminology — the John Barry Memorial Lecture', *Australian and New Zealand Journal of Criminology*, 25(1): 1–10.

Braithwaite, J. and Pettit, P. (1990) *Not Just Deserts: A Republican Theory of Criminal Justice*, Clarendon Press, Oxford.

Pettit, P. and Braithwaite, J. (1993) 'Not Just Deserts, Even in Sentencing', *Current Issues in Criminal Justice*, 4(3): 225–39.

CHAPTER 11

Critical Criminology

Introduction

The aim of this chapter is to discuss the main ideas and concepts of critical criminology. This perspective combines a wide range of concerns from across the more radical approaches, such as Marxism and feminism, and attempts to develop a type of left-wing criminology that is relevant and appropriate for the 1990s.

As with many of the perspectives in criminology, critical criminology incorporates a wide number of ideas and analytical strands. A distinguishing characteristic of critical criminology is that it is generally associated with an **oppositional** position in relation both to much of the work of conventional criminology and to many contemporary policy developments in the field of criminal justice.

Critical criminology nevertheless exhibits a number of elements which make it a natural intellectual and strategic partner of both the Left Realist and republican approaches. As will be demonstrated in this chapter, however, politically the perspective retains a strong socialist (rather than liberal-reformist) orientation. Its analytical focus emphasises the causal significance of capitalism in the generation of and responses to 'crime' (rather than relying on multi-factorial descriptions).

Social Context

As much as anything, critical criminology represents a further development of the broad radical strands within criminology. In particular, it builds upon the basic concepts and strategic concerns of the

Marxist and feminist perspectives. Generally speaking, it does so from the point of view of a broadly **anti-capitalist position**, which incorporates the ideas of creating a social and natural environment which is not associated with heterosexist, racist, and destructive practices of production and consumption.

There is some confusion and debate surrounding the term 'critical' criminology. It has been used by a wide range of writers, to describe a wide range of theoretical and political positions. In some discussions, Left Realism is regarded as part of the critical criminology perspective; in others it is not. In some instances, any critique of the existing criminal justice system from any political position other than conservative has been associated with critical criminology. This simply equates 'critical' with specific criticisms, rather than using the term to identify a particular analytical framework.

Both liberal and radical approaches may call for change to existing criminal justice practices, and they may overlap on a range of conceptual and strategic issues (e.g., unequal distribution of societal resources underpins much working class crime). However, fundamental differences in ideology and ultimate goals remain, and these must be acknowledged as they have significant implications for criminological theory and practice.

The difficulties and lack of clarity in the use of the term 'critical' are due to the blurring of boundaries between liberal and radical kinds of analysis and intervention. They are also a reflection of other changes occurring in society which have had a major impact upon prevailing attitudes and ideologies. The 1980s was a period of highly volatile politics on a world scale. The demise of Stalinism in the former Soviet Union and Eastern Europe represented not only the end of the Cold War, but also part of a general rethinking of politics and ideology around the world.

The notions of *glasnost* (openness) and *perestroika* (restructuring) signalled a far-reaching process of change, reform and transformation in the non-capitalist countries. Meanwhile, the world economy was steadily and rapidly being internationalised and globalised. Production, consumption, finance, culture, employment, debt, sport — everything was subject to processes which universalised certain ways of doing things, seeing things and engaging in things. Simultaneously, people became aware of the increasing fragmentation of their lives, as previous loyalties, communities and affiliations (e.g., links to a sporting club, to a neighbourhood, to a job) were no longer relevant or appreciated.

An age of profound uncertainty had been broached. By the late 1980s, it was clear that the world would never be the same again — politically, in terms of traditional capitalist versus communist ideologies; economically, in terms of employment and distribution of wealth; environmentally, in terms of ecological imbalance and degradation; or socially, in terms of how people relate to each other across many types of interactions. The hallmark of this period has been **rapid change**, often associated with technological innovation (in the form of the computer microchip) and the concentration of wealth and power into fewer and fewer hands on a global scale.

The world was not only an uncertain place, but increasingly an unequal one. In trying to understand the nature of the processes of inequality, the concept of **difference** was highlighted in social analysis and reflected in the ongoing presence of the 'new social movements'. Gay and lesbian rights groups, environmental and conservation movements, pro-choice and broad women's rights organisations, animal rights activists, Third World solidarity action groups, human rights advocates, anti-racist groups and so on were raising the issues, and voices, of those who had not previously been heard in mainstream political or academic circles.

The world outside criminology obviously has an impact upon what occurs within the discipline. Not surprisingly, then, a number of new strands of thought began to emerge alongside the established approaches such as those we have explored in this book so far. For example, the fascination with meaning, social difference and discourse analysis was manifest in so-called **post-modern** analysis. This describes the use of certain analytical tools to 'deconstruct' or de-code the language and meaning of law and order, and of the criminal justice system, especially 'the law'. Thus, for example, feminist jurisprudence emphasised the in-built biases against women in a legal system premised upon certain conceptions of the 'reasonable man' (see Naffine, 1990). This type of analysis uncovers the 'hidden' text of oppression as this pertains to women, ethnic minority groups, working-class people and so on.

In some cases, the method of the post-modern was elevated to the level of social theory. Thus, all meaning — every association between subject (you) and object (the world around you) — is entirely an artefact of language (e.g., signs and symbols); language in turn is relative to and determined by your particular perspective. In other words, there is no 'objective' world that is not constructed 'subjectively' by the author of a particular 'text'. There can be no privileged interpretation of reality. For some, this also means the adoption of a new neutrality which favours no particular politics (neither conservative, liberal nor radical) and which ultimately may reject the idea that there are certain dominant structures of power. Such a perspective makes it difficult to speak about and act upon oppression as a structural phenomenon (see Thompson, 1992).

If some of the new types of analysis stressed 'difference' and the relative rather than absolute nature of the social world, others emphasised 'commonality' and shared experience as the basis for criminological work. The idea of **peacemaking criminology** asks that we recognise our 'oneness' with the world around us. It views crime as essentially a consequence of a general violence toward and separation from people due to the ways in which our society responds to offenders. Its main themes include 'connectedness', 'caring' and 'mindfulness'. Ideas such as participation, peacekeeping, harmony, co-operation, reconciliation, and charity are seen as desirable and more beneficial than those of an authoritarian nature, such as retribution, control, repression or confinement (Friedrichs, 1992).

The post-modern and the peacemaking perspectives reflect in many ways the uncertainties and the hopes of the current age. Their development has been intertwined with radically altered material circumstances, and the emergence of the new social movements as political forces in society. The ideas of both these perspectives have been drawn upon to varying degrees in contemporary criminological work.

However, what really distinguishes critical criminology *per se* is its more traditional concerns with **structures of power**. These are seen to be institutionalised in particular ways, and to reflect social interests which oppress specific categories of people. While present-day critical criminology acknowledges the importance and contributions of a wide range of sources (including post-modern analysis and peacemaking sentiments), it is the legacy of the radical traditions of social-ism and anarchism which inform its central conceptual and strategic orientation.

Basic Concepts

While there are a number of different strands to critical criminology, in general it can be said that crime is defined in terms of **oppression** (see Chart 11.1). Some groups are particularly vulnerable to oppression. Members of the working class (especially its more powerless sections, including the 'underclass'), women (especially those who are poor, who are sole parents, and who are socially isolated), ethnic minority groups (especially those from non-English-speaking backgrounds and refugees), and indigenous people (especially those worst-affected by long-term colonisation processes and institutional disadvantage) are those most likely to suffer from the weight of oppressive social relations based upon class division, sexism and racism.

The focus of analysis for critical criminology is both the crimes of the powerful, and the crimes of the less powerful. In examining the **crimes of the powerful,** attention is directed at issues relating to ide-ology (e.g., the nature of 'law-and-order' politics), political economy (e.g., social impacts of privatisation) and the state (e.g., managerial rather than democratic modes of rule). The structural context of crime *vis-a-vis* capitalist development and institutional pressures is viewed as central to any explanation of crimes of the powerful.

The **crimes of the less powerful** are examined from the point of view of the specific experiences of particular sections of the popula-tion. Different forms of criminality are thus linked to specific layers of the working class, particular categories of women and men, certain ethnic minority groups, and indigenous people in a variety of rural and urban settings. There is a twofold emphasis: on the **specificity** of crime and criminal involvement (i.e., specific groups, specific kinds of activ-ity); and on the **generalist** features which unite the disparate groups (i.e., shared economic, social and political circumstances).

Crime is seen to be associated with broad processes of political economy that affect the powerful and the less powerful in quite dif-ferent ways. For the powerful, there are pressures associated with the

Chart 11.1 Critical Criminology

Definition of crime	◆ structural forms of oppression (class, gender, 'race')
Focus of analysis	◆ crimes of the powerful (the state, political economy, ideology) ◆ crimes of the less powerful (specific class, gender, ethnic, 'race' groups)
Cause of crime	◆ marginalisation, criminalisation (e.g., racialisation of crime)
Nature of offender	◆ structurally determined context, process of homogenisation, legitimation crisis
Response to crime	◆ social empowerment, redistribution of social resources, participatory democracy
Crime prevention	◆ anti-racist campaigns, human rights emphasis, public ownership under community control
Operation of criminal justice system	◆ emphasis on restorative justice, self-determination at community level, employment orientation, open and public accountability of state officials

securing and maintenance of **state power** and **specific sectional interests** in the global context of international trade and transnational corporate monopolisation. For the less powerful, the cause of crime is seen to lie in the interplay between **marginalisation** (separation from mainstream institutions) and **criminalisation** (intervention by state authorities). Of particular note is the increasing **racialisation of crime**, in which certain communities are targeted for media and police attention in the 'war against crime' and 'public disorder'.

Offending behaviour is thus linked to a social context which is structurally determined by the general allocation of societal resources and by the specific nature of police intervention in people's lives. There is a **process of homogenisation**, in which the least powerful and most vulnerable in society — the poor, the less educated, the unemployed — are filtered through the system until they constitute a disproportionate number of repeat offenders and/or recidivist prisoners.

The growing disparities between rich and poor, and the expansion in the sheer number of the poor, constitute a **legitimation crisis** for the system as a whole. One response is the swing toward 'law-and-order' politics which entrenches and exacerbates the homogenising process of identifying and punishing offenders. A particular area of concern is the repressive nature of the state in relation to particular layers of the working class and in regard to particular communities.

For critical criminology, a response to crime must be built upon a strategy of **social empowerment**. This means involving people directly in decisions about their future through direct participatory democracy. It also requires a redistribution of social resources to communities on the basis of social need and equity.

To counter crimes committed by the powerful, there must be open and public **accountability** of all state officials. Further, as part of wealth redistribution, there has to be a transfer of wealth from private hands to public ownership under community control.

As a general crime prevention measure, and to diminish the prevalence of certain crimes, there need to be anti-racist and anti-sexist campaigns (including re-education and retraining of state officials such as the police). Strong emphasis is given to extending and protecting **basic human rights** (which include economic, social, cultural and political rights), and institutionalising these by means of watchdog agencies (e.g., Children's Commissioner, Human Rights Commissioners) and developmental policies.

The criminal justice system should be based upon a model of **restorative justice**, rather than retribution and punishment. The state should not be repressive in orientation, but coercion may be required as part of the redistribution of community resources from the advantaged sectors of the population to the less advantaged. Moreover, the criminal justice system should operate openly, publicly and with full community accountability. As far as possible, its functions should reflect self-determination at the community level, within the boundaries of human rights.

Historical Development

Critical criminology is part of an important tradition of struggle and political conflict to win or defend social and human rights within a class-divided, sexist and racist social structure.

Ideologically, the perspective is most closely identified with the socialist tradition, and its emphasis on power relations, social conflict and change as a result of contest over resources. The guiding rhetoric is that of **social justice** and the importance of empowering the less powerful. The critical criminology perspective is relatively new, although as a particular theoretical model within criminology, it has continuity with both the Marxist and feminist approaches.

The initial development of critical criminology as a bona fide current within the mainstream of the discipline began with the coming to prominence of labelling theory. Sometimes referred to as 'new deviancy theorists', writers who spoke about crime as a social process challenged the discipline's conventional conceptions of, and means of dealing with, criminal justice issues. As we saw in Chapter 5, the combination of labelling and the power to label was seen to have a dramatic impact upon the person so labelled. Importantly, this perspective focused attention upon the institutions and forces of 'social reaction' and how through professional practices the process of crime actually occurred.

Left-wing critics of labelling theory argued that analysis of the processes and situations within which labelling took place is not enough. It is also essential to examine the structural relations of power in society, and to view crime in the context of the social relations, state institutions and political economy of advanced capitalism (Scraton and Chadwick, 1992). It was at this point that much work was done from a Marxist perspective to identify the causal basis of crime, and to make the link between dominant institutions and ruling-class interests. However, there was a tendency at times either to romanticise crime (as acts of rebellion or resistance) or to see crime solely in economic terms (as always reducible to material necessity). Later work was to explore in more detail the specific contexts and lived experiences of people involved with the criminal justice system (Hall and Scraton, 1981).

The issues of racism, sexism and heterosexism were by and large ignored or insufficiently explained in much of the Marxist writing. This was not simply an analytical problem; it was immediately relevant from a political point of view as well.

The diminished popularity of academic Marxism in the 1980s demanded a response which could speak to a wider range of people than a more restrictive, narrowly conceived approach. Furthermore, the rise of the New Right in the West, the tearing down of Stalinist institutions in the former communist nations according to capitalist free-market criteria, and the political mobilisation of the new social movements had implications for Left criminology generally.

The acknowledgement of differences (in terms of specific needs, experiences and histories) and recognition of commonalities (in relation to marginalisation and criminalisation processes) was translated into a concern with all forms of oppression within the critical criminology framework. Issues of class, gender and ethnicity were seen to be interrelated, and to reflect the general institutional processes of capitalism.

At the other end of the spectrum, there was a need to keep the focus on the actions of those in power, not only in relation to those marginalised in society, but more generally in the area of what has come to be known as white-collar crime. Edwin Sutherland (1983) was the first to coin this phrase in 1939, when he led a blistering attack on the actions of the respectable in society, actions which in a different context would be labelled as criminal and dealt with accordingly. Sutherland saw a need to address the inequalities in treatment of people who engaged in harmful behaviour between those with power and those without power.

This led to a steady stream of research and writing, initially in the USA and then gradually spreading worldwide, on the topic of white-collar crime (Geis and Goff, 1983). The philosophical orientation of such work was not, however, Marxist. Rather it came from Sutherland's own theorising, that of differential association (outlined in Chapter 4). Critical criminology can be seen as continuing the focus on white-collar crime, with a clearer focus on the impact of contemporary capitalism in proving opportunities for corporate criminality, and providing the justification for the lack of enforcement in the area. As such it shares a stronger legacy with Marxism than with Sutherland and his contemporaries.

The conceptual legacy of Marxism was to establish a firm interest in examining questions relating to the nature and exercise of state power. In a similar vein, and reinforced by feminist studies on the cultural and psychological basis of oppression, research was directed at the role of ideology in shaping lived experience. Racism, sexism and individualism are all bound up with certain ways in which the world is described and categorised — the definition of who is 'dangerous' and who is not, for example. The task of critical criminology was to expose the processes whereby certain groups and categories of people are deemed to be worthy of social exclusion, and to develop strategies which could open the door to a more humane and equal society.

Contemporary Examples

One of the hallmarks of critical criminology is its association with direct interventions in various law-and-order and criminal justice debates. Indeed, more than this, one of the main contributions of this strand of criminological activity has been to raise for public discussion a series of important social issues. For example, the work of critical criminologists has been crucial to ongoing critiques of the prison system and of developments relating to the privatisation of punishment (see Moyle, 1994; Mathiesen, 1990; Christie, 1993). Much of this type of research, scholarship and commentary has been informed by a concern to publicise existing injustices, and potential abuses, of our criminal justice institutions.

A key feature of critical criminology is that it is one of the few perspectives which focuses specifically on issues of racism and crime. New Right criminology tends to attribute 'blame' for crime, poverty and unemployment to particular ethnic minority communities themselves. In the conservative framework the emphasis is on the 'bad behaviour' of community members, and the 'choices' they make to be the way they are and to do the things that they do. The mainstream perspectives, such as labelling, strain and republican theories, have a more explicit concern with issues relating to racism. Here, however, the solution is often seen simply in terms of making criminal justice processes and procedures as fair and unbiased as possible. The idea is that high rates of incarceration and contact involving certain social groups are due mainly to 'discrimination' and improper use of discretion (see Cook and Hudson, 1993).

From a critical criminological perspective, the main issue is one of structural inequality. Very often this inequality has been institutionalised in a racist fashion. In such circumstances, insensitive and coercive policing, for instance, cannot be reduced to 'bad attitudes' on the part of the police; it stems from the structural role of the police in regulating the most marginalised sectors of a class-divided society. These divisions may, in turn, be associated with particular ethnic and 'race' groupings (e.g., indigenous people, non-English-speaking immigrants from South-East Asia).

An area of interest and action in recent years in Australia has been the relationship between indigenous people and the state. The routine and persistent nature of racist abuse on the part of the police and other state officials has been a constant theme, as has the double impact of marginalisation and criminalisation on the lives of Torres Strait Islander and Aboriginal people. From the point of view of theory, recent writing has attempted to situate issues relating to 'Aboriginal crime' in the context of the colonial legacy and of neo-colonial policies still apparent today (see Cunneen, 1992, 1994). Issues of under-policing and over-policing have thus been presented as flowing from broader societal pressures and divisions which have had a particularly negative impact on indigenous people.

More generally, the work of critical criminologists has been instrumental in exposing and illuminating a wide range of issues pertaining to the less powerful groups in society. The victimisation, and empowerment, of indigenous people, immigrant communities, refugees, gay men and lesbians, working-class young people and so on have been the subject of probing analysis and insightful discussion (see Brown and Hogg, 1992; White and Alder, 1994). One feature of this work has been its emphasis on explaining the specific empirical aspects of a particular phenomenon, without attempting to say that 'all crime is the same' or trying to deal with 'crime in general'. Nevertheless, the discussions of specific groups (e.g., indigenous people, female prisoners) and particular institutions (e.g., special police tactical response units, private prisons) is usually framed within a general perspective which views the state and powerful social interests (e.g., corporate sector) as problematic.

In addition to the focus on the powerless, critical criminology has also been concerned with the harm directly perpetrated by those in positions of power. Studies of white-collar crime and corporate crime

(crime specifically resulting from the action of organisations) have pointed to the enormity of harm perpetrated in the white-collar sphere. A consistent focus of this research has been to label such acts criminal, and to call for their inclusion as quintessentially criminal acts, to be dealt with accordingly (see, for example, Glasbeek and Rowland, 1979; Clinard and Yeager, 1980; Pearce and Tombs, 1990; Polk, Haines and Perrone, 1993).

Researchers in the area have pointed to the way in which the structure of capitalism itself creates opportunities for crimes of the powerful. Large corporations, most notably the multinational corporations, are in a position to reap considerable gains from their activities at the expense of the environment and of the weakest in society. In addition, certain industries such as the insurance industry may actively support crimes; for instance, an insurance company may gain from the crime of car theft through the sale of wrecked cars complete with high-value identification numbers (Brill, 1993). The market power of these large organisations gives them the opportunity to avoid effective enforcement of laws aimed at curbing their power (Barnett, 1993). Furthermore, it has been argued that law enforcement and criminalisation of these activities may in fact have limited value, because the state has an active interest in maintaining good relations with the monopoly capitalists. Those arguing for criminalisation of white-collar harm may be seen to be ignoring the problems of criminalisation as a solution to a social problem (Cohen, 1988).

Other theorists working in this area point to the nature of the dual economy, where the logic of competition pushes smaller, weaker organisations to exploit their workers and spoil the environment. While large organisations have the money to put in place extensive programmes aimed at reducing harm, smaller organisations are forced to cut corners to survive (Haines, 1995). The structure of capitalism is thus directly linked to the harm that organisations perpetrate.

There are other examples of critical criminology which illustrate the movement of the perspective beyond a Marxist base. Indeed, some theorists working from a critical standpoint actively reject Marxism as a starting point, most notably those utilising a post-modern perspective. Post-modernism stresses the plurality of knowledge, and discounts any one 'correct view'. All views, in a sense, have validity. Thus the focus is on the subjective nature of reality, rather than on objective 'truth'.

Post-modernist writers vary considerably in their opinions regarding the importance of historical context, given their focus on the plurality of existence; this contrasts with the primacy given to history by Marxists. While some post-modern authors accord it considerable importance — for example Foucault (1977) — others fix only on the (multiple) 'realities' of the present. As such, these approaches tend to negate the possibility of value in anything other than the present (since that is all that is 'knowable'), and it has been argued that past atrocities and social harms can thus melt into insignificance in the post-modernist agenda (Cohen, 1993).

Other writers, however, point to the way post-modernism, like labelling before it, empowers those with little voice (Eistadter and Henry, 1995). In this view, reality is always constituted and reconstituted in the present, but according to very specific discourses. Many post-modern authors, they argue, are concerned to give a voice to those views which are currently underplayed or ignored by those who have power — for example, the views of indigenous people, women, gay men and lesbians, and so on. Meaning is present in everything we do, but it is the task of post-modernism to unpack the complex nature of everyday 'realities', and the discourses of these realities, including those realities concerned with crime and criminality.

What unifies the many different approaches within the critical criminology perspective is a deep concern with issues of oppression and injustice. These are seen to stem from structural inequalities in resource allocation and decision-making power. Accordingly, institutional reform is not seen as an end in itself, but as part of a more profound transition toward a more equal, fairer society. To take a specific example, a call for the abolition of prisons (or at the least a radical reduction in the prison population) may reflect the position that those who end up in prison are the most vulnerable sections of the population (in terms of income, employment, education background) and hence are unfairly criminalised and further penalised for their predicament. But to abolish prisons is not enough. Until the conditions which give rise to the creation of 'surplus populations' and ethnic and racially-based social divisions are confronted, piecemeal institutional reform will not be sufficient to forestall suffering and pain in the future.

Critique

Critical criminology, since it has much in common with Marxist criminology, shares some of the same problems. In particular, it shares the problem of the definition of crime. Critical criminology, like Marxist criminology, defines crime very broadly, in terms of the oppression of a particular group (e.g., indigenous people or other minority groups) or class (e.g., working people) by those with power. In this is shares a 'human rights' definition of crime, similar to some Marxist criminologists. The problem with these definitions is how to conceive of differences in the abuse of human rights. For instance, how does one compare discrimination against a person of non-English-speaking background applying for a job to the genocide which occurred in the early 1990s in the former Yugoslavia? As previously discussed, crime/non-crime are dichotomous categories; they do not lend themselves easily to discerning different gradations of harm.

Furthermore, some critical criminology, like some Marxist criminology, tends to have a simple view of the nature of power. That is, there is a notion that some people have power (the powerful) and others do not (the powerless). There is no serious attempt to analyse the nature of power. Some argue that power works in far more complex ways than is suggested by theories which take their starting point from Marxism, as this one generally does. Foucault (1980), for example, points to the decentralisation of power within modern society: it is not held solely by the state or in one particular class or group of people. Rather, he argues that it is dispersed and that the state can act only with the support of key sections of the community. Further to this, Foucault is critical of those who always see power as negative, in that those with power will always oppress those without. Power cannot be captured simply by the term repression, as some would seem to do. He argues that power is more Machiavellian. Power when used to oppress creates resistance, which itself is a source of power. Nevertheless, a crucial point of critical criminology remains — social power is concentrated in particular directions, and it does have substantively different effects according to different groups' resources and capacities.

Given the critique of 'capitalism' which lies at the base of critical criminology, it needs to be able to spell out in more precise terms the nature of this capitalism in the light of processes of internationalisation and globalisation, and how its institutions (e.g., transnational corporations, nation-states) impact on the crime debate. Additionally, it is not always clear whether critical criminology is arguing that the basis of all crime is ultimately economic, or rather that the capitalist system merely exacerbates conflict and tension which exists independently from the economic relations inherent within capitalism. In either case, there is a need to examine the precise way in which capitalism acts to exacerbate tension and both produce and define crime.

A good example of the need for closer analysis relates to the relationship between multiculturalism and crime within Australia. While there has been some work done in the area of indigenous people and crime from a critical criminological perspective, relatively little has been done in this country to analyse the relationship between immigrant groups and crime. Unexamined are the 'criminal' activities immigrant people engage in, and more particularly the way certain activities undertaken by such groups are criminalised. One exception to this is the work done by McCoy (1980) in analysing the early drug laws, where he found that the criminalisation of opium was not so much due to the effects of the drug, but rested on the antagonism of white authorities towards immigrant Chinese, the main users of the drug. More work is needed in the contemporary context, both to document issues relating to the racialisation of conflict, and to theorise the precise nature of ethnic and 'race' relations in a criminological context.

Despite these weaknesses, critical criminology has allowed discussion of the nature and intensification of oppression against minority groups and has brought this within a discussion of crime and criminality. It has allowed insight into the diversity of groups which are progressively marginalised by contemporary capitalist societies such as Australia and further how the activities of such groups become criminalised in a way which leads to further marginalisation. In doing so, it allows for a number of new voices which have not been previously heard or listened to, such as gay men and lesbians, and indigenous people.

Critical criminology forces us to confront issues of the social interests in which the state acts. It highlights the potential long-term conflict which can be produced by a state which prioritises the interests of one group of society over and above the interests of other groups. In doing so, it gives advance warning of the likely social impact of the dismantling of the welfare state, of the 'racialisation' of public order policing, and of the social exclusion of people from basic citizenship rights. The result of such trends may be personalised in the form of high suicide rates (affecting the individual), and collective in the form of riots and general social unrest (affecting whole communities).

Conclusion

Critical criminology reflects many of the concerns of contemporary Australians. It espouses a 'liberation' philosophy which has at its centre emancipatory concerns aimed at allowing all people to participate fully in society, regardless of 'race', ethnicity, sex, class and sexual orientation. Furthermore, it includes among its concerns issues relating to the environment and animal rights. Ultimately, critical criminology views capitalism as essentially hostile to the promotion of human rights, and seeks alternative social arrangements and philosophies which can result in a more inclusive society.

In many ways critical criminology is in its infancy. It stems from and represents an amalgamation of concerns drawn essentially from a socialist or radical viewpoint. As such, it has some distance to go in analysing its own unique contribution to criminology in the face of a rapidly changing world and the dynamic nature of contemporary capitalism.

Further Reading

Brown, D. and Hogg, R. (1992) 'Essentialism, Radical Criminology and Left Realism', *Australian and New Zealand Journal of Criminology*, 25(3): 195–230.

Cook, D. and Hudson, B. (eds) (1993) *Racism and Criminology*, Sage, London.

Cunneen, C. (ed.) (1992) *Aboriginal Perspectives on Criminal Justice*, Institute of Criminology Monograph Series, No.1, Sydney.

Scraton, P. (ed.) (1987) *Law, Order and the Authoritarian State: Readings in Critical Criminology*, Open University Press, Milton Keynes.

Scraton, P. and Chadwick, K. (1991) 'The Theoretical and Political Priorities of Critical Criminology', in K. Stenson and D. Cowell (eds) *The Politics of Crime Control*, Sage, London.

CHAPTER 12

Conclusion

The aim of this book has been to provide an introduction to the main concepts and explanations of criminology. In particular, we have reviewed the many and varied ways in which the nature and causes of crime have been defined and analysed within the field. As we have seen, the way in which crime is conceived, and thus prevented and controlled, is a matter of considerable dispute. Invariably, the criminological enterprise involves issues of a theoretical, empirical and political nature. The theories and perspectives we have explored in the book focus on different and often quite specific or distinct aspects of criminal activity and behaviour. Thus, for example, some theories have concentrated attention on the individual characteristics or attributes of the offender, others on the processes whereby an action or person comes to be defined as criminal, and still others on the influence of social structure on personal and group behaviour.

The diverse explanations on offer indicate, at least in part, the interdisciplinary nature of criminology. As a field of study, criminology incorporates ideas, methodologies and theoretical contributions from disciplines such as psychology, sociology, political science, history, legal studies and forensic medicine. Different starting points and different conceptual emphases stem from the diversity of academic influences in the field. However, many of the differences within criminology also reflect broader divisions with regard to the level of analysis, and the political perspective.

This is illustrated, for instance, in the debate over whether criminal behaviour is determined or voluntary. At first glance, the debate appears to be fairly straightforward. On the one hand, there are those perspectives, such as the classical, which portray human activity as entirely voluntary, as simply a matter of individual choice. On the other hand, there are those theories which present the view that behaviour is overwhelmingly determined by factors outside the individual's control, whether these be biological, psychological or social.

Within and across this interpretive divide, however, there is considerable variation. For example, the nature, scope and extent of determinism and voluntarism often depend upon the level of analysis. A biological approach may stress individual pathology and the fixed features of an individual's genetic make-up as the reason behind certain behaviours. A strain theorist might look at aspects of social situation, and see behaviour as a result of the combination of opportunities available and immediate learning processes. A left realist approach could likewise adopt a situational analysis, but with greater emphasis on social conflict and inequality, and the role of institutions of crime control such as the police in fostering or dampening working-class criminality. For the critical criminologist, 'choice' is seen to be circumscribed by wider structural processes of marginalisation and criminalisation, or competitive market structures, and criminal activity among both the powerful and the less powerful is seen to reflect the ways in which existing social structures ultimately narrow the scope for the full exercise of human agency.

The complex ways in which the relationship between voluntarism ('free will') and determinism ('fate') is constructed in the criminological field demonstrates the existence of a series of cross-cutting analytical and political differences which transcend strict discipline boundaries.

These differences can be further highlighted by considering the underlying assumptions of criminological theory, as indicated in broad political orientation, and 'popular' conceptions of criminality and the criminal justice system. Chart 12.1 outlines how the diverse propensities (or likelihoods), motivations (or drives) and circumstances (or opportunities) underpinning criminality might be conceived according to varying political and analytical focus. The chart provides a rough guide to the different outlooks of the conservative, liberal and radical commentator, and also shows the possible divisions or emphases within each broad political persuasion.

Chart 12.1 Underlying Assumptions of Criminological Theory

Different Reform Agendas

Needs	Deeds	Greeds

Conservative political perspective

Focus on the individual's pathology and need to conform with socially accepted norms and mores. Emphasis on the need to counsel or treat the individual, which may require indeterminate sentencing.	Law and order. Focus on what the individual has done. The extent of harm to the status quo dictates the extent of punishment. Key issues are retribution, punishment and deterrence.	Motivation to offend, steal or rob, is greed. Focus is on the greed of the 'street criminal' who shirks responsibility to get work and earn money respectably. A focus on 'moral training' and reaffirmation of conservative values.

Liberal political perspective

Focus on the needs of both the victim and the offender. Needs tempered by an understanding of social conditions which influence behaviour. Emphasis on restorative justice.	Civil libertarian. Focus on individual rights, determinate sentencing and due process. Notion of equality and proportionality. All should have access to equal justice, and like offences should be treated in like manner.	Greed is more likely to be associated with those who take 'more than their fair share' from a democratic society. Discussion of white-collar crime relevant here, with a focus on regulation and moral persuasion.

Radical political perspective

Focus on the distortion of needs due to the capitalist system. This system places a priority on competition and the 'market'. The result is an emphasis on private profit, rather than social need, which dictates the priorities of the state.	Focus on the deeds of the system, in terms of systematic bias against certain classes or ethnic groups. The degree of harm perpetrated by white-collar crime is juxtaposed against the harm perpetrated by street crime.	Greed is associated with structural competitive pressures, and the widening gap between rich and poor within society. A focus on redistribution of societal resources and radical democracy.

Our presentation of 'needs', 'deeds' and 'greeds' merely indicates general tendencies and, as such, is intended to provide only a schematic conceptual map of the underlying assumptions. Nevertheless, it is useful as an analytical backdrop upon which can be placed most of the theories and perspectives discussed in this book. The relevance of studying criminological theory lies precisely in the way it informs and assists us in understanding the actual source of specific arguments and the ideas of contemporary debates over crime.

We began the book by stating that the relationship between crime and criminology is always reflected in, and reflective of, particular conceptions of society. Each theory or perspective embodies particular values regarding 'what is' the nature of present society, and 'what ought to be' the best way to deal with social issues such as crime.

As we move into a new century, the debates over crime and criminality look set to intensify as rapid social change continues to transform traditional social, economic and political relationships. Around the world, great upheavals are taking place, and more often than not these are associated with increasing social polarisation. As part of this change, and in this context, 'law-and-order' debates are now constantly at the centre of electoral politics and are standard fare for infotainment and 'serious media' alike.

In the light of current public perceptions about the 'crime threat', and general unease about the future of jobs, the environment, peace and respect for human rights, it is more essential than ever to think critically about the nature of crime, how it occurs, who it affects, and what can be done to prevent or control it.

It is our hope that this book will reinforce the fact that there are indeed alternative ways to conceptualise these issues, just as there are various options we can take to deal with them at a practical level. The doing of criminological theory, research and practical intervention is always at one and the same time a statement about the kind of world each of us would like to see, and a response to the world of which we are an integral part.

The uncertainties of the world we presently inhabit are mirrored in the limitations and uncertainties of contemporary criminological theory. In the end, each theory only fully makes sense when set within an appropriate societal context and values framework. The crucial challenge for the reader therefore is to critically question and evaluate the ethical and explanatory basis of each theory or perspective. In so doing, it is our hope that we will be better able to clarify where we stand in relation to the great issues of the day, and to determine what our specific responsibilities and interests are in building a safer, more secure and healthy future, one in which social harms such as crime are minimised.

References

Alder, C. (1985) 'Theories of Female Delinquency', in A. Borowski and J. Murray, (eds) *Juvenile Delinquency in Australia*, Methuen, North Ryde.

Alder, C. (1986) '"Unemployed Women Have Got It Heaps Worse": Exploring the Implications of Female Youth Unemployment', *Australian and New Zealand Journal of Criminology*, 19, 210–24.

Alder, C. (1991) 'Explaining Violence: Socioeconomics and Masculinity', in D. Chappell, P. Grabosky and H. Strang (eds) *Australian Violence: Contemporary Perspectives*, Australian Institute of Criminology, Canberra.

Alder, C. (1994) 'Women and the Criminal Justice System', in D. Chappell and P. Wilson (eds) *The Australian Criminal Justice System: The Mid-1990s*, Butterworths, Sydney.

Alder, C. (1996) 'Feminist Criminology in Australia', in N. Rafter and F. Heidensohn (eds) *International Perspectives in Criminology: Engendering a Discipline*, Open University Press, Milton Keynes.

Alder, C. and Wundersitz, J. (eds) (1994) *Family Conferencing and Juvenile Justice*, Australian Institute of Criminology, Canberra.

Allen, J. (1990) '"The Wild Ones": The Disavowal of Men in Criminology', in R. Graycar (ed.) *Dissenting Opinions*, Allen and Unwin, Sydney.

Barlow, H. (1993) *Introduction to Criminology*, Harper Collins College Publishers, New York.

Barnett, H. (1993) 'Wealth, Crime and Capital Accumulation', in D. Greenberg (ed.) *Crime and Capitalism: Readings in Marxist Criminology*, Temple University Press, Philadephia.

Beccaria, C. (1767) *An Essay On Crimes and Punishments*, J. Almon, London.

Becker, H. (1963) *Outsiders: Studies in the Sociology of Deviance*, Free Press, New York.

Berger, P. and Luckmann, T. (1971) *The Social Construction of Reality*, Allen Lane, London.

Bottomley, S., Gunningham, N. and Parker, S. (1991) *Law in Context*, Federation Press, Sydney.

Braithwaite, J. (1989) *Crime, Shame and Reintegration*, Cambridge University Press, Cambridge.

Braithwaite, J. (1991) 'Poverty, Power, White-Collar Crime and the Paradoxes of Criminological Theory', *Australian and New Zealand Journal of Criminology*, 24(1): 40–58.

Braithwaite, J. (1992) 'Reducing the Crime Problem: A Not So Dismal Criminology — the John Barry Memorial Lecture', *Australian and New Zealand Journal of Criminology*, 25(1): 1–10.

Braithwaite, J. and Chappell, D. (1994) 'The Job Compact and Crime: Submission to the Committee on Employment Opportunities', *Current Issues in Criminal Justice*, 5(3): 295–300.

Braithwaite, J. and Mugford, S. (1994) 'Conditions of Successful Reintegration Ceremonies: Dealing with Young Offenders', *British Journal of Criminology*, 34(2): 139–71.

Braithwaite, J. and Pettit, P. (1990) *Not Just Deserts: A Republican Theory of Criminal Justice*, Clarendon Press, Oxford.

Brake, M. (1985) *Comparative Youth Culture*, Routledge and Kegan Paul, London.

Brill, H. (1993) 'Auto Theft and the Role of Big Business', in D. Greenberg (ed.) *Crime and Capitalism: Readings in Marxist Criminology*, Temple University Press, Philadelphia.

Brown, C. (1979) *Understanding Society: An Introduction to Sociological Theory*, John Murray, London.

Brown, D. and Hogg, R. (1992) 'Essentialism, Radical Criminology and Left Realism', *Australian and New Zealand Journal of Criminology*, 25(3): 195–230.

Buchanan, C. and Hartley, P. (1992) *Criminal Choice: The Economic Theory of Crime and Its Implications for Crime Control*, Centre for Independent Studies, Sydney.

Carrington, K. (1993) *Offending Girls*, Allen and Unwin, Sydney.

Chambliss, W. (1975a) 'A Sociological Analysis of the Law of Vagrancy', in W. Carson and P. Wiles (eds) *The Sociology of Crime and Delinquency in Britain*, Vol.1, Martin Robertson, Oxford.

Chambliss, W. (1975b) 'The Political Economy of Crime: A Comparative Study of Nigeria and USA', in I. Taylor, P. Walton and J. Young (eds) *Critical Criminology*, Routledge and Kegan Paul, London.

Chambliss, W. and Mankoff, M. (1976) *Whose Law What Order? A Conflict Approach to Criminology*, John Wiley and Sons, Toronto.

Chesney-Lind, M. (1974) 'Juvenile Delinquency and the Sexualisation of Female Crime', *Psychology Today*, July: 4–7.

Chesney-Lind, M. and Seldon, R. (1992) *Girls, Delinquency and Juvenile Justice*, Brooks/Cole Publishing, California.

Christie, N. (1993) *Crime Control as Industry: Towards Gulags Western Style?*, Routledge, London.

Cicourel A. (1976) *The Social Organisation of Juvenile Justice*, Heinemann, London.

Clarke, J., Hall, S., Jefferson, T. and Roberts, B. (1976) 'Subcultures, Cultures and Class: A Theoretical Overview', in S. Hall and T. Jefferson (eds) *Resistance Through Rituals: Youth Subcultures in Post-War Britain*, Hutchinson, London.

Clarke, R. (ed.) (1992) *Situational Crime Prevention: Successful Case Studies,* Harrow and Heston, New York.

Clinard, M. and Yeager, P. (1980) *Corporate Crime*, Free Press, New York.

Cloward, R. and Ohlin, L. (1960) *Delinquency and Opportunity: A Theory of Delinquent Gangs*, Free Press, Chicago.

Cohen, A. (1955) *Delinquent Boys: The Culture of the Gang*, Free Press, Chicago.

Cohen, S. (1973) *Folk Devils and Moral Panics*, Paladin, London.

Cohen, S. (1979) 'The Punitive City: Notes on the Dispersal of Social Control', *Contemporary Crises*, 3: 339–63

Cohen, S. (1985) *Visions of Social Control*, Polity Press, Cambridge.

Cohen, S. (1988) *Against Criminology*, Transaction Books, New Brunswick.

Cohen, S. (1993) 'Human Rights and Crimes of the State: The Culture of Denial', *Australian and New Zealand Journal of Criminology*, 26(2): 97–115.

Cook, D. and Hudson, B. (eds) (1993) *Racism and Criminology*, Sage, London.

Cornforth, M. (1987) *Historical Materialism* (Vol. 2 of *Dialectical Materialism: An Introduction*), Lawrence and Wishart, London.

Coser, L. (1977) *Masters of Sociological Thought: Ideas in Historical and Social Context*, Harcourt Brace Jovanovich, New York

Cunneen, C. (ed.) (1992) *Aboriginal Perspectives on Criminal Justice*, Institute of Criminology Monograph Series No.1, University of Sydney.

Cunneen, C. (1994) 'Enforcing Genocide? Aboriginal Young People and the Police', in R. White and C. Alder (eds) *The Police and Young People in Australia*, Cambridge University Press, Melbourne.

Cunneen, C. and White, R. (1995) *Juvenile Justice: An Australian Perspective*, Oxford University Press, Melbourne.

Downes, D. (1966) *The Delinquent Solution*, Routledge and Kegan Paul, London.

Durkheim, E. (1979) *Suicide: A Study in Sociology*, Routledge and Kegan Paul, London.

Edwards, S. (1990) 'Violence Against Women: Feminism and the Law', in L. Gelsthorpe and A. Morris (eds) *Feminist Perspectives in Criminology*, Open University Press, Milton Keynes.

Eisenstein, H. (1984) *Contemporary Feminist Thought*, Unwin Paperbacks, London.

Einstadter, W. and Henry, S. (1995) *Criminological Theory: An Analysis of Its Underlying Assumptions*, Harcourt Brace, New York.

Empey, L. (1982) *American Delinquency: Its Meaning and Construction*, The Dorsey Press, Chicago.

Ericson, R., Baranek, P. and Chan, J. (1991) *Representing Order: Crime, Law and Justice in the News Media*, Open University Press, Milton Keynes.

Eysenck, H. (1984) 'Crime and Personality', in D. Muller, D. Blackmann and A. Chapmann (eds) *Psychology and Law*, John Wiley and Sons, New York.

Feldman, P. (1993) *The Psychology of Crime*, Cambridge University Press, Cambridge.

Felson, M. (1994) *Crime and Everyday Life: Insights and Implications for Society*, Pine Forge Press, London.

Feminist Anthology Collective (1981) *No Turning Back: Writings from the Women's Liberation Movement 1975-80*, The Women's Press, London.

Fine, B. (1984) *Democracy and the Rule of Law: Liberal Ideals and Marxist Critiques*, Pluto, London.

Fishbein, D. (1990) 'Biological Perspectives in Criminology', *Criminology*, 28(1): 27-72.

Fitzgerald, G. (1989) *Report of the Commission of Possible Illegal Activities and Associated Police Misconduct*, Queensland Government Printer, Brisbane.

Foucault, M. (1977) *Discipline and Punish: The Birth of the Prison*, Penguin, London.

Foucault, M. (1980) 'Truth and Power' in *Power/Knowledge: Selected Interviews and Other Writings 1972-1977*, edited by C. Gordon, Pantheon Books, New York.

Freund, J. (1969) *The Sociology of Max Weber*, Vintage Books, New York.

Friedrichs, D. (1991) 'Introduction: Peacemaking Criminology in a World Filled with Conflict', in B. MacLean and D. Milovanovic (eds) *New Directions in Critical Criminology*, The Collective Press, Vancouver.

Gamble, A. (1988) *The Free Economy and the Strong State: The Politics of Thatcherism*, Macmillan Education, London.

Garland, D. (1988) 'British Criminology Before 1935', *The British Journal of Criminology*, 28: 131-47.

Garland, D. (1990) *Punishment and Modern Society: A Study in Social Theory*, Clarendon Press, Oxford.

Garton, S. (1991) 'The Convict Origins Debate: Historians and the Problem of the 'Criminal Class'', *Australian and New Zealand Journal of Criminology*, 24(2): 66-82.

Geis, G. and Goff, C. (1983) 'Introduction' in E. Sutherland, *White-Collar Crime: The Uncut Version*, Yale University Press, New Haven.

Gelsthorpe, L. and Morris, A. (eds) (1990) *Feminist Perspectives in Criminology*, Open University Press, Milton Keynes.

Gibbons, D. (1977) *Society, Crime and Criminal Careers*, Prentice-Hall, New Jersey.

Gibbons, D. (1979) *The Criminological Enterprise: Theories and Perspectives*, Prentice Hall, New Jersey.

Glasbeek, H. and Rowland, S. (1979) 'Are Injuring and Killing at Work Crime?', *Osgoode Hall Law Journal*, 17(3): 506–94.

Goring, C. (1913) *The English Convict: A Statistical Study*, His Majesty's Stationery Office, London.

Gottfredson, M. and Hirschi, T. (1990) *A General Theory of Crime*, Stanford University Press, Stanford.

Gould, S. (1981) *The Mismeasure of Man*, W. W. Norton and Co., New York.

Grabosky, P. and Wilson, P. (1989) *Journalism and Justice: How Crime Is Reported*, Pluto Press, Leichhardt.

Graycar, R. and Morgan, J. (1990) *The Hidden Gender of Law*, Federation Press, Sydney.

Greenberg, D. (ed.) (1993) *Crime and Capitalism: Readings in Marxist Criminology*, Temple University Press, Philadelphia.

Hagan, J. (1987) *Modern Criminology: Crime, Criminal Behavior and its Control*, McGraw-Hill, Toronto.

Haines, F. (1995) 'The Show Must Go On: Organisational Responses to Traumatic Fatalities within Multiple Employer Workplaces', Unpublished Ph.D. thesis, Criminology Department, University of Melbourne.

Hall, S. (1980) 'Popular-Democratic vs. Authoritarian Populism: Two Ways of "Taking Democracy Seriously"', in A. Hunt (ed.) *Marxism and Democracy*, Lawrence and Wishart, London.

Hall, S. and Jefferson, T. (1976) *Resistance Through Rituals: Youth Subcultures in Post-War Britain*, Hutchinson, London.

Hall, S., Jefferson, T., Critcher, Roberts, B. (1978) *Policing the Crisis: Mugging, the State, and Law and Order*, Macmillan, London.

Hall, S. and McLennan, G. (1986) 'Custom and Law: Law and Crime as Historical Processes', in *Law and Disorder: Histories of Crime and Justice*, Open University Course Material, Milton Keynes.

Hall, S. and Scraton, P. (1981) 'Law, Class and Control', in M. Fitzgerald, G. McLennan and J. Pawson (eds) *Crime and Society: Readings in History and Theory*, Routledge and Kegan Paul & Open University Press, London.

Hirschi, T. (1969) *Causes of Delinquency*, University of California Press, Berkeley and Los Angeles.

Hogg, R. (1988) 'Taking Crime Seriously: Left Realism and Australian Criminology', in M. Findlay and R. Hogg (eds) *Understanding Crime and Criminal Justice*, Law Book Company, Sydney.

Howe, A. (1994) *Punish and Critique: Towards a Feminist Analysis of Penality*, Routledge, London.

Indermaur, D. and White, R. (1994) 'Juvenile Rights Given The Boot in Western Australia', *Civil Liberty*, 10(2): 12–14.

Inverarity, J., Lauderdale, P. and Feld, B. (1983) *Law and Society: Sociological Perspectives on Criminal Law*, Little, Brown and Company, Boston.

Jaggs, D. (1986) *Neglected and Criminal: Foundations of Child Welfare Legislation in Victoria*, Phillip Institute of Technology, Melbourne.

Johnston, E. (1991) *National Report, 5 Vols, Royal Commission into Aboriginal Deaths in Custody*, Australian Government Publishing Service, Canberra.

Jones, T., MacLean, B. and Young, J. (1986) *The Islington Crime Survey*, Gower, Aldershot.

Jupp, V. (1989) *Methods of Criminological Research*, Routledge, London.

Kinsey, R., Lea, J. and Young, J. (1986) *Losing the Fight Against Crime*, Blackwell, Oxford.

Lea, J. and Young, J. (1982) 'The Riots in Britain 1981: Urban Violence and Political Marginalisation', in D. Cowell, T. Jones and J. Young (eds) *Policing the Riots*, Junction Books, London.

Lea, J. and Young, J. (1984) *What is to be Done about Law and Order?*, Penguin, London.

Lees, S. (1989) 'Learning to Love', in M. Cain (ed.) *Growing Up Good*, Sage, London.

Lemert, E. (1969) 'Primary and Secondary Deviation', in D. Cressy and D. Ward (eds) *Delinquency, Crime and Social Process*, Harper and Row, New York.

Lombroso, C. (1911) *Crime: Its Causes and Remedies*, Little, Brown, Boston.

Lowman, J. and MacLean, B. (eds) (1992) *Realist Criminology: Crime Control and Policing in the 1990s*, University of Toronto Press, Toronto.

Lukes, S. (1973) *Emile Durkheim: His Life and Work*, Penguin, London.

MacLean, B. (1993) 'Left Realism, Local Crime Surveys and Policing of Racial Minorities: A Futher Analysis of Data from the First Sweep of the Islington Crime Survey', *Crime, Law and Social Change*, 19: 51–86.

MacLean, B. and Milovanovic, D. (eds) (1991) *New Directions in Critical Criminology*, The Collective Press, Vancouver.

Mathiesen, T. (1990) *Prisons On Trial: A Critical Assessment*, Sage, London.

Matthews, R. (1989) 'Alternatives To and In Prisons: A Realist Approach', in P. Carlen and D. Cook (eds) *Paying For Crime*, Open University Press, Milton Keynes.

Matza, D. (1964) *Delinquency and Drift*, John Wiley and Sons, New York.

Maxwell, G. (1993) 'Family Decision-Making in Youth Justice: The New Zealand Model', in L. Atkinson and S.-A. Gerull (eds) *National Conference on Juvenile Justice: Conference Proceedings*, Australian Institute of Criminology, Canberra.

Maxwell, G. and Morris, A. (1994) 'The New Zealand Model of Family Group Conferences', in C. Alder and J. Wundersitz (eds) *Family Conferencing and Juvenile Justice*, Australian Institute of Criminology, Canberra.

McCoy, A. (1980) *Drug Traffic: Narcotics and Organised Crime in Australia*, Harper and Row, Sydney.

Merton, R. (1957) *Social Theory and Social Structure*, Free Press, New York.

Miliband, R. (1969) *The State in Capitalist Society*, Quartet Books, London.

Miller, W. (1958) 'Lower Class Culture as a Generating Milieu of Gang Delinquency', *Journal of Social Issues*, 14: 51–119.

Moyle, P. (ed.) (1994) *Private Prisons and Police: Recent Australian Trends*, Pluto Press, Sydney.

Muncie, J. and Fitzgerald, M. (1981) 'Humanising the Deviant: Affinity and Affiliation Theories', in M. Fitzgerald, G. McLennan and J. Pawson (eds) *Crime and Society: Readings in History and Theory*, Routledge and Kegan Paul and Open University Press, London.

Naffine, N. (1987) *Female Crime: The Construction of Women in Criminology*, Allen and Unwin, Sydney.

Naffine, N. (1990) *Law and the Sexes: Explorations in Feminist Jurisprudence*, Allen and Unwin, Sydney.

Nava, M. (1984) 'Youth Service Provision, Social Order and the Question of Girls', in A. McRobbie and M. Nava (eds) *Gender and Generation*, Macmillan, London.

Nettler, G. (1984) *Explaining Crime*, McGraw-Hill, New York.

O'Malley, P. (1983) *Law, Capitalism and Democracy*, George Allen and Unwin, Sydney.

Parent, D. (1994) 'Boot Camps Failing to Achieve Goals', *Overcrowded Times*, 5(4): 8–11.

Pearce, F. (1976) *Crime of the Powerful: Marxism, Crime and Deviance*, Pluto, London.

Pearce, F. and Tombs, S. (1990) 'Ideology, Hegemony and Empiricism: Compliance Theories of Regulation', *British Journal of Criminology*, 30(4): 423–43.

Pettit, P. and Braithwaite, J. (1993) 'Not Just Deserts, Even in Sentencing', *Current Issues in Criminal Justice*, 4(3): 225–39.

Platt, A. (1977) *The Child Savers*, University of Chicago, Chicago.

Plummer, K. (1979) 'Misunderstanding Labelling Perspectives', in D. Downes and P. Rock (eds) *Deviant Interpretations*, Martin Robertson, Oxford.

Polk, K. (1993) 'Jobs, not Gaols: A New Agenda for Youth', in L. Atkinson and S.-A. Gerull (eds) *National Conference on Juvenile Justice: Conference Proceedings*, Australian Institute of Criminology, Canberra.

Polk, K. (1994) 'Family Conferencing: Theoretical and Evaluative Questions', in C. Alder and J. Wundersitz (eds) *Family Confer-*

encing and Juvenile Justice, Australian Institute of Criminology, Canberra.

Polk, K., Haines, F. and Perrone, S. (1993) 'Homicide, Negligence and Work Death: The Need for Legal Change', in M. Quinlan (ed.) *Work and Health: The Origins, Management and Regulation of Occupational Illness*, Macmillan, South Melbourne.

Potter, H. (1992) 'Crime, Shame and Reintegration: Review, Questions and Comment', *Australian and New Zealand Journal of Sociology*, 28(2): 224–32.

Poulantzas, N. (1972) 'The Problem of the Capitalist State', in R. Blackburn (ed.) *Ideology and the Social Sciences*, Fontana Books, London.

Quinney, R. (1970) *The Social Reality of Crime*, Little, Brown, Boston.

Quinney, R. (ed.) (1974) *Crime and Justice in America: A Critical Understanding*, Little, Brown, Boston.

Quinney, R. (1977) *Class, State and Crime: On the Theory and Practice of Criminal Justice*, David McKay Company, New York.

Rosenthal, R. and Jacobson, L. (1968) *Pygmalion in the Classroom*, Holt, Rinehart and Winston, New York.

Ross, D. (1985) 'A Tattoo Removal Programme in Victoria', *Medical Journal of Australia*, 142: 388.

Rubington, E. and Weinberg, M. (eds) (1978) *Deviance: The Interactionist Perspective*, Macmillan, New York.

Sarre, R. (1994) 'Violence: Patterns of Crime', in D. Chappell and P. Wilson (eds), *The Australian Criminal Justice System: The Mid-1990s*, Butterworths, Sydney.

Schur, E. (1973) *Radical Non-Intervention: Rethinking the Delinquency Problem*, Prentice-Hall, New Jersey.

Schwendinger, H. and Schwendinger, J. (1975) 'Defenders of Order or Guardians of Human Rights', in I. Taylor, P. Walton. and J. Young (eds) *Critical Criminology*, Routledge and Kegan Paul, London.

Scraton, P. (ed.) (1987) *Law, Order and the Authoritarian State: Readings in Critical Criminology*, Open University Press, Milton Keynes.

Scraton, P. and Chadwick, K. (1991) 'The Theoretical and Political Priorities of Critical Criminology', in K. Stenson and D. Cowell (eds) *The Politics of Crime Control*, Sage, London.

Scutt, J. (1990) *Women and the Law*, Law Book Company, Sydney.

Segal, L. (1987) *Is The Future Female? Troubled Thoughts on Contemporary Feminism*, Virago Press, London.

Shaw, C. and MacKay, H. (1942) *Juvenile Delinquency and Urban Areas*, Chicago University Press, Chicago.

Sheldon, W. (1940) *Varieties of Human Physique*, Harper and Row, New York.

Shoemaker, D. (1984) *Theories of Delinquency*, Oxford University Press, New York.

Smart, C. (1976) *Women, Crime and Criminology: A Feminist Critique*, Routledge and Kegan Paul, London.

Spitzer, S. (1975) 'Toward a Marxian Theory of Deviance', *Social Problems*, 22: 638–51.

Steadman, H. (1973) 'Follow-up on Baxtrom Patients Returned to Hospitals for the Criminally Insane', *American Journal of Psychology*, 3: 317–19.

Steinart, H. (1985) 'The Amazing New Left Law and Order Campaign', *Contemporary Crises*, 9: 327–33.

Sutherland, E. (1983) *White-Collar Crime: The Uncut Version*, Yale University Press, New Haven.

Sutherland, E. and Cressy, D. (1974) *Criminology*, Lippincott Company, New York.

Sykes, G. and Matza, D. (1957) 'Techniques of Neutralization: A Theory of Delinquency', *American Sociological Review*, 22: 664–70.

Tame, C. (1991) 'Freedom, Responsibility and Justice: The Criminology of the "New Right"', in K. Stenson and D. Cowell (eds) *The Politics of Crime Control*, Sage, London.

Taylor, I. (1981) *Law and Order: Arguments for Socialism*, Macmillan, London.

Taylor, I., Walton, P. and Young, J. (1973) *The New Criminology*, Routledge and Kegan Paul, London.

Thompson, A. (1992) 'Foreword: Critical Approaches to Law: Who Needs Legal Theory?', in I. Grigg-Spall and P. Ireland (eds) *The Critical Lawyers' Handbook*, Pluto Press, London.

Tong, R. (1989) *Feminist Thought: A Comprehensive Introduction*, Unwin Hyman, London.

White, R. and Alder, C. (eds) (1994) *The Police and Young People in Australia*, Cambridge University Press, Melbourne.

White, R. and van der Velden, J. (1995) 'Class and Criminality', *Social Justice*, 22(1): 51–74.

Wilson, P. and Lincoln, R. (1992) 'Young People, Economic Crisis, Social Control and Crime', *Current Issues in Criminal Justice*, 4(2): 110–16.

Wright, M. (1991) *Justice for Victims and Offenders*, Open University Press, Milton Keynes.

Young, J. (1971) 'The Role of the Police as Amplifiers of Deviancy, Negotiators of Reality and Translators of Fantasy: Some consequences of our present system of drug control as seen in Notting Hill', in S. Cohen (ed.) *Images of Deviance*, Penguin, London.

Young, J. (1981) 'Thinking Seriously About Crime: Some Models of Criminology', in M. Fitzgerald, G. McLennon and J. Pawson (eds.) *Crime and Society: Readings in History and Theory*, Routledge and Kegan Paul, London.

Young, J. (1986) 'The Failure of Criminology: The Need for a Radical Realism', in R. Matthews and J. Young (eds) *Confronting Crime*, Sage, London.

Young, J. (1991) 'Left Realism and the Priorities of Crime Control', in K. Stenson and D. Cowell (eds) *The Politics of Crime Control*, Sage, London.

Index

Aborigines 7, 77, 115, 131, 139, 164, 202
affirmative action 122
American Dream, the 66, 71, 93
American Revolution 24
androgyny 115, 127
anomie 63–4
assault 9–10
attachment 145

belief 145
bias, institutionalist approach 10–11
bio-social explanations 48, 49, 144
biochemistry 49–50
biological potentials 48
biological theories 13, 14, 44–6, 48–50, 116, 122, 123
body types 46
boot camps 147
Britain
    Brixton riots 153–4
    hybrid system 31
    Islington surveys 159
    psychological positivism 47
    rise of the state 23
    West Indian immigrants 154
bureaucratisation 40
burglary 160
business regulation 180, 185, 203

Campaign for Criminal Justice 166–7
Canada, social perspectives 2
capitalism
    globalisation 193, 197
    laws fettering 108
    mercantile 24, 193
    post-war growth 58–9, 65–6

power concentration 95, 96, 196
rise and consolidation 21–2, 25, 38, 99
state apparatuses 95, 108
technology and 40
women as commodities 117
charts, list of iv
child abuse 9
child labour 39, 40
children see youth; juvenile justice
child savers movement 119
child welfare 129–30
childhood experiences 48
Children's Aid Panels 86
Children's Court 86
choice
    class-related 98, 109
    focus of classical theory 13, 14, 26, 30
    free will 49, 210
    libertarian ethos 76, 78
    opportunities 66
    rational 141, 146
    responsibility 28, 31–2, 34, 47, 57, 135, 138, 140, 149
    self-control 50, 145, 146
    vountarism 26, 209–10
chromosome theory 46
circle, representing society 15
circular reasoning 50–1
civil rights movement 77, 93–4, 194
civilisation, European 39, 40
class
    basis of society 99–100
    central to growing up 102–3
    conflict 39, 57, 68–9, 92–110
    criminality and 97, 98, 104
    cultures 68–9

male domination and 117
see also Marxism; power
classical theory 14, 21–36, 144
  basic concepts 26–8
  challenges 31
  chart 26
  contemporary examples 31–3
  critique 33–5
  foundations 21
  historical development 29–31
  social context 21–6
Code Napoléon 23
codification 33
Cold War 66, 93, 193
collective conscience 62, 63, 117
colonialism 39
commitment 145
common law, development 23
communism 66, 100
communitarianism 178, 179, 185–6,
  187
Community Aid Panels 86
compensation 183
competitive ethos 140, 175
conditioning 48
conflict perspectives 17, 92, 93–5,
  101
conformism 67
conscience, self-sanctioning 178,
  184
consciousness-raising 117
consensus perspective 93, 101
consequentialism 181
conservatism 16, 18, 115–16, 122
  chart 143, 211
  political 136–7
  traditionalist 142–4
  v. right-wing libertarianism 135
control theory 144
corporatisation 31
correction *see* rehabilitation
correctives, biological 50, 52
counterculture 154
courts 22, 31, 189
crime
  communal evil 176–7
  culture and 60, 67–9
  denial of personal dominion 176;
    see republican theory
  distribution 34
  historical constructions 6–7, 18

measuring 10–11, 43, 79, 160
media images 7–10
natural 43, 60
opportunity and 60, 64–7
sex-related offences 128
sex-specific offences 127
socially defined phenomenon 4,
  59
unrecorded 'dark figure' 43
uselessness as concept 106–7
crime control 3
  clearance rates 8
  coercive intervention 103, 162
  collective ownership 99
  community-based 158
  dealing with causes 44
  diversion 79–80, 89
  enhancing opportunities 60
  focus on criminal act 28, 153,
    156, 160, 163
  pre-emptive action 52–3, 61,
    88–9
  resocialisation 60–1
  social transformation 99, 103
  'three strikes' policy 148
  treatment 43–4
  war on crime 137–8, 139–40,
    147, 197
  see also law and order
crime rates, persistent 58–9, 65
crime statistics 10–11, 71, 103, 161
crime waves 9
criminal anthropology 44
criminal association 68
criminal justice
  accountability 99, 182, 198
  classical perspective 31–3
  community system 158–9
  male preserve 119
  overhaul needed 122
  positive, restorative 172, 182
  private system 142
  sexualisation thesis 120
  system as sexist 112–13, 119
  system as source of positivism 47
criminal law *see* law
criminal subcultures 67–9, 70, 74,
  79
criminal typology 45
criminalisation 102, 106, 197
criminals *see* offenders

criminogenesis   3
criminologists, theorists   2
criminology
   academic discipline   1–20, 212
   analysis levels   12–14
   approaches to study   1–4, 18, 19
   causation theories   3
   critical realist approach   11
   focus areas   3
   institutionalist approach   10
   male preserve   118
   methodologies   14
   mid-range theories   19
   multidisciplinary nature   14, 209
   neglect of women   118, 119–20
   non-sexist   132
   paradigm shifts   18
   peacemaking   195
   perspectives   11–19
   political orientations   14–19, 211
   realist approach   10
   sex variable, approaches   127
   specific/generalist   196
   theoretical strands   11–19
   underlying assumptions (chart)   211
   vocational approach   2–3
critical criminology   3, 104, 133, 192–208, 210
   anti-capitalist   193
   basic concepts   196–8
   chart   197
   contemporary examples   201–5
   critique   205–7
   historical development   198–201
   oppositional   192
   social context   192–6
   socialist orientation   192
   see also Left Realism
cross-cultural universal norm   5
culpability   32
cultural feminism   118
culture   60, 67–9, 76–8, 118
curfews   8

decriminalisation   80, 141
definitions   4–10, 27–8, 60
   broadening   106
   class-based   96–7
   gender-based   120
   legal   4–6, 156

legal and sociological   4–5
   oppression-based   196
   problems reaching   107, 205
   social   4–6, 78–9
   see also charts
democratisation   99
deregulation   137
determinism   42, 59, 123, 210
deterrence   28, 29, 30, 143, 146
deviancy
   acting out   124
   amplification   103
   biological   63
   cultivated (1960s)   76
   individual   43
   new theorists   199
   primary/secondary   84–5
   self-control and   146
   socially conferred   83–4
   trauma-related   47
differential association   68
discretion see choice; judicial discretion
diversion   79–80, 89
domestic violence see violence
dominion   174, 176, 178, 180, 184
dominion status   176
drug laws   206

economic crimes   17, 97
economic dependency   120
economic efficiency   136
economic rationalism   136
egoism   63–4
environment, social   13–14, 48, 49
Equal Opportunities Board   116
equality see rights
ethnomethodology   80
Europe   39–40, 58
evolution   39, 40, 44

family conference programme   186
Family Group Conferences   86, 89, 189
fatalism   154
feminism   112–34
   basic concepts   120–2
   contemporary examples   128–32
   crime perspectives (chart)   121
   critique   132–3
   cultural   118

First Wave 113
historical development 122–8
liberal 116
Marxist 116–17
Second Wave 77, 113, 133
social context 113–20
socialist 117–18
values conflicts 71
see also women
feminist jurisprudence 194
feudalism 21–3, 99, 100
Fitzgerald inquiry 9
France 23, 77, 100
free will *see* choice
French Revolution 24
functionalist approach 93, 101

gender
criminological treatment 127
stereotypes 121, 125, 127
v. sex 113–14, 122, 124
genetics 49
genocide 205
Germany 58, 100
Great Depression, the 58, 65
greed, decade of 137

homelessness *see* vagrancy
homogenisation 197
homosexuality, activism 77, 194
hormones 123
human diversity 5
human rights 5, 96, 106, 107, 198
humans, attributes 142–3, 144–5, 154
hustling 154

ideal types, construction 12
immigration 58, 64–5
imperialism 39
individual pathology 43
industrialisation 21–2, 25, 38, 57
inequality 15, 120, 125, 201
infanticide 127
innovation 67
intelligence 45
interactionism 75
intervention, minimal 80, 85
involvement 145

judicial discretion 23, 30, 32, 33

judiciary, anti-sexist training 122
justice
administration 22
even-handedness 25, 28
fairness 34, 69
personalised and localised 23
promoting dominion 177
repressive 62
restorative 86, 180, 198
see also criminal justice
juvenile delinquency 50, 65, 82, 83
juvenile justice 85–6, 185–6
Juvenile Justice Panels 86

knowledge 1–2, 3, 7, 53

labelling 5, 72, 75–91, 129, 130, 184, 199, 201
basic concepts 78–80
central problems 90
chart 78
contemporary examples 85–7
contextual 160
critique 87–9
historical development 80–5
social context 76–8
subtlety of process 88
vulnerability to process 87–8, 92
labour
cultural exclusion 70
division 62–3
free market 25, 38
mechanical/organic solidarity 62–3
paid v. unpaid 116–17
surplus population 102, 204
working conditions 38
law
accessibililty 33, 34, 35
changes socially defined 6
crime as violation 28
defining basis for crime 4, 156, 168
formal 30, 34
formal definition of crime 4
historical contexts 6–7
intrinsic goodness 27
male-gendered 118
natural science 41
penalties predefined 30
secular v. non-secular 7

law *cont*
  substantive 34
law of the jungle 175
law and order 8, 18, 105, 133, 135,
    137, 138, 139, 147, 149, 150,
    152, 155, 167, 174, 207, 212
law-makers, bound by laws 24
learned behaviour 67, 68
left idealism 107, 152
Left Realism 2, 133, 150, 152–71,
    210
  basic concepts 156–9
  chart 157
  contemporary examples 166–8
  critique 168–9
  early versions 160–4
  historical development 159–66
  New South Wales 166
  pragmatism 153
  Second Wave 164–6
  social context 153–6
  see also critical criminology
legal aid 33
Legal Centre movement 33
legal costs 33, 108
legal definitions 4–6
legal systems, unjust 4
legitimation crisis 197–8
liberal feminism 116
liberalism 16, 18, 172, 211
libertarianism, right-wing 141
liberty 175, 176

manslaughter 33
marginalisation 154, 197, 200, 202
Marxism 92–6, 199, 203-4
Marxist criminology 92–111
  basic concepts 96–9
  chart 97
  contemporary examples 103–6
  criminal thought 100
  critique 106–10
  historical development 99–103
  social context 93–6
Marxist feminism 116–17
masculinity 114, 115, 118, 132
meaning, social process 78
media
  coverage leading to change 8, 9
  images of crime 7–10, 139, 212
  limitations re juveniles 86

symbiosis with police 8
mens rea 31–2, 107
mental illness 31, 46, 53–4, 83
metabolism 51
mitigation, extenuating circumstances
    31, 54
monarchs 22, 23, 24
monopolies 24, 203
moral consensus 43
moral danger 129–30
moral panics 7, 8, 103, 139
morality 8, 128, 138, 173
  double standard 121, 124, 129
  enforcing 119, 130
  offending against as crime 142
  social authority 144
multiculturalism 206
murder 5, 87, 101, 176

nature v. nurture 48
neo-classical reforms 31, 34
net-widening 88–9
New Right criminology 133, 135–51
  basic concepts 139–44
  contemporary examples 145–8
  critique 148–50
  historical development 144–5
  social context 136–9

occupational health and safety crimes
    9
offenders
  antisocial, destructive 157–8
  'at risk' individuals 49, 52–3, 54
  atavistic 44–5
  behaviour determined 42, 59
  biochemical factors 49–50
  biological factors 13, 44–6
  born not made 44
  designation as criminal 8, 10–11,
      13, 15, 79
  dominion recognised by 177–8,
      182
  external factors 46
  genetic factors 46, 49
  individual differences 43, 44–6
  made not born 46–7
  nature *see* charts
  product of social order 59
  psychological factors 13, 46–8

psychopharmacological factors 50
recompense to victim 177–8, 183–4
scientific study 43
'sick' 47, 52, 54
stigmatisation 79, 82–3
treatment/cure 46, 47, 50, 52
omission, statistical problem 10
opportunities, enhancing 80
opportunity 60, 64–7, 72
  illegitimate structures 68–9
  reduction 147
  response typology 66–7
  see also strain theory
opportunity theory 60
opportunity-rationality theory 135, 146
oppression 113, 117, 120, 194, 204, 205
order 143
outsiders 83–4

parsimony 182, 188
patriarchy 120, 130
peacemaking 195
penal reform 166, 168, 201, 204
penalties
  chemical castration 52
  death 23, 29, 35, 181
  determinate 28, 29, 32
  incarceration 29–30, 53, 149, 163, 181
  indeterminate sentences 44, 53
  just deserts 140, 142
  purpose 29, 30
  repressive v. restitutive 62–3
  torture 23, 29
  unequal effects 35
  v. prevention 29
  see also deterrence; punishment; sentencing
personality traits 48
phenomenology 80
phrenology 45
physiognomy 46
pleasure-pain principle 28
police
  accountability 182
  antagonistic 155, 157, 161
  cautioning programmes 186

consensus style 155
corruption 9
democratising 169
ineffective 161–2
labelling by 85, 103
mundane tasks 9
responsiveness 158
symbiosis with media 8
political orientations 14–19
  chart 211
populism 138, 139
pornography 117, 144
positivism 37–55
  basic concepts 42–4
  chart 42
  classifying and quantifying 41, 52
  contemporary examples 48–50
  critique 50–4, 55
  emergence 37–8
  historical development 44–8
  natural science and 40–1
  social context 37–42, 43
post-modernism 194–5, 204
poverty 14, 17, 34, 58, 65, 72, 101, 109, 154
power
  checking 182, 188
  conflict perpectives 94
  crime categories 17–18, 97–8, 104–5, 106, 112, 155, 196
  crimes of domination 101–2
  designing laws 101, 103, 106, 110
  double standard 121, 124, 129
  empowerment 72, 121
  gender biases 125
  institutionalised 195, 202
  limiting arbitrary uses 25–6
  opponents of classicism 31
  outside class structure 109
  to label 79, 101
  under feudalism 23
  see also class; critical criminology; feminism; Marxism
prevention
  fostering communitarianism 179
  promoting valued norms 179
  see also charts
preventivists 174
professions 430, 53, 57

proletariat *see* labour; working class
promiscuity 124, 128, 129
property 7, 8, 25
proportionality 32
prostitution 124, 127, 128
psychiatry 47, 48, 53
psychoanalytic theory 47
psychological positivism 46–8
psychopharmacology 50
punishment 43, 135, 138, 140, 142,
 143
 see also deterrence; penalties

race 17, 39, 44, 131, 132, 148
racialisation 197, 207
racism 52, 104, 201, 202
radical definition (chart) 17
radical non-intervention 80, 85
radical pluralism 95
radicalism 16–17, 211
rape 87, 104, 119, 127, 128, 129
rapists, stereotype 128–9
rationality *see* reason
reality, social construction 83
reason
 child defendant 31, 34
 classical theory 26, 27, 28, 30
 mental illness 31, 34
 scientific method 40–1
 see also choice
rebellion 67, 108, 136, 199
rebels, functional 63
recidivism 54, 197
rectangle, representing society 15
rectification 177, 181
refugees 58
rehabilitation 32, 33, 54, 61, 174
reintegration 182, 184, 185
reintegrative shaming 86, 178–9,
 184, 185, 188
religion 6, 7, 62, 142
reparation 183
reprobation 182
republican theory 133, 172–91
 basic concepts 176–9
 chart 177
 contemporary examples 183–6
 critique 186–90
 features 181
 historical development 179–82
 limits-respecting 181–2

normative theory 172, 180, 181
 social context 173–6
 symbolic and substantive 183
 wholistic view 172, 174, 190–1
resocialisation 60–1
restitution 63, 183
retreatism 67
retributivists 174, 180–1
right-wing libertarianism 140–2
rights
 equal 24–5, 28
 feudal 22
 individual 24–5, 26, 149
 movements in 1960s 77
 of victims 149, 150
 sentencing principles 32
 sexual equality 120
 universalisation 24
rights-holders, humans as 27, 125
ritualism 67
role-playing 81
rule of law 24, 26, 27, 28
Russian Revolution 57–8, 100

scientific approach *see* positivism
scientific method 40, 41, 51, 53
self, socially built 80–1
self-control *see* choice
self-fulfilling prophecies 82
sentencing
 'just deserts' 32, 33, 181
 principles 32, 54
 retribution 174, 181
 see also penalties
sex
 criminological treatment 127
 v. gender 113–14, 122, 124
sexism 52, 201
 construction of crime 125
 criminal justice system 119
 sexual bias 127
 worksites 116
sexualisation thesis 120, 129, 130–1
sexuality 114, 123, 124, 129, 144
shapes, representing society 15–16
situational analysis 13
situations, defining 81
slavery 100
small claims courts 33
social bond 144–5

social breakdown   157, 158, 168, 193–4
social contract   27, 28, 30
social control   2, 156, 162
social control theory   135
social disorganisation theory   64
social ecology   64
social empowerment   198
social facts   61
social harm   4, 5, 96, 98, 107, 203
social inequality   34, 35
social interdependency   178, 185–6
social justice   4, 199
social learning theory   60
social norms   65, 78
social order   76, 96
social pathology *see* strain theory
social problems   16
social programmes   61
social psychology   80
social reaction   83–4
social scientists   40, 41, 54
social solidarity   158
social structure, analytical approach 13, 14
social training   146
socialisation   124, 144
socialisation theories   124
socialist feminism   117–18
socialist organisations   39, 100
society
    characterised in theories   173
    classless   38–9
    consensus within   187, 190
    culturally defined goals   66, 68–9
    geometric representations   15–16
    natural science and   40–1
    pluralistic   77–8, 94
socio-cultural crimes   17
sociology   3, 57, 61, 80
solidarity, mechanical/organic   62–3
square, representing society   15
square of crime   156, 165, 168
state
    bureaucratisation   31
    intervention   141, 144
    rise of   23
    role   24, 25, 95, 108, 207
    see also social contract; social order
state crimes   17, 50, 97, 155

status, rights and   22
status offences   129
status quo   16, 57, 71, 72, 94
stigmatisation   79, 82–3, 108, 184, 188
strain theory   56–74, 201, 210
    Australian stance   70
    basic concepts   59–61
    chart   59
    contemporary examples   69–70
    critique   71–3
    historical development   61–9
    social context   56–9
street crime   8, 9, 50, 102, 104, 105, 149, 152, 156, 161, 173
subcultural theory   60
suicide   62
survivors   132
symbols   80

Tattoo Removal Scheme   86
technology   39, 40, 194
Thatcher, Margaret   136, 137, 152, 153, 159
theft   7, 98, 101, 104, 125, 128, 176
triangle, representing society   15
trivialisation   126

underclass   105
underdogs   95
unemployment   58, 65, 70, 128, 135, 154
unionisation   38, 39, 100
United States
    migration and crime   58, 64–5
    new social order 1960s   76–8
    social perspectives   2
    Un-American Activities Committee 93
utilitarianism   29, 175

vagrancy   6
values
    conflicting   71
    crime as violation of   60
    pluralism   71
victim impact statements   180
victim surveys   156, 159–60, 163, 164, 167
victimisation   202
    critical realism   10–11

victimisation *cont*
 female-specific 119, 125, 126
 Left Realism 168
 radical feminism 117
 through violence 128
victimless crimes 80, 141, 144
victimology 131, 132, 180
victims
 dominion status 178
 rights 149, 150
 street crimes 152
 v. survivors 132
 worthiness 129
Vietnam War 77, 93
violence 5–6, 50
 domestic 9, 119, 125, 126, 179,
  185
 frequency 8
 generalised 125
 hidden 120
 male, against women 120, 131–2
 metabolism connection 51
 victimisation through 128
 see also assault; child abuse;
   murder; rape
voluntarism *see* choice

war 46, 47
welfare 129, 130
white supremacy 39
white-collar crime 9, 50, 71, 108,
  160, 161, 163, 165, 179–80,
  185, 200, 202, 203
witchcraft 6–7
women
 bodies as commodities 117
 crime and 70, 118–20, 123, 124,
  125, 126
 defined in relation to men 116
 dependency 120, 124
 empowering/disempowering 120,
  121

 ethnicity/class issues 115
 female discourse 118
 gatekeepers 130
 hormones/post-natal 123
 labelling 129, 130
 manipulative 123
 neglected by criminology 118
 ordination 7
 property of men 125, 127
 rights, dignity, freedom 116
 separate culture 118
 sex-related offences 128
 sex-specific offences 127
 structurally disadvantaged 120
 unpaid labour 116–17
 witchcraft 6
 women-centred analyses 115,
  118
Women's Liberation Movement 77,
  93, 113, 194
working class
 apprehension rates 105
 crimes by 102, 112
 criminalisation 102, 106
 deprivation 157, 158
 enfranchisement 39
 overrepresentation 131
 repression by state 98
 rise 38, 57, 100
 victims of crime 152, 155, 161,
  173
 see also class; strain theory

youth
 class and 102–3
 crime rates 74
 'drifting' behaviour 85
 fingerprinting 86
 labelled by police 85
 moral panic and 7, 8, 103
 subcultures 67, 102, 103
 see also juvenile delinquency